Component Database Systems

The Morgan Kaufmann Series in Data Management Systems

Series Editor: Jim Gray, Microsoft Research

Component Database Systems

Edited by

Klaus R. Dittrich

University of Zurich

Andreas Geppert

University of Zurich

MORGAN KAUFMANN PUBLISHERS

AN IMPRINT OF ACADEMIC PRESS

A Harcourt Science and Technology Company

SAN FRANCISCO   SAN DIEGO   NEW YORK   BOSTON
LONDON   SYDNEY   TOKYO

dpunkt.verlag

dpunkt
Verlag für digitale Technologie GmbH
Heidelberg

Morgan Kaufmann Publishers

Executive Editor   Diane D. Cerra

Senior Production Editor   Cheri Palmer

Editorial Coordinator   Belinda Breyer

Cover Design   Yvo Riezebos Design

Cover Image   ©2000 PhotoDisc

Production Services   Dusty Friedman, The Book Company

Text Design   Lisa Devenish

Copyeditor   Julie Nemer

Proofreader   Martha Ghent

Composition   Nancy Logan

Illustration   Lotus Art

Indexer   Erin Taylor

Printer   Courier Corporation

dpunkt.verlag

Senior Editor   Christa Preisendanz

Designations used by companies to distinguish their products are often claimed as trademarks or registered trademarks. In all instances where Morgan Kaufmann Publishers is aware of a claim, the product names appear in initial capital or all capital letters. Readers, however, should contact the appropriate companies for more complete information regarding trademarks and registration.

ACADEMIC PRESS

A Harcourt Science and Technology Company

525 B Street, Suite 1900, San Diego, CA 92101-4495, USA

http://www.academicpress.com

Academic Press

Harcourt Place, 32 Jamestown Road, London, NW1 7BY, United Kingdom

http://www.academicpress.com

Morgan Kaufmann Publishers

340 Pine Street, Sixth Floor, San Francisco, CA 94104-3205, USA

http://www.mkp.com

05   04   03   02   01   5   4   3   2   1

Library of Congress Cataloging-in-Publication Data

Component database systems / edited by Klaus R. Dittrich, Andreas Geppert.
    p.cm
    Includes bibliographical references and index.
    ISBN 1-55860-642-4
    1. Distributed databases. 2. Database management. 3. Distributed databases.
I. Dittrich, Klaus, R. II. Geppert, Andreas.
    QA76.9.D3 C65 2001
    005.75'8--dc21   00-063407

    MKP ISBN: 1-55860-642-4
    dpunkt ISBN: 3-932588-75-4

This book is printed on acid-free paper.

Foreword

Peter C. Lockemann
Professor of Informatics
Universität Karlsruhe

I recently came across a fascinating book, *Regional Advantage—Culture and Competition in Silicon Valley and Route 128.*[1] The author compares the rise and dominance of Silicon Valley during the 1970s and 1980s with the slow decline of Route 128 during the 1980s and hypothesizes that the contrasts in development were mainly due to the large differences in industrial culture. More specifically, she claims that industrial culture in Silicon Valley is one of dense networks, close collaboration between small and highly innovative companies, low vertical integration where companies instead depend for much of their own products on the skills and expertise of neighboring companies, and companies' close relationship with their suppliers and industrial customers that ties their own success to the success of the others, and vice versa. The author makes a convincing point that such a culture is particularly capable of coping with global competition fueled by ever-shorter technology cycles.

What bearing can a study of industrial sociology possibly have on technical systems such as database management systems (DBMS)? It seems to me that indeed there are important parallels. Database systems tend to be huge monolithic systems with an internal structure that is reminiscent of tight vertical integration. One suspects that this requires the vendors themselves to follow a strategy of vertical integration. So if the study teaches us any lesson, it is that database systems should be broken up into smaller pieces that can each be procured from the best and most innovative suppliers. Many will benefit: the DBMS vendors who will have a technological edge over their slower competitors, the customers who will get the best technology for their money, and the suppliers who have a dependable partner that allows them to stay ahead of the crowd.

There remains just a small problem: What are the pieces—the components—of a DBMS, and what is the glue that holds it together? It seems that even after 30 years of DBMS development, and 20 years after the question was first posed, nobody in industry or in academia has a ready answer. To be sure, the 1980s and early 1990s saw a wealth of research flowing into extensible database system prototypes, but only one found its way into a commercial product. Other products soon followed suit. A number of chapters in this book describe the efforts of

---

[1] Saxonian, Annalee. 1996. *Regional Advantage—Culture and Competition in Silicon Valley and Route 128.* Harvard University Press, Cambridge, MA.

the vendors of these systems, with almost all based on an object-relational approach, where the objects are supposed to provide the components and the relational base system the glue.

One of the major upcoming influences comes from an entirely different direction: distributed systems and the techniques that cope with the heterogeneity and interoperability of sources. On a systems level the issues are reflected in the Intelligent Information Infrastructure (I^3) architecture, with wrappers, mediators, and facilitators. On a more technical level, middleware is the buzzword. In the context of component databases, they are candidates to provide the glue. Three of the contributions in this volume reflect efforts in this direction.

At the outset the editors set a very ambitious agenda. Some readers may feel—as I did—that the remaining chapters contribute only very modestly to the lofty goals. But we should always keep in mind that commercial products look for what is feasible at the time and solve the most pressing problems at hand. Other—seemingly esoteric—problems will have to wait until practical needs arise.

For researchers, however, there is no reason to wait. It should have become clear to all of us that, with all the new technology in processor speeds, storage capacities, transmission bandwidths, mobility, the number of database applications, and the degree of database system specializations will have to grow dramatically. Economics in database engineering have become the order of the day. And so we come full circle back to our initial, almost cultural argument in favor of componentizing database systems.

What we have in hand, then, is a wonderful book to show us how far database technology has been able to move in the direction of component databases, how limited the approaches still are when measured against the agenda, and what enormous challenges—and ensuing rewards—still lie ahead. If the book stimulates renewed efforts in research and development, then indeed it has served its purpose as a trailblazer marking the way to an information technology infrastructure that is receptive to the needs of the information society.

Contents

Preface

The recent past has witnessed an overwhelming proliferation of database technology. Without query languages, transaction management, logical data independence, and many other database functions, it is virtually impossible to run an enterprise or organization. However, now that the advantages of using database management systems are apparent, users require database technology to reach far beyond its traditional power. Nowadays database management systems must be able to handle a much broader diversity of data, such as multimedia and unstructured data. Likewise, database technology must be exported to other existing software systems, and operational existing data stores must be integrated into a coherent entirety.

Any vendor attempting to address all these new requirements in a single system would very likely end up with a dinosaur. In consequence, most vendors try to tackle this problem by making their systems extensible and by offering specialized functionality in terms of extensions. Such a goal is easier stated than achieved—prerequisites to be met are the redesign of existing database management systems to open them up for extensions, and exact and complete specification of how to add extensions in a sound way. Of course, many different ways can be devised to accommodate extensiblity. The common characteristics of the various approaches elaborated in this collection are that database functions are componentized at least to some extent and that new functions can be incorporated by adding new components or replacing existing ones.

In the first chapter, we give an in-depth overview of and introduction to the subject matter. Chapters 2 through 8 address specific aspects of component database systems, as outlined next.

Chapter 2 by Paul Brown presents the Informix perspective on distributed component database management systems based on the object-relational model. He discusses how distributed object-relational database management systems can be extended. He also discusses implications of componentization on query optimization in a distributed database management system.

Chapter 3 by Sandeepan Banerjee, Vishu Krishnamurthy, and Ravi Murthy introduces Oracle's approach to component database systems. They present a complete set of possible extensions to Oracle8*i*, including user-defined types, functions, operators, and aggregates. They also discuss extensible indexing and query optimization.

Chapter 4 by Stefan Deßloch, Weidong Chen, Jyh-Herng Chow, You-Chin (Gene) Fuh, Jean Grandbois, Michelle Jou, Nelson Mattos, Raiko Nitzsche, Brian Tran, and Yun Wang presents the IBM DB2 approach to componentization. They focus on extensible indexing and present applications of their approach to selected areas. They also discuss the integration of DB2 UDB (DB2 Universal Database) with external search engines.

Chapter 5 by José A. Blakeley and Michael J. Pizzo introduce OLE DB. They present Microsoft's component object model and show how it is used in OLE DB to accommodate componentization. They also discuss several scenarios using OLE DB, and describe how components in OLE DB can be built and managed.

Chapter 6 by Mary Tork Roth, Peter Schwarz, and Laura Haas presents the Garlic system for the integration of diverse data sources. They introduce Garlic's wrapper architecture and describe the steps necessary to build a new wrapper. They also discuss query execution and optimization in Garlic.

Chapter 7 by M. Tamer Özsu and Bin Yao discusses the Object Management Group (OMG) perspective on the subject. They introduce CORBA (Common Objects Request Broker Architecture) and CORBAservices, show how componentized applications can be built using CORBA, and show how CORBA and CORBAservices can be used to develop interoperable database management systems.

Chapter 8 by Heiko Bobzin considers database support for embedded and mobile devices. He argues that for such systems componentization is a prerequisite. He then describes POET's Navajo system and discusses the various Navajo parts that can be plugged together to form a customized database system for mobile devices.

Finally, Chapter 9 concludes the book and discusses achievements and open questions.

We are very pleased that this book, which includes the broad spectrum of covered systems, became possible. The chapter authors are leading experts in their field and key people in their companies. We are therefore very grateful that they found the time to contribute their chapters, despite the pressure due to ongoing development, product releases, and so forth.

We also appreciate the very professional support by Morgan Kaufmann. It was a pleasure to cooperate with Marilyn Alan and Diane Cerra; without their patience despite the many missed deadlines, this book would never have materialized.

Acknowledgments

Chapter 1

We gratefully acknowledge the comments by Mike Carey, Tamer Özsu, and Reinhard Riedl on previous versions of this chapter.

Chapter 3

We would like to recognize the contributions of several individuals who made the Oracle Extensibility Architecture a reality. Anil Nori, Chin Hong, Kenneth Ng, and Andy Mendelsohn helped set the direction for this technology in Oracle. There were several project leaders and developers, including the authors, who helped deliver the architecture; prominent among them are Jay Banerjee, Jags Srinivasan, Nipun Agarwal, Seema Sundara, Dinesh Das, S. Muralidhar, and Vikas Arora.

Chapter 4

This work is partially supported by DARPA Contract F33615-93-1-1339. We would like to thank the Garlic team members, both past and present, whose hard work and technical contributions made the Garlic project possible.

1

Component Database Systems: Introduction, Foundations, and Overview

Andreas Geppert
Klaus R. Dittrich
University of Zurich

1.1 Introduction

Database management systems (DBMSs) support individual applications and comprehensive information systems with modeling and long-term reliable data storage capabilities as well as with retrieval and manipulation facilities for persistent data by multiple concurrent users or transactions. The concept of data model (most notably the relational models, Codd 1970; and the object-oriented data models, Atkinson et al. 1989; Cattell & Barry 1997), the Structured Query Language (SQL, Melton & Simon 1996), and the concept of transaction (Gray & Reuter 1992) are crucial ingredients of successful data management in current enterprises. Nowadays DBMSs are well established and are, indeed, the cornerstones of virtually every enterprise.

Traditionally, data elements stored in databases have been simply structured (e.g., employee records, and product and stock information). Transactions have been of short duration and often needed to access only a few data items. Most traditional queries have been simple and the techniques used to answer them efficiently are well understood. Taking a broader view, DBMS-based information systems have been built in a rather database-centric way; that is, environment decisions such as the use of mainframe-based or client/server architectures have been typically based on what the DBMS itself requires or supports in this respect.

In the recent past, however, more and more new and demanding application domains have emerged that could also benefit from database technology, and new requirements have been posed to DBMSs. Many applications require the management of data types that are not handled well by conventional DBMSs. Examples of such new data types include multimedia data, documents, engineering artifacts, and temporal data, to name just a few.

Likewise, DBMSs are more and more often required to integrate with other infrastructure parts of their environment. For instance, instead of letting the DBMSs manage already existing data, it is often necessary to leave data where it is (possibly because there are applications that users would not want to migrate as well) and instead enhance the external data management system with some sort of database functionality (Vaskevitch 1994). It might also be necessary to integrate existing data stores with database systems in such a way that each of them is still independently operational, while users are provided with an integrated and uniform view of the entire system. In other words, often applications need support as offered by multidatabase systems or federated database systems (Elmagarmid et al. 1999; Sheth & Larson 1990), in which the federated parties might be any kind of data store. Some applications even require support for queries combining data from databases and data extracted from sources such as the World Wide Web (WWW).

In order to meet all these new requirements, DBMSs (or whatever the resulting kind of system will ultimately be called) apparently have to be extended to include new functionality. However, enhancing a single system with modules implementing all the new functions is not a viable approach for several reasons:

- DBMSs would become so large and, in consequence, complex that they could no longer be maintained at reasonable cost.

- Users would have to pay a high price for the added functionality, even if they do not need every part of it.

- Users and applications would also have to pay a performance penalty for added functionality that they actually do not need.

- A DBMS vendor might not have the expertise to perform such extensions and might not have the resources to undertake all extensions within a reasonable period of time.

Thus, beefing up a monolithic DBMS by adding more and more functions does not work. Instead, it seems attractive to consider the alternative of extending DBMSs in a piecemeal way, that is, striving to allow functionality to be added or replaced in a modular manner, as needed.

Modular extensions to a DBMS require that a well-defined software architecture is imposed on the DBMS. This architecture clearly defines the places in the system where extensions are possible. In general, extensions should be possible at a few well-defined, distinct places in the system only, and the effects of modifications on other parts should be avoided or at least minimized. To that end, DBMS architectures need to be componentized in such a way that new components can be added to it or existing components can be exchanged in a flexible yet well-defined way. Thus, the componentized architecture specifies and restricts the ways in which a DBMS can be customized. Ultimately, the componentized architecture also defines the notion of component, itself, and hence the realm of valid extensions to a DBMS.

We refer to DBMSs that have a componentized architecture and allow users to add components as component DBMSs (CDBMSs). Due to the componentized architecture, these extensions are possible without requiring other system parts to be rewritten. Components can be provided by third parties and possibly even users, thus increasing the developer base of a DBMS. Ultimately, unnecessary components do not have to be added, and applications therefore do not pay (in terms of system cost and performance) for functionality they do not use.

In the remainder of this chapter, we introduce principles and different forms of CDBMSs. In Section 1.2, we present a more detailed motivation of componentization of DBMSs. We then discuss the foundations of CDBMSs: DBMS architecture and componentware. In Section 1.4, we review past efforts regarding the extensibility of DBMSs. Section 1.5 presents a more detailed taxonomy of CDBMSs, and Section 1.6 concludes the chapter.

1.2 The Need for Componentized DBMSs

In this section, we will motivate CDBMS in more detail (see also Vaskevitch 1994, 1995). To this end, we consider DBMS support for advanced information systems (IS) with respect to the following tasks: management of new data types, adapted and new database functionality, and better integration with other IS parts and the IS environment.

1.2.1 Handling Nonstandard Data Types

In view of the success of relational database systems in supporting IS, new applications pose new requirements for database systems, and existing application areas define extended requirements. For example, many organizations offering services or products in the WWW want to manage their data in a database system. In particular, e-commerce applications need database support to manage their catalogues, product descriptions, orders, and so forth. Other areas, such as engineering (e.g., bio-engineering, mechanical engineering, or software engineering) and scientific applications (e.g., in biochemistry, geography, or meteorology), also extend the requirements of database systems. In those cases where data do not already live in existing systems, it will often be desirable to exploit database technology in order to benefit from data independence, query capabilities, transaction management, and consistency enforcement.

These applications often need support for modeling and storing data that, so far, are not supported by database systems. Examples of such nonstandard data types are images, text, spatial data, temporal data, videos, Virtual Reality Modeling Language (VRML) objects, and structured documents. Moreover, applications often need to aggregate related instances of these data types into complex objects. While some advanced data types might be supported by specialized DBMSs (e.g., temporal, spatial, or multimedia database systems), in many cases a system that offers exactly the desired set of data types does not exist. Moreover, many of these specialized DBMSs are not available commercially.

In addition to storing nonstandard data, the data also need to be retrieved. Thus, declarative queries over these nonstandard data types must be supported. However, many of them have type-specific query modes, such as content-based search in the case of images or information-retrieval-style queries in the case of text documents. Even existing applications (such as financial applications) might need more powerful query support (e.g., new forms of aggregates, such as a moving average).

Query processing, of course, must not only be possible, but it also needs to be efficient. To that end, query optimizers must be able to generate efficient plans for operations on any kind of data supported by the DBMS, including nonstandard data. Optimizers thus must know (or be taught) how to generate efficient execution plans for queries over predefined as well as nonstandard data types. Furthermore, non-standard data types often require or can at least benefit from special-ized index structures. Without exploiting these index structures, the performance of retrieval is, in many cases, suboptimal. DBMSs there-fore should be able to incorporate new index structures whenever these are needed to execute queries against nonstandard data types efficiently.

Currently, no single, off-the-shelf DBMS exists that meets all these requirements for a complete range of data types. Apparently, vendors are not interested in or able to build such a system for several reasons. Such a one-size-fits-all solution might meet the functional require-ments of most applications, but for each application it also would pro-vide functionality that this application does not need. Users would still have to pay for all the functions, regardless of what they effectively need. Moreover, adding functions usually leads to performance degra-dation, even if the new functions are not used—thus, customers have to pay a performance penalty for features they do not use.

A further reason for vendors' reluctance to build such a system is that adding too many features in parallel is not advisable and manage-able. In special cases, a vendor also might not have the expertise to add the required new features, for example, if the implementation of new query modes or optimizations requires highly specialized, type-specific knowledge.

Thus, a single DBMS supporting all the emerging and ever-more-demanding applications is not conceivable. A possible solution is to extend a DBMS on demand—that is, to provide standard, commonly needed functionality right away and to add other, more advanced fea-tures in a piecemeal way later. Customers can then purchase the core DBMS plus the extensions they require. In other words, instead of a monolithic DBMS, customers use an a la carte DBMS configuration.

1.2.2   Data Integration

The analysis just described considers cases where all the data are kept, or can be brought, under the control of a single DBMS. This, however, is not always possible because in many cases the data have existed in specialized data stores, such as image libraries or document collections, for a long time. The migration of data and application programs with-out loss is often difficult or impossible. Hence, existing and new data are to be integrated under the common roof of an integration layer. The reasons for integration typically include the facts that data in dif-ferent data stores are (semantically) related in some way and that the task of the integration layer is to store and maintain these relationships. Likewise, integration is often desired to achieve a uniform and homo-geneous view of the diverse data stores and to receive database support for the integrated system (e.g., queries against the integrated system). Thus, we face the challenge of integrating a broad diversity of data stores into a database environment.

In order to integrate disparate data stores, some kind of middleware system is needed that understands (or can be taught) the data models of the data stores. Even in the case of standardized data models (such as the relational one), each system has intricacies that require a system-specific handling and mapping. Even worse, nondatabase systems handle data in an application-specific format. Consequently, integration cannot be done just once per system, but has to be done separately for each data source.

As in the previous case, there are two options: Either a DBMS is built that knows everything (i.e., how to integrate all the possible data stores) or the integration platform is kept extensible and built in a piecemeal way. The first option is, again, not feasible because the DBMS has to know about all the interfaces and intricacies of the involved data stores.

A feasible solution to this problem is, once more, to use the principles of componentization and extensibility. Assume the middleware layer defines a (minimal) set of functions it expects from the data stores. Each extension then implements these functions using the interface of the corresponding data store to be integrated. In other words, these extensions serve as gateways or wrappers: They abstract from the intricacies of the data store, and they (instead of the data stores proper) are hooked into the middleware. The apparent advantages of this approach are that the knowledge and customization required of the middleware layer are minimized (because it only needs to know the general abstract notion of wrappers) and that ideally wrappers or gateways are written once per type of data store.

1.2.3   Downsized Database Systems

So far, we have implicitly assumed that required database functionality is provided in the form of database systems, and that nonstandard requirements are met by adding extensions. In order to use database functions, applications are implemented on top of a database system or database middleware. This, however, is not the only conceivable form of database support to meet novel requirements. Sometimes, applications need only parts of the entire spectrum of database functions or need these parts in a very specialized form. Forcing applications to always use full-fledged, entire DBMSs can turn out to be an overkill and/or to not lead to the right kind of support. As an example, suppose a document management system or a groupware system already has its own persistence mechanism to store documents. Assume further that queries are desired, but not yet supported. Query support could be achieved by moving the document management system on top of a database system. But, if, instead, query processing were available as a stand-alone service, the document management system could exploit this service.

Of course, splitting a DBMS into single, stand-alone parts is a difficult problem because the right balance between the granularity of services and the (number of) interservice relationships has to be found. Likewise, determining the right interfaces for the services is a complex task. However, feasible solutions to these questions and, in consequence, the availability of a broad range of services open up completely new ways of implementing database applications and application servers. These systems can then pick the service provider that is optimal for their problem and do not need to rely on large full-fledged DBMSs. Moreover, in cases in which services are standardized, we can envision that in such a scenario it will also be possible to mix and match services from different vendors. The objective of turning DBMSs into lightweight collections of freely combinable services can be met only if these services and their implementations are described and built as components.

1.2.4 Discussion

The general problem in the scenarios we considered is the monolithic structure of a traditional DBMS. By *monolithic structure* or *monolithic architecture*, we mean that the DBMS is a single unit whose parts are connected to one another and dependent on one another to such a degree that modifications and extensions are not easily possible. In particular, each DBMS part might make assumptions about the requirements and operations of other parts, which leads to domino effects whenever changes are made in one place. Extensions can only be made if all the interconnections and dependencies are known. The evolution of and extensions to a DBMS are only possible by the vendor, who, for each extension, also needs to make sure that other affected parts are adequately adapted.

To prevent misinterpretations, it should be stressed that monolithic architectures in their current common form have not emerged simply because developers and vendors did not know better. In the past, they have been sufficient because applications posed rather restricted requirements for DBMSs. Moreover, a monolithic DBMS can be implemented in a way that optimizes runtime performance and throughput for all applications that need just the functionality offered by the DBMS. Nevertheless, whenever extensions and customizations are considered, problems with monolithic architectures occur with respect to system complexity, system performance, system cost (production and maintenance), and complexity of system evolution.

The general idea for overcoming these problems and still providing for the needed functionality as sketched in the previous scenarios is to offer a core system and to extend it as needed. CDBMSs are meant to allow such extensions in a controlled and safe way. Although different forms of CDBMSs exist, their common basis is a componentized architecture and the support of components implementing some kind of database function. These components can be added to a DBMS or used in some other way to obtain database support.

In order to effectively allow extensions, the DBMS architecture must be made explicit and be well defined. While typically some parts of the CDBMS will need to be fixed without the possibility of altering them, others can be extended (we call this the variable part). *Explicit* means that the system structure is defined, preferably in a (formal) architecture model, and that the system structure is visible to those actors modifying it. Second, for a CDBMS the meaning of the notion of component is defined, with varieties ranging from abstract data types to implementations of internal tasks. However, the common characteristics of components are that they implement a coherent set of functions, make all restrictions concerning their use explicit in their interface, and are generally applicable across a variety of applications. Ultimately, a CDBMS architecture also defines places in the system (the variable part) where components can be added. These places can be thought of as hooks used to plug components into the enclosing system. Technically, these hooks are defined in terms of the interfaces the component can use and/or should implement.

1.3   Prerequisites and Foundations of CDBMSs

In this section, we elaborate on the principles of CDBMSs in more detail. As mentioned before, extensions to a DBMS affect its architecture and also require certain prerequisites to be met. We therefore first briefly address the issue of DBMS architecture. The subsequent section relates CDBMSs to componentware and then gives a classification of CDBMSs.

1.3.1   DBMS Architecture

Different kinds of architecture serve different purposes. For instance, the three-level-schema architecture (which distinguishes the external schemas that users work with, the internal integrated schema of the entire database, and the physical schema determining the storage and organization of databases on secondary storage) reflects the different levels of abstraction of data in a database system. The layered architecture in Figure 1.1 illustrates a hierarchy of mappings, where the topmost layer deals with data model entities and the bottommost layer deals with blocks and files. Finally, a task-oriented architecture identi-

Figure 1.1 | **Layered DBMS architecture.**

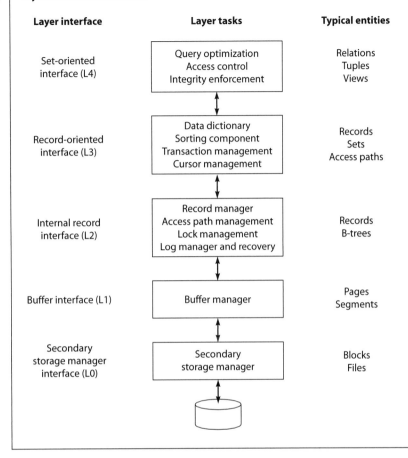

fies the relevant modules (i.e., their purpose and interface) and relationships to other modules (e.g., in the form of exported and imported interfaces). Examples of such tasks include query optimization, concurrency control, and recovery. The last two also are examples of tasks that are hard to assign to a specific layer in the layered architecture or that might even be addressed by multiple layers. Although a task-oriented architecture is much more suitable for reasoning about extensibility and DBMS construction, reference architectures rarely exist (with the strawman architecture developed by the Computer Corporation of America, CCA 1982, as a notable exception), and concrete architectures are described at a granularity too coarse to be helpful for our purposes.

For educational purposes, it is convenient to consider a DBMS architecture as consisting of a number of layers (Härder & Rahm 1999; Härder & Reuter 1983; Ramakrishnan 1997). Each layer supports a set of data types and operations at its interface and typically consists of several components (modules or managers of some concrete or abstract resource). The data types and operations defined for the modules of one layer are implemented using the concepts (data types and operations) of the next-lower level. Therefore, the layered architecture can also be considered as a stack of abstract machines. Concretely, the layered architecture model as introduced by Härder and Reuter (1983) is composed of five layers (see Figure 1.1):

1. The uppermost layer (L4) supports logical data structures such as relations, tuples, and views. Typical tasks of this layer include query processing and optimization, access control, and integrity enforcement.

2. The next layer (L3) implements a record-oriented interface. Typical entities are records and sets (e.g., as found in the Committee on Data Systems Languages, CODASYL data model) as well as logical access paths. Typical components are the data dictionary, transaction management, and cursor management.

3. The middle layer (L2) manages storage structures (internal records), physical access paths, locking, logging, and recovery. Therefore, relevant modules include the record manager, physical access path managers (e.g., a hash table manager), and modules for lock management, logging, and recovery.

4. The next layer (L1) implements (page) buffer management and implements the page replacement strategy. Typical entities are pages and segments.

5. The lowest layer (L0) implements the management of secondary storage (i.e., maps segments and pages to blocks and files).

In general, due to performance considerations, no concrete DBMS has fully obeyed the layered architecture. Note further that different layered architectures and different numbers of layers are proposed, depending on the desired interfaces at the top layer. If, for instance, only a set-oriented interface is needed, it is useful to merge the upper two layers.

From a more practical point of view, most DBMS architectures have been influenced by System R (Astrahan et al. 1976), which consists of two layers: the relational data system (RDS), providing for the relational data interface (RDI); and the relational storage system (RSS), supporting the relational storage interface (RSI). While RDS implements SQL (including query optimization, access control, triggers, etc.), RSS supports access to single tuples of base relations at its interface.

1.3.2 Components and Database Management System Architecture

When we strive for reusability, extensibility, openness, and interoperability of database systems, looking at software engineering research and practice yields helpful insights. In particular, componentware (Allen &

Frost 1998; D'Souza & Wills 1999; Griffel 1998; Hamilton 1997; Krieger & Adler 1998; Nierstrasz & Dami 1995; Nierstrasz & Meijler 1998; Orfali et al. 1996; Szyperski 1997) is a recently proposed paradigm to address these issues. This is the notion that software systems are built in a disciplined manner out of building blocks with specific properties, called components. There is currently no widely agreed-on definition of the term component; however, the following characteristics of components can be found in most definitions in the literature. A (software) component, then, is a software artifact modeling and implementing a coherent and well-defined set of functions. It consists of a component interface and a component implementation. Components are black boxes, which means that clients can use them properly without knowing their implementation. Component interface and implementation should be separated such that multiple implementations can exist for one interface and implementations can be exchanged. Defining components as black boxes also means that each component sees only the interfaces of other components; that is, access to the internal operations and structures of other components is not permitted. A component should not have an overly high number of relationships to other components because this might restrict its reuse potential.

Systems are built by putting components together to form new software systems (this principle has been referred to as reuse by composition). Systems constructed by composition can be modified or extended by replacing or adding new components. Component-based systems are expected to facilitate the addition or replacement of components without recompilation (or even without shutting down) the entire system.

In order to put the right components together to obtain complete and adequate systems, a frame (into which components are plugged) and rules governing the composition process are needed. The frame is given by the software architecture (Perry & Wolf 1992; Shaw & Garlan 1996) of the system under construction. Similar software systems are then described by architecture skeletons or generic architectures (Nierstrasz & Meijler 1998) that are successively enhanced and completed by components. Thus, as a prerequisite, the underlying generic architecture needs to be defined in terms of components (acting as placeholders) and connections in such a way that components can later be added in a meaningful and consistent way.

Components usually possess a coarser granularity than objects in object-oriented systems and models. A well-designed component supports a coherent set of tasks (e.g., in one of our scenarios, storing and retrieving textual documents), while objects and classes typically address only a part thereof. Components and objects are, however, not mutually exclusive alternatives; rather, components leverage object orientation to a higher level of abstraction and granularity. In fact, "under the hood" components are often assemblies of objects.

We use the principles of componentware to better understand, abstract, and classify the various approaches to extending and customizing DBMSs. Moreover, the characteristics of componentware (components and architecture) are crucial requirements for systematic and well-defined extensibility and integration. Extensions to a DBMS in this context are represented as components (i.e., they should meet the aforementioned properties of components). Further, DBMS should exhibit a componentized architecture, at least for those parts that are intended to be customizable.

1.4 Related Work: The Roots of CDBMSs

In this section, we review the roots of CDBMSs. In a nutshell, these roots are relational database systems, object-orientation in general and object-oriented DBMS in particular, and extensible database systems.

Extensible database systems (Carey & Haas 1990) all attempt to ease the construction of DBMSs by exploiting some kind of software reusability (Geppert & Dittrich 1994). The proposal is for a general core that can be customized or extended in some way by users, or even used to generate some DBMS parts. Here, we survey these approaches and classify them by their dominant way of extending or constructing DBMSs.

1.4.1 Kernel Systems

Kernel systems offer the common functionality required by all or most DBMS (e.g., physical object management), but typically are not fully functional DBMSs. The upper layers of a DBMS have to be implemented (i.e., programmed) by the DBMS implementor (DBI). The major question in this approach is how powerful the kernel interface is. A low-level interface (e.g., page management or unstructured records) leaves the DBI enough freedom to implement the desired concepts. On the other hand, much implementation work is necessary due to the low level of the kernel. Alternatively, if a kernel supports more powerful concepts, less implementation is required from the DBI, while the kernel will be geared toward specific kinds of systems or constructions.

The Wisconsin Storage System (WISS) (Chou et al. 1985) offers basic DBMS functionality. At its top layer interface, WISS provides for (unstructured) records and scans of files of records, where scans can contain search predicates. All necessary additional functionality has to be implemented on top of this layer.

DASDBS (Darmstadt Database System) is another kernel system (Paul et al. 1987; Schek et al. 1990) that offers a general fixed interface. The reusable part of DASDBS is the complex record manager, which handles record structures comparable to nested relations (Schek & Scholl 1986). DASDBS also supports multilevel transactions (Weikum 1991) and, therefore, provides support for implementing transaction management on upper levels. Object managers such as Bess (Biliris & Panagos 1995), EOS (Biliris 1992), the EXODUS storage manager (Carey et al. 1986), Kiosk (Nittel and Dittrich 1996), ObServer (Hornick & Zdonik 1987; Skarra et al. 1991), and Texas (Singhal et al. 1992) also fall into the class of kernel systems.

1.4.2   Pure Extensible Database Systems

Pure extensible database systems allow new parts such as abstract data types or index structures to be added to the system (note that the term "extensible database system" in the broader sense often refers to systems that support any kind of enhancing, extending, or customizing DBMS; Carey & Haas 1990).

Enhancing DBS with new Abstract Data Type (ADT) or index structures has been pioneered in the Ingres/Postgres systems (Stonebraker et al. 1983; Stonebraker 1986; Lynch & Stonebraker 1988). Ingres supports the definition of new ADTs, including operators. References to other tuples can be expressed through queries (i.e., the data type *postquel*), but otherwise ADTs and their associated relations still must be in first normal form. This restriction has been relaxed in systems that have a more powerful type system (e.g., an object-oriented data model) (Bancilhon et al. 1992; Dadam et al. 1986; Dittrich et al. 1986; Linnemann et al. 1988; Schek et al. 1990).

Another area in which extensions have been extensively considered are index structures. In Ingres/Postgres, existing indexes (such as B-trees) can be extended to also support new types (or support existing types in a better way). To extend an index mechanism, new implementations of type-specific operators of indexes have to be provided by the user. In this way, existing index structures are tailored to fit new purposes and thus have been called extended secondary indexes. Since most of the implementation of an index does not need to be changed, extensions are easier to perform than implementing a completely new index structure. The principle of extended secondary indexes has recently been applied in the DB2 UDB object-relational DBMS (Chen et al. 1999).

1.4.3   Customizable Systems

This kind of system is based on a complete DBMS that is modified or extended so that it satisfies new requirements. The basic DBMS is customized to a concrete, new DBMS. In principle, (internal) DBMS components are exchanged in order to achieve specific functionality in a different way than in the original system. Therefore, a crucial issue is the underlying architecture and the proper definition of places where exchanges can be performed.

Starburst (Haas et al. 1990; Lindsay et al. 1987) is an example of a customizable DBMS. Its query language can be extended by new operators on relations (Haas et al. 1989). Various phases of query processing in Starburst are also customizable. Queries are internally represented as query graphs, and query rewrite transforms these graphs into equivalent, better ones. The rewrite part of Starburst's query processor can be customized (Pirahesh et al. 1992) by adding new rewrite rules (where each rule is defined in the form of two C procedures). The Starburst query optimizer maps a query graph into an executable plan in a bottom-up manner. For each element of the query graph, it creates one or more alternative plans and selects the cheapest plan that meets the required properties. The mapping of query graph elements into plan operators is defined by Strategy Alternative Rules (STARS) (Lohman 1988). The optimizer can be customized by defining new STARS.

Storage methods can also be customized in Starburst in that (new) relation storage methods are plugged into the system. Relation storage methods implement the storage of relation instances and operations on them. They determine how a specific relation is represented physically (e.g., as a temporary relation or in the leaves of a B-tree). Furthermore, attachment types can be associated with relation instances. The meaning of attachments is that their operations are invoked as a side effect of relation-modification operations (operations that update a relation). Attachment types include access structures, integrity constraints, and triggers. Both relation storage methods and attachment types have to implement a collection of generic operations.

1.4.4 Toolkit Systems

Toolkit systems offer libraries of modules that implement alternative techniques for given tasks (e.g., physical access paths). The variable part of a DBMS is then built by selecting one technique from each library, and plugging together the chosen techniques.

The EXODUS (Carey et al. 1990, 1991) approach (see also Section 1.4.6) applies the idea of a toolkit for specific parts of the DBMS. A library is provided for access methods. While the library initially contains type-independent access methods such as B-trees, grid files, and linear hashing, it can also be extended by a DBI with new methods. Hereby, the DBI can use the DBMS implementation language E (Richardson & Carey 1986), a derivative of C++, for the implementation of extensions as well as for other parts of a DBMS. Furthermore, another library exists for operator methods, each of which implements an operation on a single type of storage object (e.g., selection). These operator methods are used later to realize operators of a query language (see later sections).

The Open OODB (Open Object-Oriented Database) approach (Blakeley 1994; Wells et al. 1992) supports the construction of object-oriented DBMSs. Open OODB distinguishes a meta-architecture and an extensible collection of modules implementing specific functionality (policies). The meta-architecture defines a set of kernel modules, mechanisms to define the system architecture (boundaries between components), and so forth. For some specific functional tasks, various policies can be applied (and can even be exchanged dynamically). Each domain for which multiple policies can be used is controlled by a policy manager, and all the policies of a specific domain are required to guarantee the same invariants (which ensures that they are interchangeable). In a nutshell the construction process with Open OODB consists of two major steps: defining the architecture with the means provided by the meta-architecture, and selecting policies for those required domains that allow multiple policies.

Further examples of toolkits are Trent (Unland & Schlageter 1992) for the construction of transaction managers (mainly, transaction structures and concurrency control) and A la carte (Drew et al. 1992) for the construction of heterogeneous DBMSs.

One problem in any toolkit approach is the consistency (or compatibility) of reused components. Lienert (1987) investigates conditions under which DBMSs can be configured. He first identifies the major tasks of a DBMS and generally distinguishes access (storing and retrieving data) from management (concurrency control, recovery, integrity enforcement, etc.). Furthermore, he elaborates the definition of standard techniques for these tasks and interrelationships between these techniques. Then, attributes representing certain properties of techniques are derived for the various tasks, rules are specified for deriving (deducing) some of them, and conditions are specified that have to hold for a configuration (e.g., a configuration is not correct if specific techniques have mutually contradictory values for some attributes).

1.4.5   Transformational Systems

In a transformational approach to DBMS construction, the DBI uses languages for the specification of the functions to be implemented. These functions are implemented using the interfaces of a lower layer, and DBI must also specify the mapping to that implementation base.

GENESIS (Batory et al. 1988a, 1988b) is a transformational approach that supports the implementation of data models as a sequence of layers. The interface of each layer defines its notions of files, records, and links between files. The implementation of a layer is described by the transformation of its concepts to those of the next-lower layer. Transformations themselves are collected in libraries, so that they can be reused for future layer implementations. The basic (fixed) component is the JUPITER system for file management. The sequence of transformations maps the data-model concepts to the JUPITER interface.

The approach of GENESIS has been generalized to a construction method for hierarchical software systems (Batory & O'Malley 1992). The underlying assumption is that DBMSs can be constructed as layered systems. The central notion of this approach is the component, where each component is an element of a realm. All the elements of a realm have the same interface, but possibly different implementations. Then, a software system is described as a kind of algebraic expression. Component reuse refers to referencing the same component in multiple expressions.

Another transformational approach that uses specification constructs similar to those of Acta (Chrysanthis & Ramamritham 1994) has been described by Georgakopoulos et al. (1994). The transaction specification and management environment (TSME) consists of two building blocks: a transaction specification facility (TSF) and a programmable transaction management mechanism (TMM). TSF also uses the notion of dependency between transactions. Specific dependencies are implemented through Event-Condition-Action (ECA) rules in DOMS.

1.4.6 Generators

Generator systems support the specification of (parts of) a DBMS functionality and the generation of DBMS components based on those specifications. The DBI specifies a model (e.g., an optimizer, a data model, or a transaction model), which is input to a generator. The generator then automatically creates a software component that implements the specified model based on some implementation base (e.g., a storage manager or kernel in the case of data-model software generation). The knowledge for mapping the concepts specified in the model to the implementation base is in the generator.

An example of a generator system is the EXODUS query-optimizer generator (Graefe & DeWitt 1987). Input to the generator is a model description file, which contains a set of operators, a set of methods to be considered for constructing query execution plans, transformation rules, and implementation rules. Transformation rules specify legal transformations of query trees into new ones, and implementation rules define correspondences between operators and methods (i.e., which method can be used to implement an operator); for example the join operator could have as a corresponding method a hash join. In addition to the model description, a set of C procedures has to be supplied, which, for example, determine the cost functions of the various methods. Given this information, the generator can create a query optimizer for a DBMS under construction.

Volcano (Graefe & McKenna 1993), the successor of the EXODUS optimizer generator, also falls into the group of generator systems. Volcano has been used to build the optimizer for Open OODB (Blakeley et al. 1993).

1.4.7   Frameworks

Frameworks model families of software systems with a common prescribed architecture and behavior. They model the variable parts of the considered systems as abstract classes, and a concrete system can be built by deriving new subclasses from the abstract ones (called reuse by inheritance).

Opt++ (Kabra & DeWitt 1999) is a query-optimizer framework. Abstract classes model operator trees and access plans. Further classes model the transformations of operator trees into other trees or into access plans, or of access plans into other plans. Finally, search strategies are also represented as classes. The Opt++ framework defines a general architecture of a query optimizer in terms of instances of these classes. A concrete optimizer is built by deriving concrete classes from the abstract classes prescribed by the framework.

Other frameworks for building query optimizers are the ones described in Özsu et al. (1995), Cascades (Graefe 1995), and EROC (Extensible Reusable Optimization Components) (McKenna et al. 1996). Framboise (Fritschi et al. 1998) is a framework for layering active database functionality on top of passive DBMSs.

Generalized search trees (GiST) (Hellerstein et al. 1995) allow the incorporation of new index structures into a DBMS. GiST supports tree-based indexes; their general behavior (e.g., insertion and deletion) is predefined and thus does not need to be rewritten for new instances of GiST. New index structures can be built by implementing or overriding six methods specific for concrete search trees. The GiST approach has been extended to cover a broader spectrum of search trees and search techniques (e.g., nearest neighbor) (Aoki 1998). Kornacker et al. (1997) shows how concurrency control and recovery can be implemented for instances of GiST. GiST has recently been incorporated into Informix Dynamic Server with Universal Data Option (Kornacker 1999).

1.4.8   Discussion

Many of the techniques surveyed in this section have made their way into products (user-definable types, extensible index structures, etc.). While there are some success stories (i.e., techniques having found their way into products), there are also lessons to be learned and problems to be addressed.

An interesting observation is that recent efforts have assumed a fixed data model, such as the object-relational or object-oriented model. This is in contrast to older work, in which the implementation of new data models was also investigated. The reasons for this trend are, in our opinion, that there is no significant market for new specialized data models and that the invention of new data models requires that most of the other DBMS parts (such as the query processor) as well as tools (e.g., for database design) be adapted accordingly.

Most of the recent efforts also assumed a fixed transaction model (e.g., ACID-transactions or closed nested transactions), while significantly less work has been done on extensible transaction management. Exceptions to this observation are concurrency control and recovery for extensible index structures (e.g., Kornacker et al. 1997). The probable reasons for this trend are that many of the proposed nonstandard transaction models have never been implemented and questions remain concerning their semantics and range of applicability.

Furthermore, it can be concluded from the work done in the past and the functionality available today that some techniques are more feasible than others or that they are well suited for specific cases. For instance, techniques requiring a large implementation effort (e.g., implementing a DBMS on top of object managers) are only practical for a vendor who wants to offer a suite of products and wants to share part of the codebase among products. Customization techniques require a sound understanding of the systems and of the effects that customizations have. They are therefore also only applicable for vendors, unless their specification is possible in a very high-level way and implementors are not required to know the internals of the core system.

A further noteworthy observation is that approaches in extensible database systems seem to follow trends in software engineering, but delayed a few years. For instance, while older approaches have used the principles of generators, more recent efforts have devised framework-based solutions.

Finally, another lesson is that feasible approaches to extensibility should consider the entire DBMS. Approaches concentrating on a single aspect (e.g., transaction management) tend to make assumptions that restrict other parts of the DBMS. These restrictions then raise questions of consistency and compatibility when other parts of the system should be kept extensible or customizable as well. In consequence, in order to be feasible, extension mechanisms in one area should not preclude extensions in other parts of the system.

Finally, as more and more extensions become available, we expect that problems known from software-reuse research and practice (Krueger 1992) need to be solved in our context as well. For instance, whenever there is a significant number of components to choose from, users need support for selection (i.e., finding the adequate reusable software artifact). In cases in which extensions cannot be reused as is, users need help to adapt reused extensions.

We conclude from these lessons that feasible approaches to extensibility and customizability need to rely on the componentization of DBMSs. In this way, variable parts are clearly identified, as are the component plugs used for extension and composition. This in turn significantly reduces the amount of knowledge about internals required for extensions and customizations. The notion of component used to describe possible extensions is suitable for addressing reuse problems, due mainly to their higher level of abstraction, but also due to the requirement that connections (to other system parts) be well defined.

1.5   Component Database Models

In this section, we present the various types of CDBMSs. We consider two dimensions:

- Components: What kinds of components are considered? Which kind of database functionality or DBMS task can be represented as a component? How are components defined?
- Architecture: What is the generic DBMS architecture that allows plug-in components? What are the respective fixed and variable parts? How are components and connections described?

The classification given in this section does not imply that all the categories are completely disjoint. In fact, a concrete system can belong to multiple categories, for instance, if it allows the addition of different kinds of components. We return to this issue in Section 1.5.5.

1.5.1   Plug-in Components

The first category of CDBMSs comprises universal servers. The core system in this group is formed by a fully functional DBMS that implements all the standard functionality expected from a DBMS. Nonstandard features or functionality not yet supported can be plugged into this DBMS (see Figure 1.2). Thus, such a system is functionally complete and meets basic requirements, while extensions add further functionality for specialized needs.

The components in this kind of CDBMS are typically families of base and abstract data types or implementations of some DBMS function, such as new index structures. The DBMS architecture, among others, defines a number of plugs that components can use, for example, interfaces of functions that the DBMS will invoke and that the component thus must implement. In other words, the architecture formulates

Figure 1.2 | **Principle of plug-in style CDBMSs.**

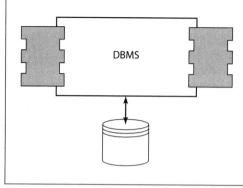

expectations concerning interfaces that the component must meet in order to be integrated successfully.

To date, all systems in this category are based on the relational data model and existing relational DBMSs, and all of them offer some object-oriented extensions. We thus discuss this type of CDBMS in an object-relational (Stonebraker et al. 1999) context, although componentization is also possible for object-oriented database systems. Example systems include IBM's DB2 UDB (IBM 1995), Informix Universal Server (Informix 1998), Oracle8 (Oracle 1999a), and Predator (Seshadri 1998). Descriptions of sample component developments can be found in (Bliujute et al. 1999; Deßloch & Mattos 1997).

The approaches we consider here aim at providing data management facilities for new nonstandard data types and for nonstandard or specialized database functionality within the DBMS. Instances of these new data types are thus stored in the database, and their manipulation and retrieval is implemented by the DBMS.

Assume an application needs support for data types not yet supported by the DBMS in use (e.g., spatial data or social security numbers). The ultimate task is to teach the DBMS how to store, manipulate, and retrieve instances of these data types.

In the first step, the designer has to model the structure of the desired new data types as well as their type-specific behavior. From a user's point of view, new data types are either complex or atomic. Complex data types possess structure and their values can thus be represented as specialized records or tuples or collections using the data definition language. Atomic data types do not have an internal structure and consist of literal values (such as numbers or characters). For atomic types, the DBMS needs basic information, such as their length in bytes, in order to store their instances.

Thus, for spatial data, we might specify points as a complex data type modeling locations in three-dimensional space. 3DPoint could be specified as a tuple type with attributes x, y, and z, each of which is of type decimal. Another example would be Region, whose structure could be defined as a pair of points `LowerLeft` and `UpperRight`. Social security numbers would be defined as an atomic type whose instances are 9 bytes long.

In addition to the structure of data types, the type-specific behavior of the new sorts of data needs to be specified. For each complex data type, its specific functions, operators, and predicates must be made known to the DBMS. In our example, a possible function would be the `move` function for points, and a typical predicate would be `overlaps`, which tests whether two regions intersect in some subregion.

Atomic types normally do not exhibit type-specific behavior. They, however, often require special treatment with respect to ordering and representation. Indeed, one reason to introduce a new type for non-standard atomic type is that existing DBMSs do not know how to sort them correctly. Thus, for new atomic types it is necessary to define operators such as <. Furthermore, the internal representation usually is not very telling for end users; thus, functions converting elements of atomic types from an internal (stored) representation to and from an external one are needed.

For each function, operator, and predicate, a signature (i.e., its name, arguments, and result) must be defined and an implementation must be provided. The implementation language in turn depends on the DBMS, possibilities ranging from DBMS-specific languages such as Oracle's PL/SQL to general-purpose programming languages such as C or C++ or Java.

The collection of data types (their definition and implementation) forms a significant part of a component, which then needs to be plugged into the DBMS. To this end, DBMSs in this category offer a facility to register new components. Component registration introduces new definitions (for types, functions, etc.), and also informs the DBMS where (i.e., in which files) implementations can be found.

After a data type has been registered, applications can, in principle, start to use them (i.e., to create and retrieve instances of them). However, efficient retrieval and processing might require further enhancements to the DBMS, particularly to the access path manager and the query optimizer. Thus, we observe that extending a DBMS by plugging in new components often has a sort of domino effect because other parts must be adapted accordingly.

Current DBMSs typically contain B-tree access paths and possibly also hash-based indexes. B-trees can handle one-dimensional keys very well and rely on the orderability of keys. New types such as spatial data types can, however, be multidimensional; thus they would not be adequately served by B-trees, and, consequently, query processing might easily become inefficient. Therefore, in some situations it will be desirable to add new access methods to the DBMS, such as one that supports multidimensional indexing (Gaede & Günther 1998). In order to integrate well with other parts of the DBMS, such a new index has to implement exactly those functions the DBMS calls for its indexes (i.e., insertion and deletion of entries, index scanning, etc.).

Furthermore, the addition of new data types also affects query processing, in particular query optimization. Cost-based optimization techniques, for instance, need information about the cost of each operator (in terms of CPU consumption and I/O-operations) to find an optimal plan. Thus, to ensure efficient query processing in this case, it is necessary to provide the optimizer with the adequate information, such as the knowledge of how it can estimate the cost of evaluating newly defined predicates.

As a typical example of the aforementioned domino effect, consider concurrency control for access paths. Many DBMSs use specialized concurrency control protocols on indexes to prevent unnecessary locking conflicts (Bayer & Schkolnick 1997; Kornacker et al. 1997), which otherwise would increase lock contention and decrease transaction throughput. Therefore, whenever a new index is introduced, concurrency control (for this new index type) should also be adapted, which is, however, not possible in current systems.

1.5.2 Database Middleware

The typical aim of systems falling into this category is to integrate existing data stores, that is, to leave data items under the control of their original (external) management systems while integrating them into a common DBMS-style framework. For instance, existing data stores should be integrated into query processing or transaction management of the entire system. External systems will in many cases exhibit different capabilities, such as query languages with varying power or no querying facilities at all. The different data stores might also have different data models (i.e., different data definition and structuring means), or no explicit data model at all. Users and applications should, nevertheless, be shielded from this kind of heterogeneity and should be provided with a uniform and integrated view of the entire system. This task is accomplished by the CDBMS acting as middleware (Orfali et al. 1996; Ferreira Rezende & Hergula 1998) between these data stores and the applications of the integration. The overall aim of systems in this group is similar to that of multidatabase systems (Sheth & Larson 1990; Elmagarmid et al. 1999), although the latter typically consider only the integration of database systems, instead of any kind of data store.

The goal of graceful integration is achieved through componentization in the following way (Figure 1.3). The architecture introduces a common (intermediate) format into which the local data formats can be translated. Components are introduced that are able to perform this kind of translation. Second, common interfaces and protocols define how the database middleware system and the components interact (e.g., in order to retrieve data from a data store). These components

Figure 1.3 | **Middleware-style CDBMSs.**

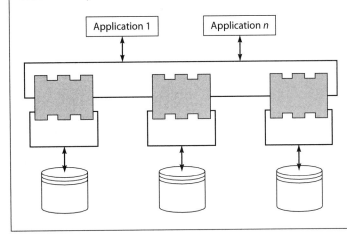

(called wrappers) are also able to transform requests issued via these interfaces (e.g., queries) into requests understandable by the external system. In other words, these components implement the functionality needed to access from, within the database middleware system, data managed by the external data store.

The underlying problem in this respect is that the database middle ware needs to understand the data formats and the functions of each data source. Two extreme alternatives exist to tackle this problem. In the first, information about the data sources' interfaces are hard-wired into the (integrating) DBMS. The realm of integrable external data stores is thus restricted, and the DBMS needs to be extended for each specific type of data store. In the other alternative, a common data model, query language, or interface to external data stores is set as a prerequisite. For instance, we might require that all data stores understand SQL and be able to return the results of SQL queries in the form of relations. Each data store that does not implement SQL right away would thus have to be extended to do so. Moreover, all the data sources and the middleware would have to agree on one specific SQL dialect.

The solution that helps to overcome the intrinsic problems of both approaches lies in the introduction of additional components. In a nutshell, a component is pushed between the DBMS and each data source. These components serve to homogenize differences in formats and functionality from the DBMS's point of view. From the data sources' perspective, they level the different data source capabilities to a common basis. Thus, each component mediates between the data sources and the DBMS, or—from the DBMS's point of view—wraps the data source.

The first prerequisite of this approach is a common data abstraction (e.g., objects). Second, the mediation components must offer a common interface. This interface is used by the DBMS to request data from the data sources. Each component should at least support the minimal interface, such as scanning a collection of data entities. Depending on the data source capabilities, its mediation component can, however, contribute more features or specialized functions, such as predicate evaluation. Whenever the DBMS executes a query and determines that it needs results from the data source, it sends a request to the corresponding component, which in turn translates the request into a form the data source can handle. Eventually, the component receives the results from the data source and converts them into the common format expected by the database middleware.

This approach requires an appropriately defined notion of components for wrapping the external data stores because it must match the requirements and characteristics of the DBMS while also using the capabilities of the data stores. Moreover, using the full potential of this approach means that a component is written once for each kind of data store (e.g., for a specific image management system) and used for all subsequent instances of the data store.

Ultimately, users should be allowed to introduce new components to integrate data stores not yet covered. To that end, the implementation of a component must be possible without the component implementor knowing the internal structure and operations of the database middleware; the requirements to be met by a component must be entirely expressed in its interface.

Examples of this approach include Disco (Tomasic et al. 1998), Garlic (Tork Roth & Schwartz 1997), OLE DB (Blakeley 1996a, 1996b; Microsoft 1996), Tsimmis (Papakonstantinou et al. 1995a), Harmony (Röhm & Böhm 1999) (which implements the CORBA query service), and Sybase Adaptive Server Enterprise (Olson et al. 1998) (which allows access to external data stores, in Sybase called specialty data stores, and other types of database systems).

1.5.3   DBMS Services

The third type of componentized DBMS is characterized by a service-oriented view of database functionality. All DBMS and related tasks are unbundled (Geppert & Dittrich 1998) into services. As a result, a monolithic DBMS is transformed into a set of stand-alone services. For instance, the unbundling process can result in persistence, query, and transaction services. Applications then no longer operate on full-fledged DBMSs, but instead use those services as needed (Figure 1.4).

Each service is defined by one or more interfaces and implemented by some software systems. Services (i.e., their interfaces) are defined in a common model or language. Services are implemented using a common platform in order to render the service implementations exchangeable and freely combinable. Services should be as indepen-

Figure 1.4 | **Principle of service-oriented architectures.**

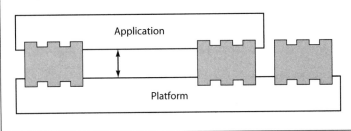

dent as possible from one another; that is, they should not rely on the
availability of a specific other service in the environment and they
should not assume that other services are implemented in a particular
way.

In this scenario, (database) services and their implementations are
viewed as components. Given that both the platform and the service
interfaces are standardized, exchangeability and compatibility are
achieved. Different implementations of a service can be exchanged,
and implementations of different services—possibly from different vendors—can be plugged together.

An example of this approach are CORBAservices (OMG 1995a),
which leverage several DBMS tasks to general object systems. These
services are standardized by the Object Management Group (OMG).
Service interfaces are defined using the Interface Definition Language.
Services related to database functionality include persistency, concurrency, and queries. Such services are implemented on top of Object
Request Brokers (ORB) (OMG 1997a).

In contrast to the other approaches discussed here, the components
(i.e., services) are not meant to extend or customize a DBMS. Rather,
the systems constructible by using services are distributed applications
located above the DBMS level. In fact, services such as persistence
could be implemented by a DBMS, and the transaction service might be
implemented by transaction processing monitors (Bernstein & Newcomer 1996).

The underlying semantics and models of services (such as the transaction model or query language) are fixed. Thus, for a transaction service, there will be distinct implementations all implementing
transactions such as flat ACID transactions, but transactions such as
cooperative or other forms of nonstandard transactions (Elmagarmid
1992) will not be supported.

A second example of this approach is the strawman architecture
developed at Computer Corporation of America (CCA 1982). The aim
of this study was to propose standard interfaces between users or applications and DBMSs as well as standards for internal interfaces (such
that different DBMS subsystems can be combined more easily). This

study identified 79 subcomponents, which are grouped together into 38 components, some of which denote internal functions, while others refer to external (i.e., visible at the DBMS interface) ones. The subcomponents are partitioned into six groups of related tasks. For each subcomponent, procedures and interfaces are proposed. Therefore, the view of DBMS architecture is more service-oriented, and concrete components are proposed to implement such services (to the best of our knowledge, however, a DBMS implementing this architecture has never been built).

1.5.4   Configurable DBMS

In the previous form of CDBMSs, the set of services have been standardized and fixed. One step further are configurable DBMSs that allow new DBMS parts to be developed and integrated into a DBMS (Figure 1.5). Thus, configurable DBMSs are similar to DBMS services in that they also rely on unbundled DBMS tasks that can be mixed and matched to obtain database support. The difference lies in the possibility of adapting service implementations to new requirements or of defining new services whenever needed. The components are DBMS subsystems, which are defined in an underlying architecture model. In this approach, the architecture model is also used to model the DBMS architecture, which is no longer fixed.

Configurable DBMSs also consider services as unbundled representations of DBMS tasks. However, the models underlying the various services and defining the semantics of the corresponding DBMS parts can now in addition be customized. As a consequence, components for the same DBMS task can vary not only in their implementations for the same standardized interface, but also in their interfaces for the same task. DBMS implementors select (or construct new) components implementing the desired functionality and obtain a DBMS by assembling the selected components (Figure 1.5). The DBMS is thus the result of a configuration process.

An example of a configurable DBMS is the KIDS project (Geppert & Dittrich 1995; Geppert et al. 1997), which aims at constructing a DBMS by developing subsystems that implement various aspects of a DBMS (such as transaction management or constraint enforcement) and by then configuring these subsystems together into a coherent and complete DBMS.

The underlying architecture model provides for constructs that are adequate for defining the architecture of DBMSs. The tasks and functionality of a DBMS and its components are modeled by means of services. Services are provided by reactive components called brokers (i.e., brokers are responsible for services). In the case of service requests, the responsible brokers react by providing the service. The functionality of

Figure 1.5 | **Principle of configurable DBMSs.**

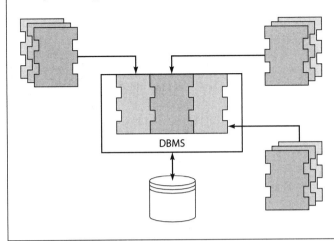

each subsystem under construction is represented as a set of services, and one or more brokers are designated as components implementing the subsystem.

The construction process defines how to proceed in order to obtain a DBMS with the desired functionality. This process consists of several phases including requirements analysis, design, implementation, and integration of multiple DBMS subsystems. Some phases of the process are common to all constructible DBMSs and are independent of subsystems (e.g., requirements analysis and architecture design). For each type of subsystem, a dedicated construction subprocess is defined and integrated into the enclosing DBMS-construction process. For each subsystem, a dedicated specification language is used to define its functionality (such as Acta in the case of transaction models, Chrysanthis & Ramamritham 1994; or Second-order Signature (SOS) in the case of data models, Güting 1993). These specifications serve as the input to subsystem-specific implementation phases, which in turn use techniques such as the generation of subsystems or the configuration of subsystems out of reusable, already existing components (Geppert & Dittrich 1995).

1.5.5 Discussion

We now summarize and discuss the elaboration of CDBMS models. Table 1.1 summarizes the characteristics of the four categories. These categories are not necessarily disjoint. For instance, it is conceivable that both plug-in components for nonstandard data and wrappers for accessing external data stores can be added to a single system. Such a system would therefore belong to the first two categories (e.g., as outlined in Stonebraker et al. 1998). Likewise, OLE DB could also be classified as a

Table 1.1 **Classification of component DBMS-models**

Category	Purpose	Architecture, Plugs	Typical Components
Plug-in DBMS	Extend existing DBMS with nonstandard functionality	Interfaces expected or provided by kernel	ADT definition and implementation, new indexes
Database middleware	Integrate existing data stores into database system	Common format and interfaces between DBMS and wrappers	Wrappers for external data sources
Service-oriented architectures	Provide database functionality in standardized, unbundled form	Service definitions	Service implementations
Configurable DBMS	Compose nonstandard DBMS out of reusable components	Service definitions	DBMS subsystems

configurable DBMS, since it in principle allows the exchange and addition of internal components, for example, to add specialized query processors. In the remainder of this book, representatives of these groups are discussed in more detail.

1.6 Summary and Conclusion

Today's users of database technology require extensibility in all conceivable forms. In order to maintain the software quality and robustness that current (monolithic) DBMS engines exhibit, yet also meet the extensibility requirements, database technology needs to adopt the principles of component technology.

This chapter has also classified approaches to componentizing DBMS and database functionality in general. The following chapters describe prominent representatives of these classes in more detail.

2

Distributed Component Database Management Systems

Paul Brown

Informix Corp.

2.1 Introduction

A component database management system (DBMS) is a systems software framework that application developers can extend by embedding modules of programming logic in it. These extensions implement database objects such as new data types, application-level object classes, analytic algorithms, and external data-access facilities. An object-relational DBMS (ORDBMS) is one kind of component DBMS. While early ORDBMSs were obliged to create their own component models and proprietary interfaces, in recent times the trend has been to adopt open standards such as Microsoft's Component Object Model (COM), SunSoft's Enterprise JavaBeans (EJB), and the Object Management Group's Common Object Request Broker Architecture (CORBA). What distinguishes an ORDBMS from other component frameworks, such as object-oriented DBMSs, middleware (e.g., transaction-processing monitors), and general-purpose application servers, is the way that, once integrated within the ORDBMS, components are organized and manipulated using a declarative database language, instead of a procedural programming language.

A distributed ORDBMS differs from a single-site ORDBMS in that the objects within it—both the persistent object data and logic implementing the extensions—are physically distributed across a set of network-connected computer systems (called nodes of the overall system). As part of its runtime operations, the distributed system moves data and logic between nodes to answer user queries as efficiently as possible. We illustrate this idea in Figure 2.1.

Ideally, the fact of this physical dispersal is not apparent to users and developers, a property known as location transparency. Queries in a distributed ORDBMS are submitted at a single node (called the local node or local site). Within this local node the query expression is decomposed into a set of lower-level operations. Some of these operations might be forwarded from the local site to remote nodes. Processing a query in a distributed ORDBMS may involve moving data between the nodes of the system, performing computational tasks on several nodes, and possibly even moving the entire implementation of some component logic between nodes. Figure 2.1 illustrates this idea by showing a single external user exchanging SQL queries for data with a local node. The arrows between the nodes of the distributed system illustrate the flow of data, code, and messages coordinating the execution of the query.

Note that this diagram is misleading in one important way. From Figure 2.1 you might conclude that the data-processing code is distinct from the database's tables. As we shall see, this is not the case. The component logic embedded in the ORDBMS is invoked using query expressions. A better way to represent this is to show the data-processing code in the columns and rows of the tables. The implications of this are far-

Figure 2.1

Topology of distributed ORDBMS.

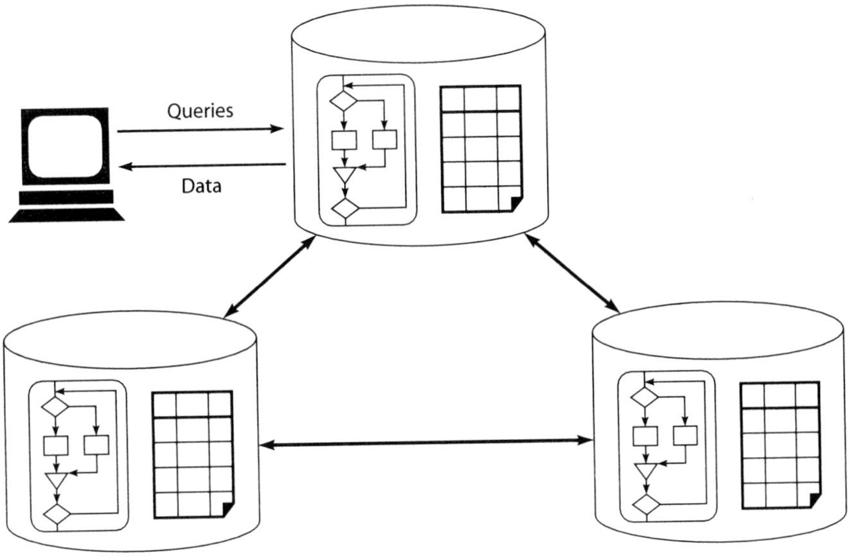

reaching. It means that the ORDBMS is more than a reliable but relatively stupid repository for data. ORDBMSs are software frameworks within which developers can store, organize, and reason about a set of software components corresponding to complex real-world entities.

2.1.1   Why Distributed ORDBMSs?

Distributed component DBMSs such as ORDBMSs are useful because they address requirements not well served by traditional distributed systems technologies. First, a distributed ORDBMS provides the means to integrate the data and logic of multiple information systems into a coherent data management infrastructure. Today, new information systems are frequently constructed by combining several preexisting systems. For example, organizations that have grown through mergers and acquisitions might need to maintain their preexisting accounting, order processing, and supply-chain software while at the same time providing global access to the information in these systems to facilitate management decision making. The kind of query-centric interface, provided by a distributed ORDBMS, is more powerful than procedural interfaces supported by other middleware technologies.

Second, in a similar fashion, certain information systems can be improved by allowing them access to remote data or logic. Transient data that reflect the current state of some functioning system—such as electronics that monitor environmental conditions or reflect the state of a security system—can be accessed through the ORDBMS and combined with persistent data in queries. E-commerce web sites interact with remote systems to process credit card transactions. The most efficient way to develop these systems is to incorporate code that understands and accesses such remote data structures and services directly into the data management framework.

Third, new systems with extreme sizing requirements—either in terms of the volume of data, number of concurrently connected users, or volume of data throughput—can be constructed using distributed ORDBMSs. Single-site ORDBMSs are limited in their capacity to handle simultaneous connections and data volumes, which forces software engineers to take a divide-and-conquer approach. Distributed ORDBMS architectures minimize internode connections while maximizing concurrent users. Partitioning data across multiple nodes facilitates parallelism. Also, these schemes can provide the basis for high availability. Such systems share many characteristics with shared-nothing DBMS architectures.

One can make a stronger claim. Distributed ORDBMSs constitute a powerful, innovative model for generalized distributed computing. ORDBMS technology is unique in that it provides a framework for managing both logic and data in an abstract data model. Traditionally, SQL queries (and in prerelational DBMSs, lower-level data access operations) were embedded in the procedural logic. Data returned by an embedded data access operation was typically subjected to further processing by the logic. And all of this was hand-coded, compiled, and deployed, so that each problem or feature of the information system had its corresponding, self-contained software module. In contrast, in an ORDBMS the logic that is integrated into the query-processing framework typically contains no data-access operations at all. Component routines can be thought of as subroutines extracted from traditional programs. Logic is bound to data using queries, dynamic-programming expressions that are processed by the ORDBMS. What this yields is tremendous flexibility at acceptable levels of performance.

Distributed ORDBMSs provide additional advantages.

- ORDBMSs include elaborate metadata management facilities. These provide a global catalogue or directory describing the contents of the entire system; its data and logic. Unlike other distributed directory services, this can be accessed by using reporting tools and graphical query-creation software, rather than by using static applications or procedural code.

- The logical data model and declarative query language mean that many high-level, conceptual operations can be expressed more or less directly in the system. Further, these expressions can be optimized at runtime to achieve goals such as computational load balancing. Other approaches rely on design time partitioning of logic based on assumptions that are often invalid at runtime.

- Distributed ORDBMSs can co-opt standard component development models to simplify software engineering. Engineers creating the system's atomic components need not know anything about the application context within which they are used. It becomes the job of the SQL-level developer to deploy them to solve a business problem.

- Component standards also make it possible to automatically move extension logic between nodes of the distributed system when necessary. This provides a mechanism for upgrading the logic in a distributed information system.

- All of the considerable virtues of the relational model apply in ORDBMS databases. Developers can use normal form theory to ensure that the databases they design are free from error and ambiguity. Three-value logic can be applied to the problem of missing information. The logical and physical abstraction inherent in the ORDBMS means developers are free to develop a variety of client applications, using a variety of programming environments, against a single schema.

However, despite the attractions of distributed computing, distributed ORDBMSs, multidatabases, and initiatives such as CORBA all have modest commercial track records. In some situations, developers have been successful building information systems based on these technologies. But more general acceptance has been slow in coming, primarily for nontechnical reasons (Gordon & Gordon 1993). It is usually considerable pressure from non-information-system (non-IS) employees and support from management that leads to their adoption. The exception to this rule has been transaction-processing monitors (or TP monitors). TP monitors are distinguished from other distributed frameworks in that they provide a single point of administration. Sharing distributed facilities requires programming against the TP monitor; with other distributed technologies, each node can evolve autonomously.

In a nutshell, the administrative burden imposed by many distributed technologies is thought to outweigh their advantages. Copies of an application's logic and some of its data must be kept local for a potentially very large community of distributed users to achieve reasonable response times. But coordinating change to this logic and data becomes exponentially more difficult as more sites are added. As a result, the human effort necessary to unravel conflicts becomes burdensome.

2.1.2   Description of the Example Application

We use a consistent application example throughout this chapter to give substance to the ideas we introduce. Figure 2.2 presents the

Figure 2.2

Extended entity-relationship (ER) model for example application.

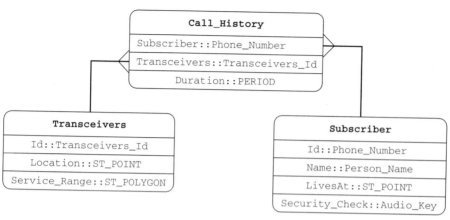

entity-relationship (ER) diagram of our example's conceptual data model. This ER model is unusual in some respects. Note that each entity attribute is specified by both a name (used to refer to the column in queries) and a data type or component name (which specifies the domain of objects the column contains). Such strongly typed schemata are characteristic of object-relational databases. It is useful to think of these domains as indivisible (or encapsulated) objects combining structure and behavior. This makes it a natural to use component approaches to software engineering to implement them. Once they are implemented and added to the ORDBMS framework, you can organize your application's domains into a logical schema corresponding to the network of facts that describe the problem domain.

In the schema in Figure 2.2, the types and domains in CAPS are standardized in SQL:99. Types with mixed upper- and lowercase are specific to our application. The schema is a highly simplified version of a database that supports the operational aspects of a cellular telephone network. Cellular networks are geographically distributed arrays of wireless transceiver stations connected by broadband wire networks. The transceivers provide voice and data connectivity for mobile-phone users, and roosts for resting birds. Our system also manages the account information about subscribers and their call history, which is used for billing. Finally, our system supports an innovative voice-activated authentication function. Subscribers record a secret password when they sign up for their service. When they power up a handheld device, they speak this word—rather than punching in a secret number—to engage the device to the wireless network. The idea is to allow the subscriber to switch freely between different devices. The audio key provides both identification and authentication for the system security.

2.1.3   Chapter Overview

In this chapter we describe how distributed ORDBMSs are constructed and how they can be used. We begin by reviewing the features, architecture, and implementation of a single-site ORDBMS. Such background is useful because the commercial versions of distributed ORDBMSs take such a system as a starting point and because detailed descriptions of ORDBMS internals are not widely available. Also, instances of these single-site ORDBMSs run on each node of the overall distributed system. In Section 2.3, we outline the architecture of a distributed ORDBMS, describing the modifications that are necessary for a single-site ORDBMS to operate in a distributed environment. We extend our example application by partitioning it across a set of computers and explain how the distributed system operates. Finally, we wrap up the chapter with a summary.

2.2   Single-Site Component DBMSs

In this section we give an overview of how a single-site ORDBMS works. In most cases, vendors implement their distributed ORDBMS products by augmenting the functionality of a single-site system. This strategy is motivated more by commercial than technical considerations. The market for distributed ORDBMSs is a subset of the broader market for single-site DBMS software. And as we shall see, much of the code in a single-site system is useful in the distributed system.

2.2.1   ORDBMS Abstract Data Model

As mentioned in the introduction, the most important difference between traditional DBMSs and ORDBMSs is that ORDBMSs manage both persistent data and logic implementing operations over to this data within an abstract data model. This permits developers to use declarative expressions to organize and manipulate the objects for which their information system is responsible. In other words, instead of creating programs wherein every user-level operation is hand-coded and compiled into an executable form, the ORDBMS encourages more flexible system architectures. With an ORDBMS, complex business questions and changes to the information system can be handled at runtime by building appropriate query expressions.

EXAMPLE 1   Figure 2.3 presents two SQL fragments illustrating this. Figure 2.3(a) creates a table to store facts about subscribers in our cellular network system, and the query in Figure 2.3(b) records the fact that a call is beginning.

Figure 2.3 | **Query data definition language (DDL) and data manipulation language (DML) examples for cellular Operational Support Systems (OSS) application.**

a.

```
CREATE TABLE Subscribers (
     Id                 Phone_Number    NOT NULL PRIMARY KEY
                            CONSTRAINT Subscriber_Primary_Key,
     Name               Person_Name     NOT NULL,
     LivesAt            ST_POINT        NOT NULL,
     Security_Check  Audio_Key          NOT NULL
);
```

b.

```
INSERT INTO Call_Record
     ( Customer, Transceivers, Duration )
  SELECT S.Id,
         :pTrCall_Transceivers,
         Period( CURRENT, FOREVER )
   FROM  Subscribers S
  WHERE  S.Security_Check MATCHES :pAudCallers_Spoken_Key;
```

Readers acquainted with relational DBMSs will find these code fragments familiar. The ORDBMS data model is loosely based on the relational data model in Codd (1970). Data are organized into relations, which correspond to classes of facts describing the state of a problem domain. All of the relational model's data integrity and consistency features, such as primary and foreign keys, can be enforced in an ORDBMS schema. The manipulation of data, their retrieval and modification, is handled through a declarative programming language. The most popular of these is SQL, which has recently appeared in its third major standard revision (ANSI 1999b). What distinguishes this revision of SQL from previous incarnations is the way that the basic language may be extended with new TYPES and FUNCTIONS. In fact, Figure 2.3 does not contain a single data type to be found in earlier versions of SQL; and it includes a predicate function, MATCHES, which, while syntactically familiar, is semantically alien. These unfamiliar types and expressions are references to modules of logic running within the ORDBMS. They represent objects of interest within the application domain: names, telephone numbers, geographic points, and audio keys. In the next section, we show how they are created.

2.2.2   Component Standards and Integration

Early ORDBMSs provided proprietary mechanisms to implement these extensions. Most relational DBMS products possessed a database procedural language that could be adapted to the new purpose. And for performance-sensitive tasks, research prototypes, such as Postgres (Stonebraker & Kemnitz 1991) and Starburst (Haas et al. 1990), and commercial systems, such as Illustra (Illustra Information Technologies 1995), INFORMIX (Informix 2000), and IBM's DB2 (Chamberlin 1998), all implemented mechanisms allowing developers to integrate logic programmed using C. C extensibility relies on standard operating system dynamic linking to handle the mechanics of loading and unloading compiled libraries and invoking the functions compiled within them.

In recent times we have seen a rush of component-development standards. Most of these are designed with frameworks other than an ORDBMS in mind. They describe how to implement logic so that it can be linked into other programs in a way that overcomes some of the limitations of the minimal operating system support. For example, Microsoft COM (Box 1998) specifies how to build C++ class libraries in such a way that they can be reused consistently across all Windows platforms. The standard explains how to interrogate a COM class to find out what interface methods the class implements and how they are called. Another popular component standards is the Sun Soft EJB standard. JavaBeans are components written in the Java programming language. The standard describes how to implement a Java class and how to use certain facilities in the Java language environment to get information about what the class consists of.

In this section we provide several examples showing how an ORDBMS can be extended. In order to keep this presentation general we adhere as closely as possible to standard languages and syntax.

Stored Procedure Languages. As we mention earlier, all commercial DBMSs support a proprietary procedural language. These were developed for database procedures, which are a primitive kind of database extensibility. Database procedure languages are attractive to DBMS vendors because their implementation is entirely under the vendor's control. Such languages tend to be simple and robust: They support scoped variables, looping and branching, subprocedure calls, and exception handling. Initially designed as procedural extensions to support complex multistatement transactions, stored procedure languages provide an excellent mechanism for rapidly prototyping component logic.

But stored procedure languages have their drawbacks. They do not execute as quickly as equivalent extensions created using compiled languages. This is because procedural languages are compiled into an intermediate form that is interpreted by a module in the ORDBMS. For

CPU-intensive tasks, interpretation is a slower execution strategy than running machine code generated by native compilers. Also, stored procedures were not designed to be invoked hundreds or thousands of times during query execution. Whereas properly implemented compiled language extensibility allows the engine to invoke an extension through a local procedure call within the engine address space (roughly 100 machine code instructions or 1.0×10^{-8} seconds) invoking stored procedure language interpreters is much more expensive (perhaps 10,000 instructions or 1.0×10^{-5} seconds). This makes stored procedures a poor choice for lightweight extensions that are invoked many times during query processing.

EXAMPLE 2

Figure 2.4 illustrates how a data type such as `Person_Name` from Figure 2.4 might be defined. In it we illustrate how the SQL:99 language standard's CREATE TYPE DDL statement is used to define a data structure and an interface method. Note that the method in this example is called "Equal" and it returns a Boolean result. The ORDBMS can infer from this that the method corresponds to the SQL language operator symbol =.

The biggest drawback to implementing components with stored procedure languages is that you can only run them in a single kind of ORDBMS. Being able to deploy your components elsewhere—in a middleware server, in another DBMS, or in a client user-interface program—is highly desirable.

Compiled Languages (C and C++). Another approach to writing extensions is to use general-purpose programming languages such as C or C++. These languages compile down into object code or assembler,

Figure 2.4 | **Example of component implemented using a stored procedure language.**

```
CREATE TYPE Person_Name AS

(       First_Name   VARCHAR(48)        NOT NULL,

        Surname      VARCHAR(48)        NOT NULL,

        Middle_Name  VARCHAR(48)        NOT NULL,

        Title        CHAR(5)

)

INSTANCE METHOD Equal ( Other_Name Person_Name )

RETURNS BOOLEAN

        RETURN (( Other_Name.First_Name  = this.First_Name) AND

                ( Other_Name.Surname     = this.Surname ) AND

                ( Other_Name.Middle_Name = this.Middle_Name ));

END METHOD;
```

low-level instructions executed in computer hardware. Compiled languages provide the fastest possible execution, and developers using languages such as C or C++ can make use of the functions included with standard language libraries. The SQL:99 language standard refers to this kind of extension as an EXTERNAL FUNCTION.

EXAMPLE 3   Figure 2.5 presents code samples illustrating how implementing such an extension might look.

However, compiled languages have drawbacks of their own. Implementing C or C++ extensions that can be moved easily between ORDBMS instances or used in non-DBMS software frameworks is difficult. Compiled libraries are portable only if you assume a homogenous hardware and operating system environment. For example, we have already mentioned that it is possible to develop components on Microsoft Windows platforms using the COM standard. Other developers

Figure 2.5   **Example of component implemented using a C compiled language.**

```
#include <math.h>

BOOLEAN geo_within  (
      geo_point      *    pGeoPnt,
      geo_circle     *    pGeoCirc,

      /* ORDBMS specific context information */
)
{
      DOUBLE       dx, dy;
      dx = pGeoPnt->X - pGeoCirc->Center.X;
      dy = pGeoPnt->Y - pGeoCirc->Center.Y;

      if (pGeoCirc->radius < sqrt((dx*dx)+(dy*dy)))
            return TRUE;

      return FALSE;
}

CREATE FUNCTION Within (  Geo_Point, Geo_Circle )
RETURNS boolean
EXTERNALNAME'/home/external_routines/Geo.c(geo_within)'
LANGUAGE C;
```

using the same hardware and operating system can reuse the library, but developers using a flavor of UNIX or non-Intel hardware cannot.

Second, illegal operations in compiled programs are difficult for the ORDBMS to recover from gracefully. Such bugs can halt the running server, which is a highly undesirable behavior in systems required to provide high availability. This problem is made worse by the fact that compiled languages such as C and C++ are notoriously hard to work with. The pragmatic solutions to this problem are to isolate the binary object in a separate address space or to test your code exhaustively. The first of these dilutes the performance advantages of using compiled code in the first place, and the second is extremely laborious. Another alternative is to compile safe languages, such as FORTRAN, Perl or LISP, into executable binaries.

Java. Semicompiled languages such as Java have all of the advantages of general-purpose programming languages without some of the drawbacks that accrue from the immobility of compiled code. Java is compiled into a terse, portable format. Java's runtime environment, which is implemented on almost all varieties of hardware and operating systems, is responsible for actually executing this byte-code. More importantly, Java's runtime environment has been designed to work in a broad variety of computer system contexts. In fact, the entire Java execution engine or virtual machine can be linked into the address space of a correctly implemented ORDBMS just like any other compiled library. Then the virtual machine running inside the ORDBMS can load byte-code files and execute them.

EXAMPLE 4

Figure 2.6 illustrates how a Java class is implemented and integrated into the ORDBMS. In this example we follow the SQL-J Part 2 standard, which has recently been combined with the Java DataBase Connectivity (JDBC) standard.

Figure 2.6

Example of component implemented using Java.

```
//
//      File:      PersonName.java
//      About:
//
//      Compile:        javac [ -g ] PersonName.java
//      Create Jar:  jar -cf PersonName.jar PersonName.class
//
import java.sql.*;

public class PersonName implements SQLData
{
```

```
    private String   Surname;
    private String   FirstName;
    private String   TypeName;

    public String getSQLTypeName() { return TypeName; }

    public void readSQL  ( SQLInput stream,
                             String typename )
         throws SQLException
    {
        Surname   = stream.readString();
        FirstName = stream.readString();
        TypeName  = typename;
    }
    public void writeSQL ( SQLOutput stream )
          throws SQLException
    {
      stream.writeString( this.Surname );
      stream.writeString( this.FirstName );
    }
    public static PersonName PersonName (
                                 String  Surname,
                                 String  FirstName )
    {

         PersonName p = new PersonName();
         p.Surname   = Surname;
         p.FirstName = FirstName;
         return p;

    }
}
--  SQL-J extensions to install the .jar, and to use it
--  when you declare a new SQL expression.
--
execute procedure install_jar(
"file:D:\informix\extend\examples\PersonName\PersonName.jar",
"personname_jar");
--
```

continued

```
create function personname ( lvarchar, lvarchar )
returns personname
external name
'personname_jar:PersonName.PersonName(java.lang.String,
                                    java.lang.String )'
language java;
```

Java's greatest virtue is its runtime mobility. Logic implemented in Java can be moved from site to site within a distributed system built using heterogeneous hardware and operating systems. Achieving this in a consistent way is the goal of the JavaBeans standard. The Java-Beans standard is a collection of APIs describing the means by which a JavaBeans instance interacts with its environment and the means by which the environment can find out about the properties of a Java-Beans component.

Single-site ORDBMSs can support all of these component extensibility mechanisms simultaneously. End users submitting a query to the system have no idea how the extension logic they invoke is actually implemented. This abstraction turns out to be doubly useful in the distributed-systems case. As we see later, it means that in a distributed ORDBMS the query-processing module can pick the site location on which the logic is executed based on some optimization goal. Key to this is the system's ability to move both data and logic between nodes.

2.2.3 Query-Processing Overview

All ORDBMS data access is done through queries. There is no low-level record-at-a-time or navigational interface to the objects in the ORDBMS stores. Queries can come from external programs or from logic running inside the ORDBMS that implements an application-level object. (The implementation of a JavaBeans class that corresponds to an application-level object such as Work_Order can run entirely within the ORDBMS. This same class logic can be moved to a client or middleware program. Java code implementing this JavaBean might include SQL queries over a database schema.) So far as the query-processing aspects of the ORDBMS are concerned, there is no difference between queries with external and internal sources. When it receives a SQL expression, the ORDBMS decomposes it into an ordered sequence of low-level operations, called a query plan. Then it executes this plan, returning its results to the software module that submitted the query in the first place.

EXAMPLE 5   Consider the relatively simple query: Show me the ids and size of coverage areas of all transceivers within 13 miles of the geographic point located at longitude –127.513, latitude 35.362, ordered by the size of the coverage area. This is illustrated in Figure 2.7 and might be submitted by an external report writer program. Alternatively, it might be part of some logic implementing an application-level object's constructor. For example, our information system might include an object that corresponds to a service request. Such an object is probably transient. It only exists until the work order is complete. This object's state—which might include the list of transceivers returned by this query—is derived from a series of SQL queries that run against the persistent database. The ORDBMS framework can accommodate this class of object, which is traditionally associated with midtier application servers. And like other kinds of components, application objects can be made mobile within the distributed ORDBMS.

This query will probably be decomposed in the ORDBMS engine into a series of simple operations, shown in Figure 2.8. An approximate translation of this plan is as follows. First, examine the Transceivers table and extract those rows that are located in the circle supplied to the query as an argument. Then strip away the first attribute from these matching rows, adding an additional attribute value by executing some logic over ST_POLYGON data in the Service_Range attribute. Finally, order the resulting rows using the values in that second, computed attribute.

Figure 2.7   **Simple ORDBMS query.**

```
SELECT T.Id,
       Area ( T.Service_Range ) AS Area
  FROM Transceivers T
 WHERE Within ( T.Location,
                Circle ( -127.513, 35.362, '13 Miles' ) )
 ORDER BY 2;
```

Figure 2.8   **Plan illustrating decomposition of query in Figure 2.7 into discrete operations.**

1. RESTRICT [Transceivers, Within (Location, Circle (–127.513, 35.362, '13 Miles'))]
2. PROJECT [1, < Id, Area (Service_Range) >]
3. SORT [2, 2]

The automatic decomposition of declarative queries into this kind of plan is the key to understanding how relational and object-relational engines work. In Table 2.1, we present an incomplete list of the low-level data management operations implemented in DBMS engines.

Table 2.1 **Several data management operations implemented in RDBMSs and ORDBMSs.**

Abstract Operation Name	Algorithms Used
RESTRICT (Input_Data, Boolean_Expression)	Table scan
	Index scan
PROJECT (Input_Data, Column_List)	Restrict
JOIN (Input_Data, Input_Data, Boolean_Expression)	Nest loop
	Merge join
	Hash join
SORT (Input_Data, Column_List)	Various sorting algorithms

They all take as input at least one set of row data, and all of them return a set of row data as a result. The results of one operation can become the input to another. An important goal for vendors and academic researchers working in DBMS is to create efficient algorithms to implement these operations.

What distinguishes relational DBMS (RDBMS) from ORDBMS engines is the way that these low-level operations are generalized in the ORDBMSs. For example, the query in Example 5 and Figure 2.7 requires that the ORDBMS sort its results according to coverage area (step 3 in Figure 2.8). Strictly speaking, measurements of area combine quantities (number values) and units (square miles or square kilometers or square degrees). Such objects cannot be represented directly with a single built-in SQL-92-data type. Information systems that use SQL-92-style RDBMSs rely on application logic in an external program to convert each user's data entry into a consistent form for storage. The problem is that each new application using this data must re-implement the conversion logic, and bug fixes, upgrades, and evolutionary changes to the system's functionality are thereby made more difficult. A better solution is to create a component to encapsulate area data and the operations over it (for example, a JavaBean or COM object) and to embed this in the ORDBMS.

To clarify what we mean by generalized, let us look more closely at the SORT operation. Algorithms used to sort data are almost all looping and branching constructs around two operations: swap and compare (Knuth 1998). The ORDBMS knows the size of each object, so swapping them is straightforward. To sort a set of component instances, the ORDBMS requires that the component's developer supply the compare logic to tell it if one instance of the object is less than, equal to, or greater than another. Based on what this logic reports, the ORDBMS's sort algorithms can take the appropriate action (swapping or not swapping them). All of the data management operations supported by the ORDBMS—access methods such as B-trees, client-server communication, and page management—can be generalized in this way.

Metadata is the key to supporting this kind of functionality. Traditional RDBMSs stored information about database schema objects such as tables, columns, and indices in a special set of tables called system catalogues. This information was used by SQL-92 RDBMSs to identify what data (table and column) a query was addressing. An ORDBMS's system catalogues include additional tables storing information about whatever components it manages: the size of their persistent form in bytes (or whether they are of a variable length), the logic that can be applied to them, and information about how this logic is best handled in a query. Parsing in an ORDBMS is therefore considerably more sophisticated than in an RDBMS. Data structures used to represent operations in query plans include substructures containing references to the component's C, C++, or Java code to be invoked in the generalized RESTRICT, JOIN, or SORT operations. As it parses a query the ORDBMS populates these structures with appropriate values.

System catalogues document all of a database's contents. They can be used to reconstruct entire schema definitions and to answer questions such as

- What interface methods can be applied to ST_POINT object instances?
- What other entities in the schema can be combined with Transceivers (what other tables have columns of component types also present in the Transceivers table)?

This reliance on query-able system catalogues is another way in which an ORDBMS can be distinguished from other component frameworks. And it provides a valuable resource in the distributed ORDBMS. Modules of programming logic can be updated or upgraded, and new modules added to a running system without bringing the whole system down.

2.2.4   ORDBMS Query Optimization

ORDBMS query processing is based on classic RDBMS techniques. Query expressions are parsed into a set of data structures, each of which corresponds to a data management operation of the kind in Table 2.1. An important property of these operations is that they may be re-arranged, subject to certain rules, without affecting their result. Although each arrangement is equivalent with respect to the result, they are not necessarily equal with respect to the computational resources they consume. This means that the ORDBMS is free to examine every alternative arrangement and to pick the one it estimates is best according to some optimization goal—usually whichever plan consumes the least resources or returns a result the most quickly. In this section we explore how this is done in more detail.

It is useful to introduce some semiformal notation when reasoning about query plans. One of the better ways to visualize physical query-execution plans is using trees. The lowest level nodes of the tree represent the ultimate data sources (tables). Within each node of the tree, input data is subjected to some processing to produce some output. Note that these nodes correspond to the operations introduced in Table 2.1. Nodes in the higher levels of the tree represent operations that consume data produced by lower nodes. Edges connecting nodes in the tree represent data flowing from the ultimate data sources upward to the single result node.

EXAMPLE 6

For example, consider the query: Show me the name and all calls longer than an hour for subscribers living in California. This is illustrated in Figure 2.9.

Figure 2.10 presents three alternative physical plans to compute the results of the query. Plans A and B swap the inner and outer data source as they feed into the join. Depending on the circumstances—the number of rows passing through the filters from S and C—either plan might be preferable. If the number of rows passed through the "Contains (California, S.LivesAt)" filter is large, and the number of rows passed through the "Length (C.Duration) > 1 HOUR" filter is small, then plan B will probably outperform plan A because the ORDBMS can cache the smaller amount of data in memory as it reads in all the rows stored on disk from the larger.

Figure 2.9 | **Query.**

```
SELECT   S.Name,
         C.Duration
  FROM   Subscribers S, Call_History C
 WHERE   C.Subscriber = S.Id
   AND   Length( C.Duration ) > 1 HOUR
   AND   Contains ('California'::ST_POLYGON, S.LivesAt);
```

To pick the best plan among the alternatives, RDBMSs calculate a cost for each of them according to a cost function. For single-site RDBMSs, the most common approach is to calculate the total computational resources consumed by the query as follows.

Total_Cost = CPU_Cost + I/O_Cost

I/O_Cost = Data_Page_Disk_I/Os * I/O_Weighting

CPU_Cost = Tuples_Processed * CPU_Weighting

Figure 2.10

Alternative query plans for query in Figure 2.9.

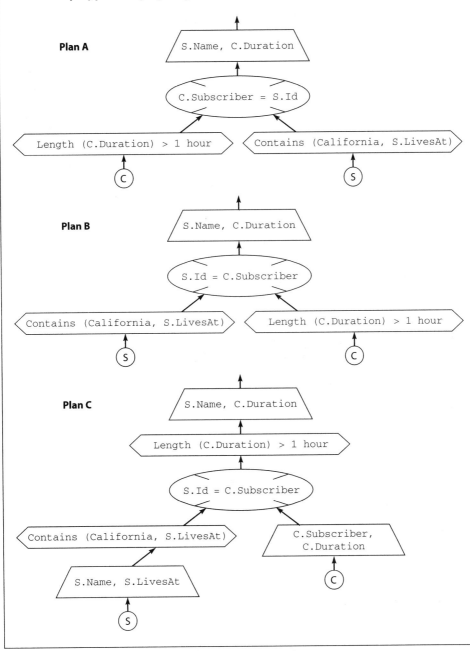

For each plan, the total cost can be computed by aggregating the costs for each suboperation. This cost is at best an accurate estimate of the real cost of the query. Factors such as the amount of memory the

DBMS can use and the weightings assigned to I/O and CPU costs affect the outcome of the query-planning phase.

ORDBMS optimizers modify and extend these techniques in several ways. These modifications amount to a generalization of RDBMS techniques. The basic problem is that RDBMS optimizers make a set of assumptions that are highly unrealistic in ORDBMS databases. For instance, in plan C (Figure 2.10), we defer executing the Length() predicate to the very end. In this particular case, such a plan makes little sense. Length(PERIOD) is a relatively inexpensive operation (i.e., it consumes few CPU resources) and in this query it is likely to dramatically reduce the number of records read from the Call_History table. RDBMS optimizers assume that the CPU and I/O cost of processing each tuple is equivalent. In Example 6, an unmodified RDBMS optimizer would assume that Length(PERIOD) and Contains (ST_POINT, ST_POLYGON) use an equal amount of computer resources. But in an extensible DBMS, the user-defined logic of the kind implementing Length() might consume considerable CPU and memory resources. In addition, the data object to which the logic is applied might be very large, which means it will incur additional I/O costs. Clearly, ORDBMSs optimizers must handle extension logic with care.

Suppose the Duration attribute did not store 16-byte Period objects, but was in fact a digital recording of the entire call. Length() might compute the time during which there was an active conversation going on in a call by examining the recording and counting up the seconds of nonwhite noise. Intuitively, an ORDBMS performing this query should try to minimize the number of times the Length() logic is invoked because this is computationally expensive and each time it is invoked a large data object must be read from disk. This insight has led to techniques referred to as expensive predicate migration (Hellerstein & Stonebraker 1993). An ORDBMS optimizer needs to be informed about the relative cost of each extension. Knowing that Length() is expensive will mitigate against plans A and B because they invoke the expensive Length() logic for every row in the Call_History table. Under these circumstances, plan C might make the most sense.

This leads to a modification of the previous formulas. If each query includes n expressions, then calculating the total cost for a query requires something similar to the following.

$$\text{I/O\_Cost} = \text{I/O\_Weight} * (\text{Data\_Page\_Disk\_I/Os} +$$
$$\Sigma_n (\text{Expression\_I/O\_Cost}_I * \text{Number\_of\_Invocations}_I))$$
$$\text{CPU\_Cost} = \text{CPU\_Weight} *$$
$$\Sigma_n (\text{Expression\_CPU\_Cost}_I * \text{Number\_of\_Invocations}_I)$$

That is, rather than simply assuming that each expression has an invariant CPU cost and no additional disk I/O cost, an ORDBMS optimizer must cater to the diverse possibilities implied by running user-defined extension logic in the engine. In certain ORDBMS applications, I/O and CPU within extensions dwarf the costs of traditional tuple-oriented query processing.

Second, the ORDBMS cannot determine the cost of alternative query plans accurately without help. Consider the join operation that appears in each plan in Figure 2.10. As we have mentioned earlier, one efficient way to compute the answer to this query is to read all of the rows from the smaller data set into memory and scan these cached rows for matches as each row is read once from the larger one. (Note than in ORDBMSs, where join predicates are frequently expressions other than the ordinal operators <, <=, =, and so on, this nested-loop join algorithm is quite popular.) But which data set is the smaller one? As another example, consider the problem of deciding whether or not to use an index. If a predicate does not identify only a few rows in a table, then the ORDBMS will read the majority of the index data and the majority of the table data from disk. It might be better simply to scan all of the table data in this case.

RDBMSs store information about data sources (such as row counts and row sizes) in system catalogues. Sophisticated RDBMSs also store a statistical characterization of the data in each table's columns, usually a range of values (Selinger et al. 1979) or a frequency histogram. An RDBMS optimizer can use this information to estimate what proportion of rows a query predicate will filter out. We call this selectivity estimation. Enormous efforts have been made to improve the performance and accuracy of these techniques for SQL's built-in data types. But in an ORDBMS, the optimizer needs a mechanism to estimate selectivity for the user-defined logic in predicates, so the ORDBMS allows developers implementing the extensions to integrate logic that creates a statistical characterization of the data in a column and code that lets the optimizer estimate an expression's selectivity based on this characterization.

Developers can register support functions, such as the per-function call costs, and selectivity estimators when they integrate their components into the ORDBMS. In terms more familiar to object-oriented software engineering, support functions are interface templates that generally remain private for the use of the ORDBMS. Other examples of support functions include mechanisms to copy data to a neutral format for backup and to send and receive data value instances across a network.

2.2.5 Internal Architecture of ORDBMS

Once it has decided on a query plan, the ORDBMS's final task is to execute each of the plan's operations in the appropriate order and return the results to the user who submitted the query. Sometimes the interval of time between when a query is submitted to the ORDBMS and when it is executed can be considerable. Queries can be prepared long before the query's results are requested. This fact encourages us to divide the ORDBMS into two functional halves. The first, top half of the ORDBMS engine is responsible for the query-processing tasks described in the previous few sections: parsing the query string into an internal form, optimizing this internal form into a plan, and scheduling the execution of the optimized plan. The second, lower half of the ORDBMS is responsible for each of the low-level data management operations such as RESTRICT, JOIN, and SORT. As it executes each of the operations in a query plan, the ORDBMS's top half calls upon facilities implemented in the lower half, such as buffer management (I/O and caching); transaction support (locking, logging, etc.); and scheduling, memory management, and other low-level operations.

Looking at the ORDBMS in this way highlights the extent of the changes needed to transform an RDBMS into an ORDBMS. All of the functional components labeled in Figure 2.11 must be generalized in the same way that the ORDBMS's sorting algorithms are generalized. Over and above these modifications, managing certain kinds of components efficiently makes it necessary to add to the list of data management algorithms and techniques in the engine. For example, indexing spatial data requires something like an R-tree (Guttman 1984), and recently several researchers have developed algorithms to compute joins over spatial data that are more efficient than the simple nest loop (Patel & DeWitt 1996). Further, joins involving expensive predicates make the case for techniques such as join indices (Valduriez 1987) more compelling than it was for SQL-92 DBMSs.

Figure 2.11 | **Internal architecture of ORDBMS.**

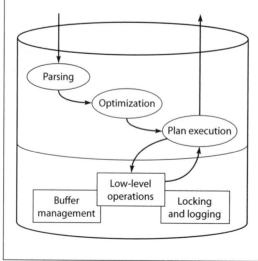

2.2.6   Function Manager

An important objective of ORDBMS engineering is to provide equivalent support for all component extensibility mechanisms. In other words, we wish to create a system where end users are unaware of how the extensions specified in their queries are actually implemented. For example, the query in Example 1 and Figure 2.3 includes SQL expressions that invoke the Period constructor and logic that compares audio keys. These might be implemented using any of the mechanisms introduced in Section 2.2.2: stored procedure language, C, Java, or a COM library. Such agnosticism is highly desirable from a commercial point of view. It gives customers and developers freedom of choice. In certain, homogenous hardware environments, COM or C might be preferred, but when the code must be mobile—for example, when it might make sense to push the audio-key comparison down into the handheld device—languages such as Java have their advantages.

Achieving this agnosticism requires that the ORDBMS include an internal facility for managing the dispatch (invocation) of extension logic and an associated mechanism to add different language environments to the ORDBMS. Such facilities need to be quite sophisticated. For example, programming logic routinely requires blocks of memory for its private use, but letting an integrated component acquire memory directly from the operating system creates problems for the ORDBMS. When an exception causes a transaction to roll back, the ORDBMS should clean up any memory allocated for the temporary use of any logic invoked in the query. But this is impossible if the ORDBMS has no record of what was allocated in the first place. Inevitably, this leads to memory leaks and system instability. Other resources traditionally provided to programs by the operating system—file management, interprocess communication, scheduling, and exception handling—face similar problems.

Operating system techniques for memory management, scheduling, and exception handling can be adapted for use in the ORDBMS, and the functionality of common system calls can be implemented by the ORDBMS itself. Dynamic linking resolves any references made to these services from within compiled libraries. Such low-level plumbing can in turn be used to provide support for environments such as Java's virtual machine because these language environments are designed to be fairly neutral with respect to the operating system context in which they are deployed. An ORDBMS language manager needs to map any operating system calls that such environments make to their ORDBMS equivalents. Thus, whenever the on-board Java virtual machine asks for memory, it receives it from the ORDBMS (rather than from the operating system). In addition, the ORDBMS needs to know what low-level facilities in the new environment it must invoke to perform tasks such as data value conversion, logic invocation, and return results locating.

Figure 2.12 | **Illustration of function manager and language manager.**

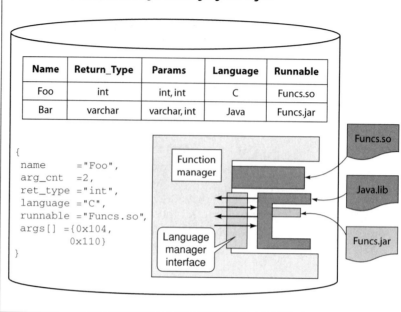

Name	Return_Type	Params	Language	Runnable
Foo	int	int, int	C	Funcs.so
Bar	varchar	varchar, int	Java	Funcs.jar

```
{
  name     ="Foo",
  arg_cnt  =2,
  ret_type ="int",
  language ="C",
  runnable ="Funcs.so",
  args[]   ={0x104,
            0x110}
}
```

We illustrate these ideas in Figure 2.12. Dark gray represents binary objects. These can be linked to the ORDBMS's function manager using the operating system dynamic-linking mechanisms. If the binary object itself implements a language environment—as the Java.lib file does in this figure—then appropriate entry points within it must be identified for the language manager interface. The lighter gray object is a Java archive or jar file. In the diagram, we show it being loaded into the Java language environment using standard Java techniques. When the function manager seeks to invoke some logic implemented in Java, it does so through the language manager. When the Java environment requires resources, these are made available from the ORDBMS.

The ability to link compiled binary files into the ORDBMS, to allow the code in those files to access the kinds of resources they need, and to invoke the logic within these files is the most fundamental aspect of ORDBMS engineering. Generalized algorithms for performing RDBMS operations can use logic written to address a specific problem domain. Once achieved, this becomes the foundation on which the other features of the engine can be built.

2.3 Distributed Component DBMSs

In this section we describe how to modify a single-site ORDBMS to make it work across a network of computers. With distributed

ORDBMSs we face many of the same challenges as with distributed RDBMSs: How do we ensure transactional guarantees for distributed operations?; How do we present users with a global schema name space while providing for local autonomy?; and How do we optimize queries that require data movement over the network? In addition, a distributed ORDBMS must address a set of challenges that are the consequence of introducing programmatic, user-defined extensions into the data model. Depending on how it is implemented, extension logic may be mobile (which means it can be copied across the network to wherever it makes the most sense to invoke it) or fixed (which means it can be run only on a particular node of the distributed system). Distributed RDBMS products can assume that every node in the system has identical functionality or, in the case of a federation of different RDBMS products, very similar (i.e., mapable) functionality. But with a distributed component DBMS, each node might contain disjoint sets of component extensions.

Fortunately, many of the mechanisms developed for distributed data management in RDBMSs can also be applied in distributed ORDBMSs. For example, the theoretical models and engineering techniques used to implement distributed transactions can be reused. Therefore, we focus our attention here on topics related to query processing rather than lower-level data management. Also, we assume that within our distributed ORDBMS the same server software runs at each site; that is, we ignore the multidatabase problem. It is certainly feasible to use gateways and a variety of user-defined access methods (see later) to build a federated or multidatabase system using an ORDBMS. But such systems can be thought of as constrained cases of the more ideal designs we describe in this section. In addition, many multidatabase vendors require that developers run an instance of the vendor's software as a co-server adjacent to the system being federated (Cohera 1999) converting the overall system into a homogeneous distributed ORDBMS.

To investigate these ideas, we modify our cellular network example slightly by running it over three nodes arranged in a fashion similar to that shown in Figure 2.1. We use the site names Billing, Foundation, and History when referring to these nodes. Each entity in Figure 2.2 is stored on separate nodes: Transceivers (T) is stored on Foundation, Call_History (C) is stored on History, and Subscribers (S) is stored on Billing. Certain operations are limited to single nodes in the system. For example, adding new subscribers inserts a row in the Subscribers table on Billing. Other operations, such as the query in Example 1 and Figure 2.3, mix data and operations from different nodes. We illustrate this configuration in Figure 2.13.

Figure 2.13

Distributed query processing flows.

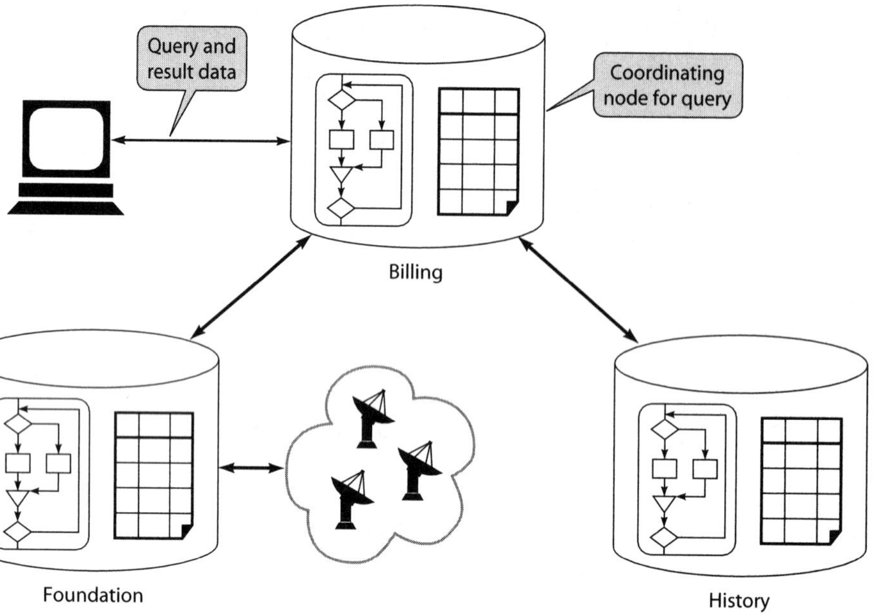

2.3.1 Overview of Query Processing in Distributed ORDBMS

Distributed ORDBMSs adopt the same query-processing strategy as distributed RDBMS (Özsu & Valduriez 1999). Each node in the system connects to the other nodes with which it interacts. These connections are used to exchange messages and data between nodes. The client-server infrastructure developed to transfer SQL queries and data between the DBMS and external programs can be reused for this purpose. Creating these connections can take several seconds, and each connection requires a significant amount of main memory for data buffering and state management. To limit the resources they are consuming, ORDBMS nodes typically maintain a pool of several open connections to other sites that are shared among locally connected users. For example, we might have several hundred users connected to the Billing node multiplexed over 10 or 20 connections to the History and Foundation nodes.

Users submit their distributed queries to a local node, which becomes the coordinating node for all the subsequent activity. The coordinating node parses the query and prepares an execution plan that may involve several subordinate (remote) nodes. At parsing time, the local node resolves names in the global schema name-space into references to shared data or logic.

Producing the physical plan requires that the coordinating node access metadata describing things such as the amount of data in tables, the selectivity and computational cost of user-defined logic, and whether a module of logic can be moved between sites. Based on this information, the ORDBMS can evaluate a list of possible query plans and pick the one that consumes the least resources. When the query is executed, the nodes involved in the query plan each performs its localized task, passing its results back to the coordinating node. As all of the distributed query's subtasks are completed, the data they produce are combined on the local node, and the query's results are passed back to the user.

This description should not surprise readers familiar with distributed RDBMS technology. However, because a distributed ORDBMS is a framework for both logic and data, it can be deployed in configurations that are quite different from what was typical for distributed RDBMSs. Most distributed RDBMS applications typically involve a few—almost always fewer than 10—large DBMS instances. The application logic applied to this data is embedded in client-side programs or midtier application servers. Because the ORDBMS can host embedded logic, it is possible to replace many of these midtier programs with ORDBMS instances. These probably store very little data, although they can cache intermediate results and the state of transient objects. We illustrate this kind of distributed architecture in Figure 2.14. With this approach the overall system can scale extremely well in terms of the number of simultaneously connected users and the total amount of data that a user's query may address. Application servers and TP monitors use a similar strategy to achieve the same goal. In fact, there is little difference between the functionality of a single-site node in an ORDBMS that stores no data but embeds component logic and a server in one of the more conventional middleware systems. Both are scalable data-processing frameworks with external APIs, security services, and support for distributed transactions. They provide connectivity management to a variety of distributed data management services. And both permit the integration of software modules that do work involving multiple sites. Further, the techniques used in these systems (e.g., queues and transactional messaging; Gray & Reuter 1992), can be incorporated in the ORDBMS and used to sustain performance and reliability behind the data model and query language abstraction.

The chief difference is that using distributed ORDBMS in this way provides a declarative query language interface in the midtier in addition to these other facilities. Unlike conventional application servers or client programs, these midtier ORDBMS nodes can take advantage of SQL query-processing techniques to improve developer productivity and overall performance. It is impossible, for example, to use a graphical report writer with a TP monitor or application server middleware. However, it is perfectly possible with a distributed ORDBMS. Developers building applications that are amenable to being handled in

Figure 2.14

Architectural alternative for distributed ORDBMS.

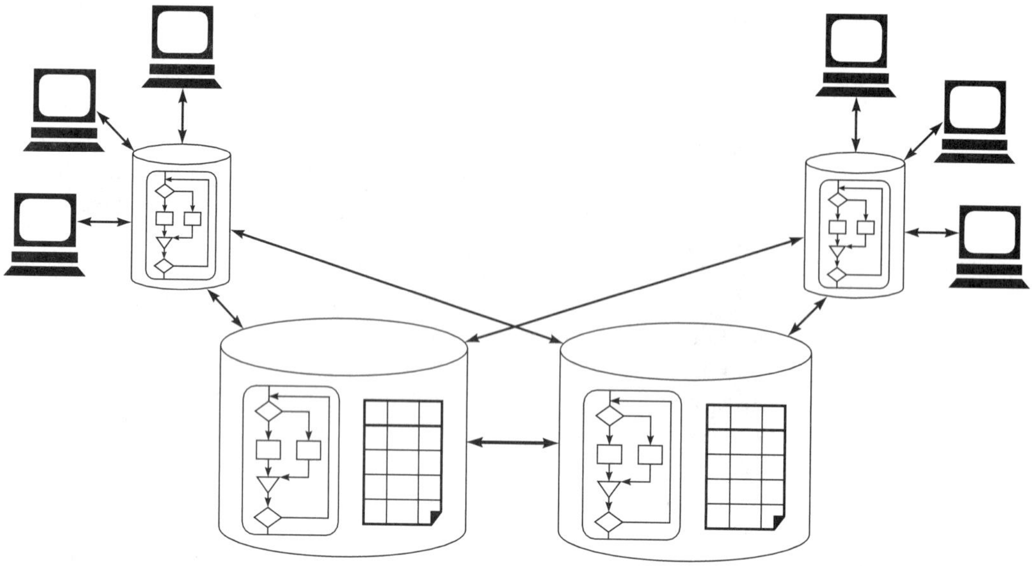

parallel—e-commerce web sites selling goods and services from a cata-logue or making markets—could make most immediate use of such architectures. Each web-server machine could store a replicated copy of shared data and could record offers, bids, and sales independently. A single point of failure is thereby avoided. Global queries can be han-dled using distributed query-processing techniques.

2.3.2 Distributed Extensions to SQL

In distributed RDBMSs, the SQL language is modified by adding site names to schema object names. Schema objects in a distributed sys-tem—tables, views, and expressions referencing component logic—are fully named by a combination of their site-local name and the name of the site from which they originate. If an object name is not fully quali-fied, then the local site name is substituted by default. At first glance this would seem to be contrary to the objective of location transpar-ency because developers will need to know the site on which an object resides when they write queries. But this strategy is a necessary com-promise between location transparency and the need for local site autonomy. Creating a global name-space might imply unacceptable limitations on local site policies.

In distributed RDBMS products, this technique was applied to nam-ing tables and views. In distributed ORDBMSs it is also applied to component logic. This allows an extension integrated into one site to be referenced from all other connected sites.

EXAMPLE 7 | The queries we introduced in Example 1 (Figure 2.3b) and Example 5 (Figure 2.7) are represented in the distributed system as shown in Figure 2.15.

If location transparency is desired, it can be achieved with synonym or alias techniques. These associate each fully named schema object with a unique, site-local label. If a single global name-space is desired—for example, if the distributed system allows for the mobility of application-level objects between nodes—these alias mappings must be identical on every site. Thus every node in the example system in Example 7 and Figure 2.15 would use an alias to associate a local label Subscribers with the global table name Subscribers@Billing. Properly administered, this would permit us to replace the queries in Example 7 and Figure 2.15 with their original versions. Regardless of which node in our distributed system these queries were submitted to, consistent synonym mapping would ensure that the same data and logic were always invoked. Parsers on each node can detect errors and ambiguities in queries, and distributed ORDBMS vendors provide utilities to detect inconsistencies between sites.

Figure 2.15 | **Using fully qualified object names in distributed ORDBMSs.**

a.

```
INSERT  INTO Call_History@History
        ( Customer, Transceivers, Duration )
   SELECT   S.Id,
            :pTrCall_Transceivers,
            Period@History ( CURRENT, FOREVER )
     FROM   Subscribers@Billing S
    WHERE   Matches@Billing (S.Security_Check,
            :pAudCallers_Spoken_Key);
```

b.

```
SELECT  T.Id,
        Area@Foundation ( T.Service_Range ) AS Area
   FROM Transceivers@Foundation T
  WHERE Within@Foundation ( T.Location, Circle@Foundation
                            (-127.513,35.362,'13 Miles')
                          )
  ORDER  BY 2;
```

As we show earlier in this chapter, the key to ORDBMS query processing is metadata. When it receives a query, the local ORDBMS needs to create an efficient schedule of operations to compute an answer. In distributed ORDBMSs, a local site might need to access information about data and logic residing on multiple remote sites. At the very least, the coordinating node needs to verify that certain objects actually exist, and that it has permission to access them. In more advanced systems, it might also be able to discover a locally available version of some component logic or a copy of some data replicated from its original site.

Proposals for managing distributed catalogues include centralizing all catalogue information in a canonical store, replicating it among all participating sites, or performing remote lookups at the time that queries are received at the coordinating node. All of these approaches are deficient in some way. The first two techniques require that changes to local sites be propagated to the central store or broadcast to the entire set of inter-connected sites. This turns every local DDL statement into a distributed transaction and implies an explosion in the number of messages as the number of sites increases. However, reading from remote catalogues each time a query is parsed and optimized makes query compilation more expensive.

In practice, different distributed relational systems have adopted different strategies. Many research systems and early commercial systems opted for globally replicated schema because, it was reasoned, schema changes were relatively rare events. However, in distributed ORDBMSs there is a greater variety and number of schema objects, and application development calls for fairly regular upgrades and additions of new components. Both of these indicate that the frequency of schema changes in distributed ORDBMSs will be higher and argue for the parse-time remote lookup strategy (Hong 1993).

It should be emphasized that so far we have only considered the problem of object naming. The fact that a site name is included in the query specification does not imply that that is the site on which the named logic is actually run. In the first place, an equivalent implementation of the function might be available on another node (this equivalency needs to be noted in the system catalogues). Moving data to that node and invoking the specified logic there might be a better way to process the query. And second, as we mention earlier in this chapter, distributed ORDBMSs can co-opt component technologies to move the implementation of component logic among nodes of the system. Decisions about where the named logic is actually invoked for some data can be deferred to later in the query processing. The principle of location transparency applies not only to where the distributed system's data are located, but also to where the logic specified in a query statement is actually run.

2.3.3   **Query Processing in Distributed ORDBMSs**

Although it adopts the same basic strategy, distributed query planning is considerably more complex than the same task in a single site. Distributed queries are compiled into schedules of lower-level operations, just like single-site queries. And these schedules can be re-arranged, subject to certain rules, into more or less computationally efficient plans. The extra complexity of distributed query planning is due to the physical dispersal of data and logic. When a query addresses data and logic on two machines, then the only way to answer the query is to bring the data and logic together on one of them. But which one? To answer this question, a distributed optimizer must consider the overhead of moving data across a network when it determines the costs for each alternative query plan.

Networking overhead can be modeled by assigning a cost to each edge of the query-execution plan trees we introduced in Section 2.2.4. This cost factor is estimated by calculating the volume of data moving along the edge. As in the single-site case, the total cost of a distributed query plan can be found by aggregating the costs of each suboperation in the plan and including the cost of the edges. Distributed RDBMS optimizers use a similar approach. An important difference between distributed RDBMS optimizers and distributed ORDBMSs is that the data management costs of user-defined objects must also be considered, for much the same reasons as single-site ORDBMSs (see Section 2.2.4). If a distributed query includes n instances of user-defined logic, the cost of a distributed ORDBMS query can be calculated as follows.

$$\text{Total\_Cost} = \text{CPU\_Cost} + \text{I/O\_Cost} + \text{Network\_Cost}$$

$$\text{I/O\_Cost} = \text{I/O\_Weight} * (\text{Table\_Data\_Disk\_I/Os} + \sum_n (\text{Expression\_I/O\_Cost}_I * \text{Number\_of\_Invocations}_I))$$

$$\text{CPU\_Cost} = \text{CPU\_Weight} * \sum_n (\text{Expression\_CPU\_Cost}_I * \text{Number\_of\_Invocations}_I)$$

$$\text{Network\_Cost} = \text{Network\_Weight} * (\text{Message\_Transfers} + \text{Data\_Transfers} + \sum_n (\text{Expression\_Data\_Size}_I * \text{Number\_of\_Invocations}_I))$$

In simple distributed ORDBMSs, the coordinating node's optimizer prepares an initial query plan using single-site techniques; then a special module within the coordinating node determines the most efficient data movement strategy given this plan. This first phase of query processing is sometimes referred to as global optimization. At runtime, the query plan's distributed operations are forwarded to the appropriate remote sites. Remote operations are often entire SQL queries that each site is free to optimize according to local priorities. To understand why this works, recall that the result of a SQL query is a set of rows and columns that looks much like a table. Internal to the coordinating node, the entire remote SELECT query can be treated as though it were a scan of a local table. This second phase of a distributed query is sometimes called local optimization, because its scope is typically contained within a single node.

EXAMPLE 8

To explain these ideas in more detail, consider the query: What are the billing line-items for each subscriber in the 555 area code for calls over the last month? It joins data from two sites and invokes component logic on both of them. Let us assume that this query is submitted at the Billing node. This is illustrated in Figure 2.16.

As it parses this query, the coordinating node at Billing identifies what data are local, what data are remote, and what logic can run on which sites. But it ignores this information until it considers what work to pass to the remote History node. In this case, there are (at least) two possibilities: The coordinating node can retrieve all of the matching Call_History records from the History node or it can request each subscriber's matching records as it needs them. We illustrate these alternatives using the trees in Figure 2.17.

When it arrives on the History node either of the queries we show in bubbles is parsed, optimized, and executed at that local site. This allows the distributed ORDBMS to take advantage of each local node's physical configuration. Then the result of the query is returned to the coordinating node, where it can be treated as if it came from a local table. Such a strategy is extremely flexible. If the ORDBMS optimizer is clever enough, it can even make use of SQL features such as ORDER BY and SELECT DISTINCT to employ more sophisticated join algorithms on the coordinating node. Queries passed to remote nodes can be relatively simple, single-table lookups or elaborate multitable joins.

Figure 2.16 | **Join query in distributed ORDBMS.**

```
SELECT    S.Name,
          Calculate_Billing_Line_Item@History ( C.Duration )
   FROM   Subscribers@Billing S,
          Call_History@History C
  WHERE   C.Subscriber = S.Id
    AND   Contains (Start@History ( C.Duration ),
              Period@History ('LAST MONTH'))
    AND   AreaCode@Billing ( S.Id ) = '555';
```

Other factors complicate distributed query planning. Distributed ORDBMSs needs to cope with the fact that, in contrast to distributed RDBMSs, some logical query plans are physically impossible because not all logic can run at all sites. If the temporal Contains() restriction cannot be run on the History node, then neither of these plans is possi-

Figure 2.17

Query plans for distributed join query in Figure 2.16.

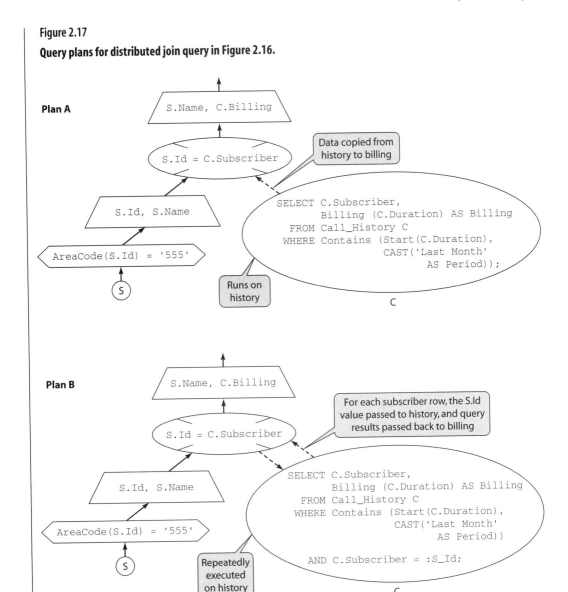

ble. We say that, as the optimizer evaluates the query-plan alternatives in its plan space, it must be able to detect such impossible plans and ignore them. Later in this section we see how this affects the information that the ORDBMS must keep about extension logic.

2.3.4 External Storage Interfaces

Unlike the situation with RDBMSs, data accessed through an ORDBMS need not be stored in a database. It has been observed that less than

20% of the data on which modern organizations depend is stored in structured repositories. The rest is found in personal computer file formats or in legacy applications where the data management and programming logic are tightly intertwined. In addition, organizations are increasingly making use of network and wireless connectivity to deploy command and control systems to monitor real-world environmental conditions. Distributed ORDBMSs provide the means whereby external data and processes may be integrated within the database and accessed using its query language. We illustrate this later in Figure 2.20 by showing access to the actual transceiver devices integrated into the Foundation schema. Because the query language represents the only means by which data in these systems is manipulated, these external data appear in the schema as a table.

There are obvious business advantages to integrating the spreadsheets on which sales forecasting is done into a business's financial management systems. But other possibilities present themselves. In our cellular network application, it would be useful to create an interface to data that is essentially transient—current calls. Current call data—literally the calls in progress at the moment that this information is wanted—lists the calling subscriber, transceiver, and current signal strength.

EXAMPLE 9

Current call data might be used in the query: What is the average signal strength of current calls by each transceiver? This is illustrated in Figure 2.18.

Figure 2.18

Query using external data source for analysis.

```
SELECT C.Transceivers,
       AVG( C.Signal_Strength )
  FROM Current_Calls C
 GROUP BY C.Transceivers;
```

In Figure 2.11, we present the internal architecture of a DBMS. This allows us to explain how extension components interact with the various modules making up the engine. But a more radical possibility presents itself. In an extensible DBMS, it is possible to replace one of these modules entirely.

EXAMPLE 10

Consider the query plan introduced in Example 5 and Figure 2.8. In the simplest case, the first of these operations (the restriction) needs to examine each of the rows in the Subscribers table. Such a facility might be implemented as shown in Figure 2.19.

By implementing the routines shown in bold, a developer can create an interface that makes an external data source available in the database. That is, instead of calling the engine's built-in implementation of OpenTable, BeginScan, and so on (which use the buffering and storage management facilities built into the ORDBMS), the ORDBMS instead invokes logic implemented by a developer. This logic can access external data using file management or interprocess communication facilities. So far as the rest of the engine is concerned, it has no idea how the data it is processing is stored. Such an interface provides a very flexible, lowest-common-denominator way to access external data. It provides an ideal mechanism for unstructured data and data stored in nonrelational data stores because it allows a developer to use procedural code to unravel non-normalized data structures.

Figure 2.19 | **Pseudocode for restriction operation.**

```
Function Restriction (
STRING              TableName,
PREDICATE           Predicate
)
{
     TABLE_DESCRIPTION          Table;
     SCAN_DESCRIPTION           Scan;
     ROW                        Record;

     Table   :=  OpenTable(TableName);
     Scan    :=  BeginScan(Table);
     while (( Record := GetNext(Scan)) != END_OF_SCAN)
     {
         if  Check_Predicate ( Record, Predicate ) == TRUE
         {
             Add_Row_to_Result_List ( Record );
         }
     }
     EndScan(Scan);
     CloseTable(Table);
}
```

It is useful to think of the implementation of these external data interfaces as creating new kinds of access methods (in addition to the ORDBMS's built-in heap, B-tree, hash, and R-tree access methods).

EXAMPLE 11

Figure 2.20 illustrates how to use a SQL data definition statement to create a new access method, and then use it in the declaration of a table. Within the body of this declaration, various aspects of the access method interface (appearing on the left) are associated with their respective user-defined functions (named on the right). Figure 2.20 illustrates how write operations—UPDATE, INSERTs, and DELETEs—can also be incorporated in this abstraction. In practical terms, you might use the DELETE operation to terminate a cellular phone call in progress. This mapping is stored in the ORDBMS's system catalogues.

The second statement in Figure 2.20 illustrates how the new access method may be employed. Current_Calls is the table presenting the external data within the schema. Queries with Current_Calls invoke the user-defined routines specified in the CREATE ACCESS METHOD statement, instead of the ORDBMS's built-in methods. Access methods may even be parameterized. Parameter values such as the machine-port combination used here are made available to the extension logic. Therefore, the same access method logic may be used to implement interfaces to multiple, different external data instances.

Figure 2.20 | **SQL data definition statements for user-defined access method.**

```
CREATE PRIMARY ACCESS_METHOD Transceivers_Access (

    am_create          =   Transceivers_create_access,

    am_open            =   Transceivers_open_access,

    am_close           =   Transceivers_close_access,

    am_beginscan       =   Transceivers_beginscan,

    am_endscan         =   Transceivers_endscan,

    am_getnext         =   Transceivers_getnext,

    am_delete          =   call_hangup,

    am_perscan_cost    =   Transceivers_latency
);


CREATE TABLE Current_Calls (

    Transceivers        Transceivers_Id   NOT NULL,
    Subscriber          Phone_Number      NOT NULL,
    Signal_Strength     FLOAT             NOT NULL
)

USING ACCESS METHOD
Transceivers_Access(Addr='machine:port');
```

This interface can be improved on in several ways. When the external data source can do more than simply store data, which is the case when it is another DBMS, an obvious optimization would be to push any predicates included in the query to the external source. For example, were we to query for current calls on a particular transceiver, it makes sense to avoid bringing all current calls back to the ORDBMS and performing the check there. To do this, we would augment the BeginScan function in Figure 2.19 with an additional parameter and pass any predicates from the query. Checking predicates locally to the remote data minimizes the volume of data brought back to the local node and helps to balance the CPU load. This kind of interface can provide the foundation for more sophisticated interfaces directed at external data sources capable of accepting declarative queries. However, extracting predicates from queries significantly complicates the interface.

Another improvement involves providing statistical information about these tables. It is possible to incorporate routines into the new access method that return information such as total row counts and row widths. This is especially helpful to the ORDBMS query processor because it estimates the resources needed for alternative query plans. The interface also needs to deal with an important difference between external data sources and internally stored data. Single-site optimizers can assume that the cost of scanning an unchanging table does not vary over time. This might not be the case for external data. For instance, the time taken to perform a read from a tertiary or hierarchical storage device varies tremendously, depending on where the data resides (e.g., racked tape, mounted tape, disk cache, or memory). To overcome this, the access method interface includes a function that computes a multiplier value. If the data is on disk or in memory, this value might be 1. If the data is on mounted tape it might be 100. If the tape must be fetched from racks by a robot, the multiplier value might be as high as 10,000.

2.3.5 Distributed Processing

In this subsection, we describe changes that can be made to the ORDBMS function manager to allow the ORDBMS to invoke logic on remote computer systems. The first of these extensions simply invokes logic integrated into another node of the distributed ORDBMS. This is necessary because, as we mention in the introduction, some component logic might be immobile. Also, in most organizations you will find a diverse ecology of information systems already developed and not amenable to being run inside an ORDBMS. Interoperability standards already exist to permit these systems to exchange messages. Therefore, it makes sense to add support for these standards within the ORDBMS so that logic in these systems can be invoked from within the ORDBMS (and vice versa).

When it is integrated into the ORDBMS, most component logic can be marked as execute anywhere. Either an equivalent version of the logic is installed on all sites of the distributed ORDBMS or the runable logic is copied between compatible nodes by the distributed system at runtime. Immobile logic, which is taken to be the default, only runs at a single node. This might be because a particular computer uses a different hardware or operating system than all of the others or because of software licensing restrictions. But the fact that the logic is immobile does not mean it cannot be addressed from other nodes. Integrated component logic can be invoked directly, without the use of queries.

EXAMPLE 12

Developers can use the syntax in Figure 2.21 to invoke integrated component logic directly. Just like a query, this expression might be submitted from an external program or from some application-level logic embedded in the ORDBMS. It specifies that a particular module of logic should be invoked and what argument values should be used. The coordinating node receiving this expression might discover that the runable logic implementing this extension is not available at its site (i.e., it exchanges messages with the remote site to ascertain the status of the integrated component and is informed that the logic cannot be executed anywhere). Under such circumstances, the coordinating node can send a message to the remote node and have it invoke the logic locally. This requires an extension to the language manager introduced in Section 2.2.6. Data structures describing an expression must be modified to include a notion of the site on which the logic must be invoked. Then the ORDBMS function manager can be modified to employ the same SQL-centric mechanism used for distributed queries to send messages to function managers on remote sites.

The need for this kind of remote procedure call (RPC) functionality is well understood in other software engineering contexts. In fact, there is a set of system interoperability standards that rely on it. Object Management Group's (OMG's) CORBA, Microsoft's Distributed COM (DCOM), and SunSoft's Remote Method Invocation (RMI) and EJB standards are the best known of these. Although these models relate to different language and operating system environments, which somewhat dilutes their promises of heterogeneous interoperability, they all share certain properties. All of them define how messages can be exchanged between logic embedded in separated programs. Allowing

Figure 2.21 | **Direct invocation of component logic.**

```
EXECUTE FUNCTION Matches@Billing (:First_Audio_Key,
                                  :Second_Audio_Key );
```

ORDBMS developers access to remote procedure call facilities and interoperability frameworks is a good idea.

Achieving this requires that the ORDBMS integrate code managing the dispatch of RPCs into its function manager. Several vendors ship libraries implementing either simple RPC functionality or a fully functional Object Request Broker (ORB). These libraries can be integrated into the ORDBMS using the same techniques that were used to integrate the Java environment.

We illustrate this idea in Figure 2.22. Allowing external systems to invoke logic within the ORDBMS using an RPC mechanism requires more substantial changes. To become an RPC server, which means that a program can become the recipient of RPC calls in addition to being the sender, requires that the ORDBMS register the facility with the operating system. When an external program directs an RPC call to the ORDBMS, the operating system interrupts the ORDBMS, which must handle the interrupt before continuing normal processing.

It should be pointed out that the interoperability standards introduced earlier in this subsection also specify object models—the means by which an object's interfaces are described. SQL defines its own interface specification standard, and the ORDBMS's system catalogues constitute a repository or registry. Therefore, the naming services provided by other interoperability frameworks are of little value. That said, it is highly desirable to allow different systems to exchange this kind of information. Using the external access methods interface to provide query-centric interrogation of an ORB's naming services or the Windows NT registry is fairly straightforward.

The most important difference between these standards and the ORDBMS approach is philosophical. ORDBMSs integrate data instances and logic into an abstract framework that is profoundly dynamic in its

Figure 2.22 | **Remote logic invocation from RPC handler within language manager.**

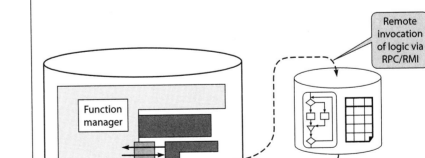

character. Logic is applied to data with queries in an ORDBMS, whereas all of the standards mentioned here handle this within the programming logic.

2.3.6   Distributed Data Movement

Distributed ORDBMSs frequently copy data between nodes. This is fairly straightforward for distributed RDBMSs, which include a fixed set of predefined data types. They can implement logic to deal with issues such as variable binary formats for data types. In contrast, distributed ORDBMSs need mechanisms to move copies of arbitrary, user-defined data structures between different hardware and operating systems. In the simplest case, our cellular support system might employ the same hardware and operating system at all sites. Under these circumstances, the distributed ORDBMS can distribute binary versions of data directly. But when the distributed ORDBMS is built on heterogeneous local systems, the problem becomes considerably more difficult. Sometimes in fact, data instances cannot be distributed at all.

One solution is to require the component developer to provide logic to facilitate data movement. For example, the Java language includes mechanisms to serialize instances of Java components into an efficient, hardware-neutral format. Data might be stored everywhere in this canonical format, or the mechanism can be used to move data between dissimilar computer systems. The drawback of storing data in such a format is that it must be converted to a format suitable for each local computer at runtime. If each system stores data in a different binary format, then as a last resort a developer might choose to implement send and symmetrical receive logic. These support functions process the local binary data into a neutral form, such as an ASCII string, and from the neutral form back into binary. Of course, this scheme assumes equivalent versions of the C or C++ component exist on both sites.

Component data can be very large. For example, our audio key might be several kilobytes in size. A digitized audio recording might be several megabytes. Most ORDBMSs use a system whereby the large object data is stored separately from a table's row data and a large object handle is placed in the row. Queries that do not access large object data thereby avoid reading it from disk as they scan the table. When a module of logic needs to access the large object data, the handle is passed into it as the internal reference. Server interfaces that open large objects and access their contents take large object handles as arguments. Corresponding facilities in operating systems use file names instead of handles. Figure 2.23 illustrates the basic idea.

The computational cost of reading large objects from disk, copying them across the network, and applying logic to them is often a significant factor in query planning. It would be very inefficient to move

Figure 2.23

Large object data management in ORDBMS.

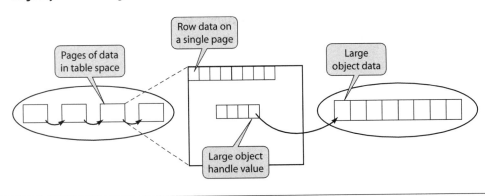

large object instances unnecessarily. But the size of a large object handle is quite small relative to the size of large object data, so moving handles is generally not a problem. Therefore, efficiently supporting large object data in a distributed ORDBMS environment requires that the following modifications be made.

1. Augment the structure of the large object handle to include the identity of the site on which it is stored. In detail, something similar to the Open Software Foundation's (OSF's) Distributed Computing Environment (DCE) specification describes an opaque Universal Unique IDentifier (UUID) value that can be used.

2. Augment the ORDBMS's internal facilities to ensure that its facilities for accessing large object data operate across a network.

Using this strategy, the distributed ORDBMS avoids unnecessarily copying large objects across the network. In fact, because logic that accesses large object data frequently uses only a fraction of the entire object, buffering and caching techniques from network file systems can be used. Rather than bring the entire object across the wire when it is to be accessed, only those portions of the large object that are actually read by the remote logic need to be moved.

2.4 Summary

In this chapter we show how a distributed ORDBMS, a kind of component DBMS, works. We begin by describing how a single-site ORDBMS functions and how it differs from RDBMSs. Then we explain how such a single-site ORDBMS system can be modified to allow it to participate in a distributed multisite system. The chief technical benefit of this approach is that the distributed ORDBMS provides a framework for the mobility of both data and programming logic. In economic terms, such a system provides a foundation for code reuse, scalability, and the flexibility that comes from combining these features in a dynamic SQL language environment.

3

All Your Data: The Oracle Extensibility Architecture

Sandeepan Banerjee
Vishu Krishnamurthy
Ravi Murthy
Oracle Corp.

3.1 Overview

The new Internet computing environment has brought new kinds of data to a huge number of users across the globe. Multimedia data types such as images, maps, video clips, and audio clips were once rarely seen outside of specialty software. Today, many web-based applications require their database servers to manage such data. Other software solutions need to store data dealing with financial instruments, engineering diagrams, or molecular structures. An increasingly large number of database applications demand content-rich data types and associated content-specific business logic.

With the addition of object-relational extensions, the Oracle8*i* Server (Oracle 1999b, 1999d) can be enhanced by developers to create their own application-domain-specific data types. For example, one can create new data types representing customers, financial portfolios, photographs, or telephone networks—and thus ensure that database programs deal with the same level of abstraction as their corresponding application domain. In many cases, it is desirable to integrate these new domain types as closely as possible with the server so they are treated at par with the built-in types such as NUMBER or VARCHAR. With such integration, the database server can be readily extended for new domains.

Oracle8*i* gives application developers greater control over user-defined data types, not only by enabling the capture of domain logic and processes associated with the data, but also by providing control over the manner in which the server stores, retrieves, or interprets this data. The Oracle8*i* database contains a series of database extensibility services, which enable the packaging and integration of content-rich domain types and behavior into server-based managed components. Such components are called data cartridges (Oracle 1999d). They are developed and managed by means of a set of database interfaces called the Oracle Data Cartridge Interfaces (ODCI). Let us look at the issues involved in creating data cartridges in more detail.

Relational databases, so far, are widely known for efficiently managing and manipulating simple, structured business data. The business data of the early 1990s mostly consisted of flat, row-oriented data (i.e., tabular data with no nested or structured columns). Also, databases did not maintain unstructured data such as text associated with records, voice clips, or spatial data. With advances in both computer hardware and software technologies, applications are becoming more sophisticated, and they desire the efficient integration of heterogeneous, multimedia data sources. For example, it is quite reasonable to store and manipulate data about an employee's salary (structured relational data) with the employee's resume (textual nonrelational data), and correlate the results with the location of employees on a map: How many employees who know database management systems (DBMSs) and make less than $50 thousand live within 50 miles of San Francisco? Surely they deserve raises.

Until recently, the burden of integrating heterogeneous data types and data sources fell on the applications rather than the underlying DBMS. This happened for three reasons:

1. Databases did not have the capability to store the unstructured or semistructured data, such as free-form text resumes.

2. Databases could not perform specialized querying on high-dimensional data, such as spatial queries on geographic locations.

3. Databases did not provide adequate performance for the efficient manipulation of a large amount of content-rich data, so that queries such as the employee query finished in reasonable time.

Specialized applications became available from various vendors to provide middle tiers that perform spatial searches, free text searches, and so forth. However, such loosely integrated specialty middle tiers have several disadvantages.

● Many functions have to be built repeatedly.

● Applications become too large, too complex, and far too customized.

● Even though these midtier products can exploit special access and storage methods to manipulate multimedia data, they run outside the DBMS server, causing performance to degrade as interactions with the database server increase.

● Optimizations across data sources cannot be performed efficiently. For instance, a spatial data server knows nothing about text searches, and vice versa.

● Each specialty server comes with its own utilities and practices for administering data, causing severe complexity in the backup, restore, and monitor functions necessary to guarantee high availability.

Because processing for content-rich data is beset with problems when done outside the database, the next question that arises is whether databases can support specific rich types inside them. Because it is not clear what constitutes a full set of such types, it seems inefficient to provide, on an ad hoc basis, support for each new type that comes along. The DBMS would have to be re-architected each time a new type is encountered. In other words, unless all the content-rich types belong to some comprehensive architecture, they will continue to be bedeviled by issues of re-architecture, cross-type query optimization, uniform programmatic access, and so on.

Oracle approached the content-rich data problem from the standpoint of creating such an architecture. Databases must be dynamically extended to be able to efficiently handle various rich, application-domain-specific data types. Extensibility is the component architecture that enables vendors to integrate components dealing, say, with rich-content data, efficiently into the DBMS, thereby dynamically extending its capabilities. Such components, called data cartridges, typically include a definition of a structured or unstructured data type, user-defined operations (operators and functions) on the data type, user-defined storage and access structures for efficient storage and retrieval of the data type instances, and query-ability on the datatype instances.

EXAMPLE 1

Consider the following example.

```
CREATE TABLE patients (

            patient_id        PersonID,

            age               INTEGER,

            medhistory        Text,

            catscan           Image,

            loc               Location

);

CREATE TABLE cities (

            name          CHAR(20),

            loc           Location,

            population    INTEGER

);
```

Given these definitions, it should be possible to formulate queries on the different data types in the tables. For instance, find the number of patients older than 50, who live within 50 miles of San Francisco, who have a family medical history of cancer, and for whom there is a probability greater than 0.6 of finding a tumor in their CAT scan.

```
SELECT      count(p), p.age

  FROM      patients p, cities c

  WHERE     p.age > 50 AND

            c.name = 'San Francisco' AND

            Distance(p.loc, c.loc, 50) AND

            TumorProb(p.catscan) >= 0.6 AND

            Contains(p.medical_history, 'cancer')

  GROUP     BY p.age;
```

Example 1 illustrates the query-ability we desire of an assortment of multimedia data types. In order to support such a query, it is clear that significant extensions to the services normally provided by the DBMS are required. The steps involved in making these extensions are as follows.

- Creation of user-defined types: the ability to define text, image, and location data types.
- Storage of user-defined type instances: the ability to store and manipulate multimedia-type instances.
- Creation of domain-specific operations: support for user-defined functions and operators such as `Contains()`, `Distance()`, and `TumorProb()`.
- Implementation of domain-specific indexes: support for indexes specific to text data (to evaluate `Contains()`), spatial data (`Distance()`), and so on, which can be used to speed the query.
- Providing optimizer extensibility: support for intelligent ordering of query predicates during evaluation. In the query in Example 1, it is critical to decide the order in which to evaluate the where clauses, so that the most restrictive clause can be applied first. The `Contains` operator evaluation involves a text index search; the `Distance` evaluation involves a spatial index lookup. The most efficient order of evaluation of these various operators and functions depends on the CPU and I/O costs of the operations. The `TumorProb()` function call should be evaluated last if there is no index on it. Because all these operators and functions are user-defined, the optimizer has to be extended to allow type-designers to specify the costs of various operations on the types.

In each case where a service is an extensible one, an interface or API provides access to the service. Figure 3.1 shows this extensibility architecture. Next, we take a look at the functionality of each extensible service in more detail.

Figure 3.1 | **The Oracle Extensibility Architecture.**

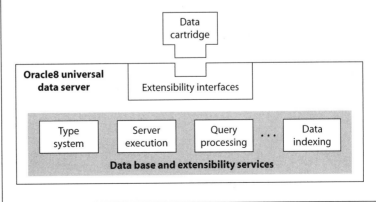

3.2   Extensible Type System

The Oracle Type System (OTS) (Oracle 1997, 1999c), based on the SQL:99 type system, provides a declarative interface for defining types. The behavior for these types can be implemented in Java, C, C++, PL/SQL. The DBMS automatically provides the low-level infrastructure services needed for I/O, heterogeneous client-side access for new data types, optimizations for data transfers between the application and the database, and so on. Let us examine the constituents of OTS.

3.2.1   Object Types

An object type, distinct from native SQL data types such as NUMBER, VARCHAR, or DATE, is user-defined. It specifies both the underlying persistent data (called attributes of the object type) and the related behavior (called methods of the object type). Object types are used to extend the modeling capabilities provided by the native data types. They can be used to make better models of complex entities in the real world by binding data attributes to semantic behavior.

There can be one or more attributes in an object type. The attributes of an object type can be the native data types, large objects (LOBs), collections, other object types, or reference (REF) types (see the following).

A method is a procedure or a function that is part of an object-type definition. Methods can access and manipulate attributes of the related object type. Methods can be run within the execution environment of the Oracle8*i* Server. In addition, methods can be dispatched to run outside the database as part of the Extensible Server Execution service.

3.2.2   Collection Types

Collections are SQL data types that contain multiple elements. Each element or value for a collection is an instance of the same data type. In Oracle8*i* there are two collection types—variable arrays (VARRAYs) and nested tables. A VARRAY contains a variable number of ordered elements. VARRAY data types can be used as a column of a table or as an attribute of an object type. Also, the element type of a VARRAY may be either a native data type such as NUMBER or an object type.

Using Oracle8*i* SQL, a named table type can be created. These can be used as nested tables to provide the semantics of an unordered collection. As with VARRAY, a nested table type can be used as a column of a table or as an attribute of an object type.

3.2.3   Relationship Types

It is possible to obtain a reference (or the database pointer) to a stand-alone instance of an object type. References are important for navigating among object instances, particularly in client-side applications. A special REF operator is used to obtain a reference to a row object.

3.2.4   Large Objects

Oracle8*i* provides LOB types to handle the storage demands of images, video clips, documents, and other such forms of data. LOBs are stored in a manner that optimizes space use and provides efficient access. More specifically, LOBs are composed of locators and the related binary or character data. A locator is an opaque handle or proxy to a LOB that is retrieved by the application and is then used to read and manipulate the LOB data. The LOB locators are stored in-line with other table record columns, and, for internal LOBs (binary larger objects, BLOBs; character large objects, CLOBs; and national character large objects, NCLOBs), the data can reside in a separate storage area and even on a different secondary storage device. For external LOBs (binary files, BFILEs), the data are stored outside the database table spaces in operating system files.

There are SQL data definition language (DDL) extensions to create and delete tables and object types that contain LOB types. The Oracle8*i* Server provides SQL data manipulation language (DML) commands to INSERT and DELETE complete LOBs. In addition, there is an extensive set of commands for piecewise reading, writing, and manipulating LOBs via Java, PL/SQL, OLE DB or the Oracle Call Interface (OCI).

For internal LOB types, the locators and related data participate fully in the transactional model of the Oracle8*i* Server. The data for BFILEs does not participate in transactions. However, the BFILE locators themselves are fully supported by server transactions.

With respect to SQL, the data residing within Oracle8*i* LOBs is opaque and not query-able. One can write functions (including methods of object types) to access and manipulate parts of LOBs. In this way the structure and semantics of data residing in large objects can be supplied by application developers.

3.2.5   Opaque Types

The opaque type mechanism provides a way to create new basic types in the database whose internal structure is not known to the DBMS. The internal structure is modeled in some 3GL languages (such as C). The database provides storage for the type instances that can be bounded by a certain size with a varying length or a fixed one. The storage requirement is specified in the type definition. The type methods or functions that access the internal structure are external methods or external procedures in the same 3GL language used to model the structure.

3.3 Server Execution Environments

The OTS decouples the choice of implementation language for the member method of an object type from its specification. Thus, components of an Oracle8i data cartridge can be developed using any of the popular programming languages. In Oracle8i, methods, functions, and procedures can be developed using Java, PL/SQL, or external C language routines. Indeed, a type developer can mix and match multiple languages. Thus, the database server runtime environment can be extended by user-defined methods, functions, and procedures.

3.3.1 Java

Java is one of the available choices for server-based execution. Oracle8i provides a high performance Java Virtual Machine (JVM) to enable the use of Java in developing stored procedures, object-type methods, stand-alone functions, and constraints (Oracle 1999g). This scalable, multiuser JVM runs in the address space of the database server and can be used to run standard Java behavior inside the database. There are multiple programming models available with the JVM. Java Data Base Connectivity (JDBC) allows object-relational statement-wise access to data (Oracle 1999h). SQLJ, a standard precompiler technology, allows SQL to be embedded directly in Java code (Oracle 1999j). Associated with the JVM is a server-based Object Request Broker (ORB), which enables an Enterprise JavaBeans (EJB) programming model (Oracle 1999e). The server ORB is fully compliant with the Common Object Request Broker (CORBA) specification. Finally, it is possible to perform ahead-of-time compilation on server-based Java code, so that the costs of interpreting this code are not taken at each invocation. Such native compilation capabilities make it possible to write computationally intensive data-cartridge behavior in Java.

In addition to server-based Java execution, Oracle8i also provides client-side Java access to the JVM, as well as the SQL and PL/SQL engines, by means of JDBC. Figure 3.2 shows how these fit schematically into the overall database architecture.

Figure 3.2 | **Java and Oracle8*i*.**

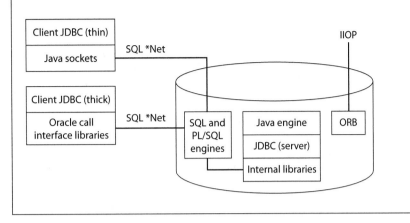

3.3.2 PL/SQL

In Oracle8*i*, PL/SQL offers a data-cartridge developer a powerful procedural language that supports all the object extensions for SQL (Oracle 1999l). With PL/SQL, program logic can execute on the server performing traditional procedural language operations such as loops, if-then-else clauses, and array access. All of this processing occurs in a transactional SQL environment where DML statements can be executed to retrieve and modify object data.

3.3.3 C and C++

While PL/SQL and Java are comprehensive languages, certain computations such as a Fast Fourier Transform or an image format conversion are handled more efficiently by C programs. With the Oracle8*i* Server, C language programs can be called from PL/SQL. As shown in Figure 3.3, external programs are executed in an address space separate from the server. This ensures that the database server is insulated from any program failures that might occur in external procedures and that under no circumstances can an Oracle database be corrupted by such failures.

In general, the Extensible Server Execution Environment enables an external C routine to be used wherever a PL/SQL subprogram could be called, such as the body of a PL/SQL method for an object type, a database trigger, or a PL/SQL function embedded in an SQL statement. Figure 3.3 shows the process of dispatching an external routine.

External routines need not be confined to C; in fact, any external language that is capable of generating a dynamically linked library or

Figure 3.3 | **Dispatching external routines.**

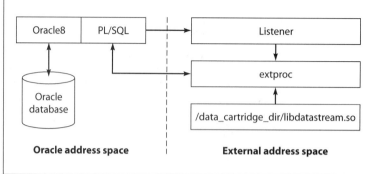

shared object file can be used to implement behavior in the Extensible Server Execution service. C++, Pascal, and other languages are all available as implementation choices.

With certain reasonable restrictions, external routines can call back to the Oracle Server using Oracle Call Interface (OCI). Callbacks are particularly useful for processing LOBs. For example, by using callbacks an external routine can perform piecewise reads or writes of LOBs stored in the database. External routines can also use callbacks to manipulate domain indexes stored as index-organized tables (see Section 3.4) in the database. External routines can be procedures or functions (the difference is that functions have a return value and procedures do not.)

3.3.4   Safe Execution

Opening up the server-execution environment creates a new problem for component databases. As long as all the operating parts of a database came from one vendor, safety and operational reliability of the data can be achieved relatively easily. However, as database systems evolve into platforms for hosting specialized data and behavior, the end user could see reliability reduced because the least reliable vendor component becomes the weakest link in the chain.

One key characteristic of the Oracle Extensibility architecture is that it is always safe for an end user to run cartridges created by third parties on the Oracle platform. PL/SQL and Java are interpreted and therefore safe to run in the server's address space. Even in the case where Java code is compiled, the native compiler performs various bounds-checking operations to ensure that the generated compilable code is safe to run. Unsafe cartridge code (written in C or C++) is run outside the address space of the database using the extproc mechanism.

3.4 Extensible Indexing and Operators

Typical database management systems support a few types of access methods (e.g., B+-trees and hash indexes) on some set of data types (e.g., numbers and strings). In recent years, databases have been used to store many different types of data such as text, spatial, image, video, and audio. In these complex domains, there is a need for the indexing of complex data types and for specialized indexing techniques. For simple data types such as integers and small strings, all aspects of indexing can be easily handled by the database system. This is not the case for documents, images, video clips, and other complex data types that require content-based retrieval. Complex data types have application-specific formats, indexing requirements, and selection predicates. For example, there are many different document encodings (e.g., Open Document Architecture, ODA; Standard Generalized Markup Language, SGML; and plain text) and information retrieval techniques (e.g., keyword, full-text Boolean, similarity, and probabilistic). Similarly, R-trees are an efficient method of indexing spatial data. No database server can be built with support for all the possible kinds of complex data and indexing. Oracle's solution is to build an extensible server that provides the application developer with the ability to define new index types (Oracle 1999d).

The framework to develop new index types is based on the concept of cooperative indexing where a data cartridge and the Oracle Server cooperate to build and maintain indexes for data types including text, spatial, and Online Analytical Processing (OLAP). The cartridge is responsible for defining the index structure, maintaining the index content during load and update operations, and searching the index during query processing. The index structure itself can either be stored in the Oracle database (e.g,. in heap or index-organized tables) or externally (e.g., in operating system files). However, it is highly desirable for reasons of concurrency control and recovery to have the physical storage of the domain indexes be in the Oracle database.

To this end, Oracle8*i* introduces the concept of an Indextype. The purpose of an Indextype is to enable efficient search and retrieval functions for complex domains such as text, spatial, image, and OLAP. An Indextype is analogous to the sorted or bit-mapped index types that are built into the Oracle Server. The difference is that the routines implementing an Indextype are provided by the cartridge developer, whereas the Oracle Server kernel implements the built-in indexes. Once a new Indextype has been implemented by a data-cartridge developer, end users of the data cartridge can use it just as they would the built-in index types.

With extensible indexing, the application defines the structure of the domain index as a new Indextype; stores the index data either inside the Oracle database (in the form of tables) or outside the Oracle database; and manages, retrieves, and uses the index data to evaluate user queries. When the database server handles the physical storage of domain indexes, cartridges must be able to do the following.

- Define the format and content of an index. This enables cartridges to define an index structure that can accommodate a complex data object.

- Build, delete, and update a domain index. The cartridge handles the building and maintenance of the index structures. Note that this is a significant departure from the automatic indexing features provided for simple SQL data types. Also, because an index is modeled as a collection of tuples, in-place updating is directly supported.

- Access and interpret the content of an index. This capability enables the data cartridge to become an integral component of query processing. That is, the content-related clauses for database queries are handled by the data cartridge.

Traditional database systems do not support extensible indexing. Many applications maintain file-based indexes for complex data residing in relational database tables. A considerable amount of code and effort is required to maintain consistency between external indexes and the related relational data, to support compound queries (involving tabular values and external indexes), and to manage a system (backup, recovery, allocate storage, etc.) with multiple forms of persistent storage (files and databases). By supporting extensible indexes, the Oracle8*i* Server significantly reduces the level of effort needed to develop solutions involving high-performance access to complex data types. Table 3.1 lists the functionality of the ODCIIndex interface.

Before we provide an example of extensible indexing, we introduce a few additional constructs, all necessary to add power and flexibility to the database indexing service. We discuss index-organized tables and function-based indexes, followed by a discussion of user-defined operators, before presenting the example of extensible indexing.

3.4.1   Index-Organized Tables

An index-organized table (IOT) is a useful tool in the armory of a cartridge developer using extensible indexing. An IOT differs from an ordinary table in that the data for the table are held in their associated index. In fact, the table and the index are one and the same such that changing the table data, such as adding new rows, updating rows, or deleting rows, is tantamount to updating the index.

The IOT is like an ordinary table with an index on one or more of its columns, but instead of maintaining two separate storages for the table and the B*-tree index, the database system only maintains a single B*-tree index, which contains both the encoded key value and the

Table 3.1 **ODCIIndex interface.**

	Interface Routine	Description
Index create	ODCIIndexCreate	Creates the domain index according to user-specified parameters
Index drop	ODCIIndexDrop	Drops the domain index
Index scan	ODCIIndexStart	Initializes the scan of the domain index
	ODCIIndexFetch	Fetches from the domain index: returns the rowid of each successive row satisfying the operator predicate
	ODCIIndexClose	Ends the current use of the index
Insert	ODCIIndexInsert	Maintains the domain index structure when a row is inserted in the indexed table
Delete	ODCIIndexDelete	Maintains the domain index structure when a row is deleted
Update	ODCIIndexUpdate	Maintains the domain index structure when a row is updated
Truncate	ODCIIndexTruncate	Deletes the domain index data preserving the structure
Alter	ODCIIndexAlter	Alters the domain index
Metadata	ODCIIndexGetMetaData	Allow import and export of domain-index-specific metadata

associated column values for the corresponding row. Rather than having a row's rowid as the second element of the index entry, the actual data row is stored in the B*-tree index. The data rows are built on the primary key for the table, and each B*-tree index entry contains the pairs <primary_key_value, non_primary _key_column_values>.

IOTs are suitable for accessing data by the primary key or any key that is a valid prefix of the primary key. There is no duplication of key values because only nonkey column values are stored with the key. One can build secondary indexes to provide efficient access to other columns.

Applications manipulate the IOT just like an ordinary table, using SQL statements. However, the database system performs all operations by manipulating the corresponding B*-tree index. Table 3.2 summarizes the main distinctions between access of ordinary tables and IOTs. IOTs can be very useful to developers of domain indexes in that they provide a canned B*-tree index in which to store their data.

3.4.2 Function-Based Indexing

So far, we have discussed indexing data in various ways. Another intriguing possibility open to data-cartridge developers is the ability to index on behavior.

Table 3.2   Ordinary tables versus index-organized table.

Ordinary Table	Index-Organized Table
Rowid-based access	Primary key–based access
Physical rowid in `ROWID` pseudocolumn allows building secondary indexes	Logical rowid in `ROWID` pseudocolumn allows building secondary indexes
Rowid uniquely identifies a row; primary key can be optionally specified	Primary key uniquely identifies a row; primary key must be specified
Sequential scan returns all rows	Full-index scan returns all rows in primary-key order
`UNIQUE` constraint and triggers allowed	`UNIQUE` constraint not allowed; triggers allowed
Can be stored in a cluster with other tables	Cannot be stored in a cluster

To address the efficient evaluation of a query when the predicate is based on an object method, Oracle8*i* supports function-based indexes. Users can create indexes on functions (object methods) and expressions that involve one or more columns in the table being indexed. A function-based index precomputes the value of the function or expression and stores it in the index. A function-based index is created as either a B*-tree or bit-map index. The function used for building the index can be an arithmetic expression or an expression that contains an object type method or a stand-alone SQL function. In order for the function to be indexed, it must be declared deterministic; that is, it must return the same result when invoked with the same set of parameter values.

Function-based indexes provide an efficient mechanism for evaluating SQL statements that contain functions in their `WHERE` clauses. One can create a function-based index to materialize computational-intensive expressions in the index, so that Oracle does not need to compute the value of the expression when processing `SELECT` or `DELETE` statements. However, when processing `INSERT` and `UPDATE` statements, Oracle must still evaluate the function to process the statement.

Suppose a table contains all purchase-order objects, and suppose `TotalValue` is a method defined for `purchase_order` type that returned the total value of a purchase-order object by summing up the values of the individual line-items of the purchase order. Then the index

```
CREATE INDEX TotalValueIndx ON purchase_order_table p
p.TotalValue();
```

can be used instead of evaluating the `TotalValue` method, for example, when processing queries such as

```
SELECT   p.order_id
  FROM   purchase_order_table p
 WHERE   p.TotalValue() > 10000;
```

The ability to build functional indexes thus extends the database indexing service in a fundamental way.

3.4.3 User-Defined Operators

Data-cartridge developers find it useful to define domain-specific operators and integrate them into the Oracle8*i* Server along with extensible indexing schemes that such operators take advantage of while accessing data. The ability to increase the semantics of the query language by adding such domain-specific operators is akin to extending the query service of the database.

Oracle8*i* provides a set of predefined operators that include arithmetic operators (+, −, *, /), comparison operators (=, >, <), and logical operators (NOT, AND, OR). These operators take as input one or more arguments (or operands) and return a result.

Oracle8*i* allows users to extend the set of operators by defining new ones with user specified behavior. Like built-in operators, they take a set of operands as input and return a result. The implementation of the operator is provided by the user. After a user has defined a new operator, it can be used in SQL statements like any other built-in operator.

For example, if the user defines a new operator Contains, which takes as input a text document and a query string and returns TRUE if the document satisfies the specified query string, we can write an SQL query as

```
SELECT   *
  FROM   Employees
 WHERE   Contains(resume, 'Oracle AND Unix');
```

Oracle8*i* uses indexes to efficiently evaluate some built-in operators—for example, a B-tree index can be used to evaluate the comparison operators =, >, and <. Similarly, in Oracle8*i,* user-defined domain indexes can be used to efficiently evaluate user-defined operators.

In general, user-defined operators are bound to functions. However, operators can also be evaluated using indexes. For instance, the equality operator can be evaluated using a hash index. An Indextype provides index-based implementation for the operators listed in the Indextype definition.

An operator binding identifies the operator with a unique signature (via argument data types) and allows associating with it a function that provides an implementation for the operator. The Oracle8*i* Server executes the function when the operator is invoked. Multiple operator bindings can be defined as long as they differ in their signatures. Thus, any operator can have an associated set of zero or more bindings. Each of these bindings can be evaluated using a user-defined function, which could be stand-alone functions, package functions, or object member methods. User-defined operators can be invoked anywhere built-in operators can be used, that is, wherever expressions can occur. For example, user-defined operators can be used in the SELECT list of a select command, the condition of a WHERE clause, or ORDER BY and GROUP BY clauses. When an operator is invoked, its evaluation is transformed into the execution of one of the functions bound to it. This transformation is based on the data types of the arguments to the operator. If none of the functions bound to the operator satisfies the signature with which the operator is invoked, an error occurs. There might be some implicit type conversions present during the transformation process. Example 2 illustrates the extensible indexing and user-defined operator framework.

EXAMPLE 2 | **Extensible Indexing and Operators**

Consider a text-retrieval application. For such applications, indexing involves parsing the text and inserting the words or tokens into an inverted index. Such index entries typically have the following logical form:

```
(token, <docid, data>)
```

where token is a word or stem that is a term in searches, docid is a unique identifier for a document this word occurs in, and data is a segment containing information on how many times or where in the document the word occurs.

A sample index entry for such an application would look like

```
(Ulysses, <5, 3, [7 62 225]>, <26, 2, [33, 49]>, ...)
```

In this sample index entry, the token Ulysses appears in document 5 at 3 locations (7, 62, and 225) and in document 26 at 2 locations (33 and 49). Note that the index would contain one entry for every document with the word Ulysses.

3.5 Defining a Text-Indexing Scheme

The sequence of four steps is required to define a text indexing scheme using a text Indextype.

First, define and code functions to support the functional implementation of operators that eventually would be supported by the text Indextype. Suppose our text-indexing scheme is in the context of a text data cartridge that intends to support an operator Contains. The operator Contains takes as parameters a text value and a key, and returns a

Boolean value indicating whether the text contains the key. The functional implementation of this operator is a SQL function defined as

```
CREATE FUNCTION TextContains(Text IN VARCHAR2,
                        Key IN VARCHAR2) RETURN BOOLEAN AS
        BEGIN
                .......
        END TextContains;
```

Second, create a new operator and define its specification, namely the argument and return data types, and the functional implementation:

```
CREATE OPERATOR Contains
BINDING (VARCHAR2, VARCHAR2) RETURN BOOLEAN
USING TextContains;
```

Third, define a type or package that implements ODCIIndex. This involves implementing routines for index definition, index maintenance, and index scan operations. The index definition routines (ODCIIndexCreate, ODCIIndexAlter, ODCIIndexDrop, and ODCIIndexTruncate) build the text index when the index is created, alter the index information when the index is altered, remove the index information when the index is dropped, and truncate the text index when the base table is truncated. The index maintenance routines (ODCIIndexInsert, ODCIIndexDelete, and ODCIIndexUpdate) maintain the text index when the table rows are inserted, deleted, or updated.

The index scan routines (ODCIIndexStart, ODCIIndexFetch, ODCIIndexClose) implement access to the text index to retrieve rows of the base table that satisfy the operator predicate. In this case, Contains(...) forms a Boolean predicate whose arguments are passed into the index scan routines. The index scan routines scan the text index and return the qualifying rows to the system.

```
CREATE TYPE TextIndexMethods (
        FUNCTION ODCIIndexCreate(...)
        ...
);

CREATE TYPE BODY TextIndexMethods  (
            ...
);
```

Fourth, create the text Indextype schema object. The Indextype definition also specifies all the operators supported by the new Indextype and the type that implements the index interface.

```
CREATE INDEXTYPE TextIndexType
FOR Contains(VARCHAR2, VARCHAR2)
USING TextIndexMethods;
```

3.5.1 Using the Text-Indexing Scheme

Suppose that the text Indextype presented in the previous section has been defined in the system. The user can define text indexes on text columns and use the associated Contains operator to query the text data. Further, suppose an Employees table is defined as follows:

```
CREATE TABLE Employees (name VARCHAR2(64), id INTEGER,
                        resume VARCHAR2(2000));
```

A text-domain index can be built on the resume column as follows:

```
CREATE INDEX ResumeIndex ON Employees(resume)
INDEXTYPE IS TextIndex;
```

The text data in the resume column can be queried as

```
SELECT * FROM Employees WHERE Contains(resume, 'Oracle');
```

The query execution will use the text index on resume to efficiently evaluate the Contains() predicate.

3.6 Extensible Optimizer

The extensible optimizer functionality enables the authors of user-defined functions and indexes to create statistics collection, selectivity, and cost functions (Oracle 1999d). This information is used by the optimizer in choosing a query plan. The cost-based optimizer is thus extended to use the user-supplied information.

The optimizer generates an execution plan for a SQL statement (for simplicity, consider a SELECT statement—this also applies to other statements). An execution plan includes an access method for each table in the FROM clause, and an ordering (called the join order) of the tables in the FROM clause. System-defined access methods include indexes, hash clusters, and table scans. The optimizer chooses a plan by generating a set of join orders or permutations, computing the cost of each, and selecting the one with the lowest cost. For each table in the join order, the optimizer computes the cost of each possible access and join method, choosing the one with the lowest cost. The cost of the join order is the sum of the access method and join method costs. The costs are calculated using algorithms that together compose the cost model. A cost model can include varying levels of detail about the physical environment in which the query is executed. Oracle's present cost model includes only the number of disk accesses with minor adjustments to compensate for the lack of detail. The optimizer uses statistics about the objects referenced in the query to compute the costs. The statistics are gathered using the `ANALYZE` command. The optimizer uses these statistics to calculate cost and selectivity. The selectivity of a predicate is the fraction of rows in a table that will be chosen by the predicate.

Extensible indexing functionality enables users to define new operators, index types, and domain indexes. For such user-defined operators and domain indexes, the extensible optimizer gives data-cartridge developers control over the three main components used by the optimizer to select an execution plan: statistics, selectivity, and cost. We look at each of these components in more detail.

3.6.1 Statistics

The `ANALYZE` command is extended so that whenever a domain index is to be analyzed, a call is made to the cartridge-specified statistics collection function. The representation and meaning of these user-collected statistics is not known to the database.

In addition to domain indexes, cartridge-defined statistics collection functions are also supported for individual columns of a table and data types (whether built-in types or object types). In the former case, whenever a column is analyzed, in addition to the standard statistics collected by the database, the user-defined statistics collection function is called to collect additional statistics. If a statistics collection function exists for a data type, it is called for each column of the table being analyzed of the specified type. For example, the following statement associates a statistics type `ImgStats_t`, which implements the statistics collection function ODCIStatsCollect, with the image column `imgcol` of the table `tab`.

```
ASSOCIATE STATISTICS WITH COLUMNS tab.imgcol
      USING ImgStats_t;
```

The following `ANALYZE` command collects statistics for the tab table. In addition to the usual statistics collected by Oracle, the ODCIStatsCollect function is invoked to collect extra statistics for the `imgcol` column.

```
ANALYZE TABLE tab COMPUTE STATISTICS;
```

EXAMPLE 3 | **Statistics**

Consider images stored in a BLOB column in a table created as

```
CREATE TABLE ImgTab (
            name VARCHAR2(100),
            imgcol BLOB
);
```

The following statement associates a statistics type ImgStats_t, which implements the statistics collection function ODCIStatsCollect, with the image column imgcol of the table tab.

```
ASSOCIATE STATISTICS WITH COLUMNS ImgTab.imgcol
    USING ImgStats_t;
```

The type ImgStats_t implements the ODCIStats interface.

```
CREATE TYPE ImgStats_t AS OBJECT
(
            STATIC FUNCTION ODCIStatsCollect(...) ...
            ...
);
```

The following ANALYZE command collects statistics for the ImgTab table. In addition to the usual statistics collected by Oracle, the ODCIStatsCollect function is invoked to collect extra statistics for the imgcol column. It could collect any relevant information regarding the images. For example, the average size of the images is a useful indicator of the time required to process the images.

```
ANALYZE TABLE ImgTab COMPUTE STATISTICS;
```

3.6.2 Selectivity

The optimizer uses statistics to calculate the selectivity of predicates. The selectivity is the fraction of rows in a table that will be chosen by the predicate and is a number between 0 and 1. The selectivity of a predicate is used to estimate the cost of a particular access method. It is also used to determine the optimal join order. A poor choice of join order by the optimizer could result in a very expensive execution plan.

By default, the optimizer uses a standard algorithm to estimate the selectivity of selection and join predicates. However, the algorithm does not work very well when predicates contain functions or type methods. In addition, in Oracle8*i* predicates can contain user-defined operators about which the optimizer does not have any information and so cannot compute an accurate selectivity.

For greater control over the optimizer's selectivity estimation, the extensible optimizer enables data-cartridge developers to specify user-defined selectivity functions for predicates containing user-defined operators, stand-alone functions, package functions, or type methods. The user-defined selectivity function will be called by the optimizer whenever it encounters a predicate with one of the following forms:

```
op(...) relop <constant>
<constant> relop op(...)
op(...) LIKE <constant>
```

where `op(...)` is a user-defined operator, stand-alone function, package function, or type method; `relop` is any of the standard comparison operators (<, <=, =, >=, >); and `<constant>` is a constant value expression. For such cases, data cartridges can define selectivity functions that will be associated with `op(...)`. The arguments to `op` can be columns, constants, bind variables, or attribute references. When such a predicate is encountered, the optimizer will call the user-defined selectivity function and pass the entire predicate as an argument including the operator, function, or type method and its arguments; the relational operator `relop`; and the constant expression or bind variable. The return value of the user-defined selectivity function must be between 0 and 1, inclusive; values outside this range are ignored by the optimizer. Typically, the arguments and the statistics collected are used to estimate the selectivity of an operation.

EXAMPLE 4 | **Selectivity**

Consider a function `Brightness()` defined on images that returns a value between 0 and 100 to indicate the level of brightness. A selectivity function can be associated by implementing the ODCIStatsSelectivity function within a type, say `ImgStats_t`, and executing the following statement:

```
ASSOCIATE STATISTICS WITH FUNCTIONS Brightness
USING ImgStats_t;
```

Now, if a user executes a query of the form:

```
SELECT * FROM ImgTab
WHERE Brightness(imgcol) BETWEEN 50 and 60;
```

the selectivity of the predicate is computed by invoking the user-supplied implementation of the ODCIStatsSelectivity function.

3.6.3   Cost

The optimizer estimates the cost of various access paths to choose an optimal plan. For example, it may compute the cost of using an index and a full table scan in order to choose between the two. However, for data-cartridge defined-domain indexes, the optimizer does not know the internal storage structure of the index. Thus, the optimizer cannot make a good estimate of the cost of using such an index. Similarly, the default optimizer model assumes that the cost of I/O dominates and that other activities such as function evaluations have zero cost. This is only true when functions include relatively inexpensive built-in functions. User-defined functions can be very expensive because they can be CPU-intensive. User-defined functions can invoke recursive SQL. When the function argument is a file LOB, there may be substantial I/O cost.

For superior optimization, the cost model is extended to enable users to define costs for domain indexes, user-defined functions, standard stand-alone functions, package functions, and type methods. The user-defined costs can be in the form of default costs that the optimizer simply looks up, or can be full-blown cost functions that the optimizer calls to compute the cost.

User-defined cost, like user-defined selectivity, is optional on the part of a data cartridge. If no user-defined cost is available, the optimizer uses its internal heuristics to compute an estimate. However, in the absence of useful information about the storage structures in user-defined domain indexes and functions, such estimates can be very inaccurate and may result in the choice of a suboptimal execution plan.

User-defined cost functions for domain indexes are called by the optimizer only if a domain index is a valid access path for a user-defined operator. User-defined cost functions can return three parameters. Each parameter represents the cost of a single execution of a function or domain index implementation:

1. *cpu*—Number of machine instructions executed by the function or domain index implementation.

2. *I/O*—Number of data blocks read by the function or domain index implementation.

3. *network*—Number of data blocks transmitted. This is valid for distributed queries as well as functions and domain index implementations.

EXAMPLE 5 | **Cost**

Consider again the query involving the `Brightness()` function introduced in Example 4.

```
SELECT * FROM ImgTab
WHERE Brightness(imgcol) BETWEEN 50 and 60;
```

The optimizer will invoke the `ODCIStatsFunctionCost()` function implemented within `ImgStats_t` to estimate the cost of executing the `Brightness()` function. Typically, the cost function retrieves the user-collected statistics (e.g., in this case, average length of the image column) and computes the cost of one invocation of the function. Table 3.3 describes the ODCIStats interface.

Table 3.3   ODCIStats interface.

	Interface Routine	Description
Statistics	ODCIStatsCollect	Collects statistics for column and index data
	ODCIStatsDelete	Drops statistics
Selectivity	ODCIStatsSelectivity	Estimates the selectivity of a predicate involving user-defined functions or operators
Cost	ODCIStatsFunctionCost	Accepts information about the function parameters and computes the cost of a single execution
	ODCIStatsIndexCost	Accepts information about the operator predicate and computes the cost of the domain index scan

3.7   User-Defined Aggregates

Typical database systems support a small number of aggregate operators (e.g., `MAX` and `MIN`) over scalar data types such as number and character strings. However, it is desirable to provide the capability of adding new aggregate operators to the DBMS. For instance, a new aggregate operator `SecondMax()`, which ignores the highest value and returns the second highest, might be necessary in some application. Further, in complex domains, the semantics of aggregation is not known to the DBMS and has to be provided by the domain code. For instance, `MAX()` in the spatial domain may refer to the geometry with the largest enclosed area.

User-defined aggregate operators (UDAGs) are the mechanisms that incorporate new aggregate operators with user-specified aggregation semantics. Users can specify a set of routines that implements the aggregation logic. Once the aggregate operator is registered with Oracle, it can be used by users wherever built-in aggregates can be used.

An aggregate operator operates over a set of rows and returns a single value. The sets of rows for aggregation are typically identified using a `GROUP BY` clause. For example,

```
SELECT AVG(T.Sales) FROM AnnualSales T
GROUP BY T.State
```

Conceptually, an aggregate value is computed in three steps. Using the example AVG(), the steps are as follows.

1. `Initialize`: Initialize the computation.
   Action: Assign 0 to `runningSum` and `runningCount` variables.
2. `Iterate`: Iteratively examine each of the tuples and perform necessary computations.
   Action: Add input number value to `runningSum` variable, and increase `runningCount` variable by 1.
3. `Terminate`: Compute the resulting value.
   Action: Compute the average as (`runningSum`/`runningCount`).

New aggregate operators can be registered by providing the implementations for these aggregation steps.

The variables `runningSum` and `runningCount` in the steps determine the state of the aggregation. We can think of the state as a state variable, an object that contains `runningSum` and `runningCount` as elements. Thus, the `Initialize` function initializes the state variable, `Iterate` updates it, and `Terminate` uses the state variable to return the resultant value. Note that the state variable completely determines the state of the aggregation. In the presence of a GROUP BY clause in the query, this sequence of steps is performed for every group.

Thus, with user-defined aggregate operators, the application defines the set of implementations of the UDAG and specifies each of the implementations in terms of the implementation routines and the data types of the argument values and return value. The application then creates the implementation routines in C++ or Java. Finally, the application uses the UDAG in SQL query statements.

EXAMPLE 6 | **User-Defined Aggregates**

An application requires the use of a `TopTen` aggregate operator, which has the behavior: The aggregate operator, computed over a set of values, determines the 10 largest values and returns a single object having the 10 values as its components.

The end user would like to use the `TopTen` operator in queries such as the following.

```
SELECT TopTen(A1.DollarSales) FROM AnnualSales A1
GROUP BY A1.State
```

The `TopTen` aggregate operator is implemented in the following steps.
1. Specify the aggregate operator in terms of its implementations, and specify the data types of the argument values and return value for each implementation as follows.

```
CREATE OPERATOR TopTen AS AGGREGATE

BINDING (NUMBER) RETURN TenNUMBER USING TopTenNumber;
```

Where `TenNUMBER` is a collection type capable of holding 10 values and is the return type of the aggregate operator implementation.

2. Implement the aggregate operator implementation routines in any language supported by Oracle for type methods (e.g., PL/SQL, C, C++, or Java). The implementation routines for aggregation are member methods of the `TopTenNumber` object type.

```
CREATE TYPE TopTenNumber
(
        FUNCTION ODCIAggregateInitialize(...)
        . . .
);
CREATE TYPE BODY TopTenNumber
(
        FUNCTION ODCIAggregateInitialize() AS
        BEGIN
        . . . . . .
        END ODCIAggregateInitialize;
. . .
);
```

Table 3.4 describes the ODCIAggregate interface.

Table 3.4   **ODCIAggregate interface.**

Action	Interface Routines	Description
Serial aggregation	ODCIAggregateInitialize	Initializes aggregation context
	ODCIAggregateIterate	Accepts next batch of rows and updates aggregation context
	ODCIAggregateTerminate	Returns aggregate value
Parallel aggregation	ODCIAggregateParInit	Initializes parallel aggregation context
	ODCIAggregateParIter	Accepts next batch of rows and updates the parallel aggregation context
	ODCIAggregateParTerm	Returns the final parallel aggregation context
	ODCIAggregateSuperAggr	Accepts set of aggregation context and returns aggregate value

3.7.1   Using the User-Defined Aggregates

User-defined aggregate operators can be used in DML statements much like built-in aggregates. The evaluation of the UDAG triggers the invocation of the underlying user-supplied routines to compute the aggregate value. For example,

```
SELECT TopTen(A1.DollarSales) FROM AnnualSales A1
GROUP BY A1.State
```

triggers the invocation of the initialization routine followed by one or more invocations of the iteration routine followed by an invocation of the termination routine.

3.8 Abstract Tables

A user might occasionally need to access data that is outside any database. Such data may have a certain structure, albeit different from the structure of relational or object-relational databases. For example, some data may be stored as Extensible Markup Language (XML) files on a file system. As part of data-cartridge operations, it is sometimes important to perform composite operations that span such external data as well as internal, tabular data. The best way to combine such different structures is by providing data-cartridge developers the ability to create a uniform table metaphor over all data by constructing abstract tables corresponding to the external sources.

An abstract table is a virtual table whose data are retrieved by invoking user-registered functions. In its simplest form, the user implements iteration routines to scan the rows of the table. However, abstract tables provide a firm framework for supporting user-defined data manipulation as well. The user can implement routines that will be invoked when the abstract table is created or dropped and when its rows are inserted, deleted, or updated. Abstract tables also support other table features such as building secondary indexes and defining constraints and triggers.

An abstract table is created in a manner similar to regular tables, the difference being that the name of the underlying implementation type is specified. The implementation type contains the implementations of the ODCITable interface—consisting of the table scan and manipulation routines. The ODCITable interface is listed in Table 3.5.

EXAMPLE 7

Abstract Tables

Suppose we want to read employee data that originates from a set of operating system files.

```
CREATE ABSTRACT TABLE emps_filetab
(
name VARCHAR2(30),
  id NUMBER,
 mgr VARCHAR2(30)
)
```

```
USING LoaderFileReader

PARAMETERS ('/tmp/emp.dat');
```

The abstract table definition of `emps_filetab` specifies the name of the object type `LoaderFileReader` that implements the ODCITable interface routines. The ODCITable interface includes the create, drop, DML, and scan routines. The `PARAMETERS` clause can be used to pass user-defined parameters to the ODCITableCreate routine—in this example, the path to the loader file is specified. Once the abstract table has been created, it can be used exactly like regular tables—creating indexes, performing DML operations and queries, and so forth.

The ODCITable interface contains the definitions of all the routines that need to implemented by the abstract table implementor. Note that the definitions are static and are specified by Oracle, but their actual implementations must be provided by the user. The ODCITable interface consists of three classes of routines.

- Query routines. These are the set of routines that are invoked by Oracle while querying abstract table data. These are also the same set of routines that are implemented for table functions.
- DML routines. These are the set of routines that are invoked by Oracle to insert, delete, and update rows of the abstract table.
- DDL routines. These are the set of routines that are invoked by Oracle when an abstract table is created or dropped.

The implementations of all the ODCITable interface routines are provided by the user in the form of an object type. For example, the type `LoaderFileReader` contains the implementation of the DDL and query routines for the `emps_filetab` abstract table.

```
CREATE TYPE LoaderFileReader AS OBJECT

(

      MEMBER FUNCTION ODCITableStart(...) RETURN NUMBER;

      MEMBER FUNCTION ODCITableFetch(...) RETURN NUMBER;

      MEMBER FUNCTION ODCITableClose(...) RETURN NUMBER;

);

CREATE TYPE BODY LoaderFileReader AS

...

END;
```

When the user executes a query over the abstract table, a scan is set up to iterate over the rows of the table.

```
SELECT * FROM emps_filetab;
```

The integrity and consistency constraints across the external data sources can be enforced through additional sets of extensible APIs, which are not elaborated in this chapter.

Table 3.5   **ODCITable interface.**

	Interface Routine	Description
Table scan	ODCITableStart	Initializes a full scan of an abstract table
	ODCITableFetch	Accepts the scan context and returns the next set of rows
	ODCITableClose	Performs cleanup at the end of scan
Rowid access	ODCITableLookup	Retrieves row corresponding to the specified row identifier
Describe row	ODCITableDescribe	Returns the metadata descriptor of a row
Query rewrite	ODCITableRewrite	Returns a SQL query string that can be plugged into original query in place of the abstract table
Data manipulation	ODCITableInsert	Inserts a new row into the table
	ODCITableDelete	Deletes a row from the table
	ODCITableUpdate	Updates a row of the table
Data definition	ODCITableCreate	Processes parameters specified while creating the abstract table
	ODCITableDrop	Performs cleanup when abstract table dropped

3.8.1   Table Functions

Data-cartridge developers may also need to generate table data dynamically. The extensibility architecture provides this capability through iterative table functions that are complementary to abstract tables.

There are scenarios in which data are inherently dynamic and depend on user-supplied parameters. Such data cannot be modeled easily using abstract tables. For example, one might want to access data present in an external web site (identified by a uniform resource locator, URL). A function ReadURL() can be implemented to take in the URL as input and return a collection representing the read data.

```
SELECT * FROM TABLE(ReadURL("www.oracle.com"));
```

This solution has some drawbacks. The entire result set is returned from ReadURL() as a single collection. This not only affects the response time of the query, but also consumes more resources. Table functions are the right answer to this problem. They are similar to regular functions returning collections, except that the result is returned iteratively (i.e., in subsets). This is accomplished by implementing the table scan routines in the ODCITable interface.

E X A M P L E   8 | **Table Functions**

The following statement creates a table function `GetURL()`, which is implemented to return the result collection iteratively.

```
CREATE FUNCTION GetURL(url VARCHAR2) RETURN ROWSET
ITERATE USING GetURLMethods;
```

The type `GetURLMethods` implements the table scan routines of the ODCITable interface.

```
CREATE TYPE GetURLMethods AS OBJECT
(
          STATIC FUNCTION ODCITableStart(...)...
          MEMBER FUNCTION ODCITableFetch(...)...
          MEMBER FUNCTION ODCITableClose(...)..
);
```

Now, when the user executes a query of the form,

```
SELECT * FROM TABLE(GetURL("www.oracle.com"));
```

the table scan routines are appropriately invoked by Oracle to retrieve the rows representing the data contained in the web site.

The differences between abstract tables and table functions lie in the dynamism of data and the set of allowed operations. Table 3.6 shows some of the key differences. In other words, abstract tables are a more general mechanism, but do not provide the user the ability to specify parameters at query time. Table functions are a simplified mechanism to provide user-defined iterators in such cases.

Table 3.6   **Table functions versus abstract tables.**

	Table Functions	Abstract Tables
Query-time parameters	Yes	No
Create-time parameters	No	Yes
Indexes	No	Yes
Constraints and triggers	No	Yes
Inserts/deletes/updates	No	Yes
Partitioning specification	No	Yes

3.9   Cartridge Basic Services

In order to develop and deploy full-fledged cartridges, Oracle's Extensibility Architecture provides a set of commonly useful routines. They represent a very useful library, which not only assists in the development of data cartridges, but also facilitates intercartridge coordination. Typically, these basic services are exposed as OCI routines that can be invoked by a cartridge.

These cartridge service interfaces include memory management, parameter management, internationalization, error reporting, context management, and file I/O.

3.9.1   Memory Management

The Memory Management Interfaces contain support for allocating permanent and freeable memory of several durations (session, statement, user call to server, and server call to cartridge), re-allocating memory, allocating subduration memories, allocating large contiguous memory, and so forth.

3.9.2   Parameter Management

The parameter manager provides a set of routines to process parameters from a file or a string. Routines are provided to process the input and to obtain key and value pairs. These key and value pairs are stored in memory and can be accessed via certain routines.

The input-processing routines match the contents of the file or the string against an existing grammar and compare the key names found in the input against the list of known keys that the user has registered. The behavior of the input-processing routines can also be configured.

3.9.3   Internationalization

To support multilingual applications, national language support (NLS) functionality is required by the cartridges. The National Language Support Run-Time Library (NLSRTL) is a multiplatform and multilingual library that is currently used by Oracle object-relational database management systems (ORDBMSs) and provides consistent NLS behavior to all Oracle products. The basic NLS services are available to cartridge developers in the form of interfaces for the following functionalities: locale-information retrieval; string manipulation in the format of multibyte and wide-char; character-set conversion, including Unicode; and messaging.

3.9.4 Error Reporting

The cartridge code can return errors or raise exceptions that are handed back to the Oracle server. There are service routines to raise errors, register error messages, and manipulate the error stack.

3.9.5 Context Management

Context management allows clients to maintain context across calls to a cartridge. The context maintained by a cartridge could be based on a duration such as SESSION, STATEMENT, or CALL. The cartridge services provide a mechanism for saving and retrieving contexts.

3.9.6 File I/O

The OCI file I/O package is designed to make it easier to write portable code that interacts with the file system by providing a consistent view of file I/O across multiple platforms.

3.10 Case Studies

The extensibility services and interfaces available in Oracle8*i* have been used by Oracle to create some commonly useful data cartridges. This section discusses the implementations of these data cartridges with a view to shedding more light on the Extensibility Architecture and its benefits.

3.10.1 The Oracle8*i inter*Media Text Data Cartridge

The Oracle8*i inter*Media Text Cartridge supports full-text indexing of text documents (Oracle 1999f). The text index is an inverted index storing the occurrence list for each token in each of the text documents. The inverted index is stored in an index-organized table and is maintained by performing insert, update, and delete on the table whenever the table on which the text index is defined is modified. The text cartridge defines an operator Contains, which takes as input a text column and a keyword and returns true or false depending on whether the keyword is contained in the text column. The benefits of the extensible indexing framework can be seen by analyzing the execution of the same text query before and in Oracle8*i*.

EXAMPLE 9 | Consider the query:

```
SELECT * FROM docs WHERE Contains(resume, 'Oracle');
```

In releases prior to Oracle8*i*, the text-indexing code, although logically a part of the Oracle Server, was not known by the query optimizer to be a valid access path. As a result, text queries were evaluated as a two-step process:

1. The text predicate is evaluated. The text index is scanned and all the rows satisfying the predicate are identified. The row identifiers of all the relevant rows are written out into a temporary result table, say `results`.

2. The original query is rewritten as a join of the original query (minus the text operator) and the temporary result table containing row identifiers for rows that satisfy the text operator, as follows:

```
SELECT d.* FROM docs d, results r WHERE d.rowid = r.rid;
```

In Oracle8*i*, using the extensible indexing framework, the query is now executed in a single step in a pipelined fashion. The text-indexing code is invoked at the appropriate times by the kernel. There is no need for a temporary result table because the relevant row identifiers are streamed back to the server via the ODCI interfaces. This also implies that there are no extra joins to be performed in this execution model. Further, all rows that satisfy the text predicate do not have to be identified before the first result row can be returned to the user.

The performance of text queries has improved due to reduced I/O because of no temporary result table; improved response time because the row satisfying the text predicate can be identified on demand; and better query plans because the number of joins is reduced, as there are no extra joins with temporary result tables—a decrease in the number of joins typically improves the effectiveness of the optimizer due to reduced search space. We have observed as much as a 10-fold improvement in performance for certain search-intensive queries after the integration using the extensible indexing framework.

3.10.2   The Oracle8*i* Spatial Data Cartridge

The Oracle 8*i* Spatial cartridge allows users to store, spatially index, and query spatial data (Oracle 1999i). The spatial data is modeled as an object type `SDO_GEOMETRY`. The coordinate values describing a geometry are stored as a collection attribute within the object type.

A spatial index can be built on a `SDO_GEOMETRY` column. The spatial index consists of a collection of tiles corresponding to every spatial object and is stored in an Oracle table. The spatial index is an instance of a spatial Indextype that defines the routines for creating, maintaining, and querying the spatial index. The spatial Indextype supports an operator called `Overlaps`, which determines which geometries in two given layers overlap with each other.

EXAMPLE 10 A spatial query is of the form

```
SELECT   r.gid, p.gid
  FROM   roads r, parks p
 WHERE   Overlaps(r,p);
```

The extensible indexing framework has greatly improved the usability of the Oracle spatial cartridge. Prior to Oracle *8i*, the user had to explicitly invoke PL/SQL package routines to create an index or to maintain the spatial index following a DML operation to the base spatial table. With this framework, the spatial index is maintained implicitly by the server just like a built-in index.

Also, with the extensible indexing framework the logic of using the index to process the queries is encapsulated in the Indextype routines and the end user is not burdened with any details of the index implementation. Prior to Oracle *8i* the spatial query had to be formulated as follows:

```
SELECT   DISTINCT r.gid, p.gid
  FROM   roads_sdoindex r,parks_sdoindex p
 WHERE   (r.grpcode = p.grpcode) AND
         (r.sdo_code BETWEEN p.sdo_code AND p.sdo_maxcode
         OR p.sdo_code BETWEEN r.sdo_code
         AND r.sdo_maxcode)
```

The drawback of this approach is that the querying algorithm, which may be proprietary, has to be exposed to the user, the entire logic has to be expressed as a single SQL statement, and the user is expected to learn the details of the storage structures for the index. In addition to vastly simplifying the queries, the Oracle *8i* framework allows changing the underlying spatial indexing algorithms without requiring the end users to change their queries. The performance of spatial queries using the extensible indexing framework has been as good as the performance of the prior implementation.

3.10.3   The Oracle8*i* Visual Information Retrieval Data Cartridge

The Oracle8*i* Visual Information Retrieval (VIR) cartridge supports content-based retrieval of images (Oracle 1999k). An image is modeled as the `ORDImage` object type. A BLOB attribute stores the raw bytes of the image. The image cartridge supports building image indexes. For the purposes of building an index, each image is transformed into a signature, which is an abstraction of the contents of the image in terms of its visual attributes. A set of numbers that is a coarse representation of the signature is then stored in a table representing the index data. The cartridge supports an operator `Similar` that searches for images similar to a query image. The benefits of extensible indexing can be seen by analyzing the execution of the same image query before and in Oracle8*i*.

EXAMPLE 11

Consider the query:

```
SELECT  *
  FROM  images T
 WHERE  VIRSimilar(T.img.Signature, querySignature,
                   'globalcolor=0.5, localcolor=0.0,
                    texture=0.5, structure=0.0', 10,1);
```

In releases prior to Oracle8*i*, the image cartridge had no indexing support. Hence, the operator was evaluated as a table scan, and the image comparison had to be done for every row.

In Oracle8*i*, using the extensible indexing framework, the `VIRSimilar` operator can be evaluated in three phases—the first phase is a filter that does a range query on the index data table, the second phase is another filter that is a computation of the distance measure, and the third phase does the actual image comparison. Thus, the complex problem of high-dimensional indexing is broken down into several simpler components. Also, the first two passes of filtering are very selective and greatly reduce the data set on which the image comparisons need to be performed.

The performance of image queries has improved due to the multilevel filtering process instead of doing the image comparison for every row and the optimization of the range query on the index data table using indexes. Thus, in Oracle8*i*, it is now possible to do image comparisons on tables storing millions of rows, something that was not possible in prior releases.

3.11 Conclusion

Oracle8*i* provides a framework for database extensibility so that complex, content-rich types can be supported and managed natively in the database. This framework provides the infrastructure needed to allow extensions of the database server by creating domain-specific components called data cartridges. The major services provided by the database (type system, server execution environment, indexing, query optimization, aggregation, etc.) are all capable of being customized through a special set of interfaces. These DCIs help the close integration of all kinds of data into the Oracle8*i* platform.

4

Extensible Indexing Support in DB2 Universal Database

Stefan Deßloch
Santa Teresa Lab, IBM Corp.

Weidong Chen
LinkAir Communications, Inc.

Jyh-Herng Chow
Oblix, Inc.

You-Chin (Gene) Fuh
Santa Teresa Lab, IBM Corp.

Jean Grandbois
Environmental Systems Research, Inc.

Michelle Jou
Santa Teresa Lab, IBM Corp.

Nelson Mattos
Santa Teresa Lab, IBM Corp.

Raiko Nitzsche
Universitat Rostock

Brian Tran
Santa Teresa Lab, IBM Corp.

Yun Wang
Santa Teresa Lab, IBM Corp.

4.1 Introduction

Emerging database (DB) applications require the scalable management of a large quantity of complex data together with traditional business data and flexible querying capabilities for business intelligence. Such applications are called universal applications (Stonebraker et al. 1999). Object-relational databases or universal servers are component database management systems (DBMSs) that have been developed to support such applications. They leverage the mature relational database technology, which provides scalability, reliability, and recovery. More important, they enable users to introduce application-specific types and methods into a database. These extensibility features can be seen as infrastructure for providing plug-in components that extend the built-in repertoire of database types and functions with support for additional, nonstandard data types. Tables in a database may now contain such user-defined objects as geographical shapes, images, and semi-structured or unstructured text documents.

IBM's DB2 Universal Database product (Chamberlin 1998; Davis 2000) implements important object-relational concepts that have been standardized in SQL:99 (ANSI 1999a), such as structured types with subtyping, inheritance, and value substitutability (Fuh et al. 1999); typed tables, table hierarchies, and object views (Carey et al. 1999); and user-defined functions and methods. With the object-relational features provided by DB2, the content-based search capabilities of DB2 can be extended to new data types such as text, image, video, audio, and spatial. To make this not only possible but also easy, IBM (working with customers and software vendors) has created the Relational Extenders—prepackaged collections of user-defined types, user-defined functions, triggers, constraints, and stored procedures that can easily be plugged into DB2's SQL engine to support integrated content search. This has enabled DB2 customers to quickly develop customized applications by using the functionality provided by DB2 and its Relational Extenders as parts that can be easily assembled to create powerful applications that meet the search requirements of today.

The business value of complex data and nonstandard content cannot be fully realized unless efficient searching and querying can be provided on user-defined objects together with the traditional business data. In order to achieve this, component database management systems have to support a plug-in architecture that goes beyond the support of merely adding new data types. The concept of plug-in components also has to be supported at the index-management level to allow for the definition of new data-access methods for user-defined types. Unfortunately, existing commercial databases are rather primitive in their support of access and indexing of user-defined objects. B-trees (Bayer & McCreight 1972; Comer 1979) often serve as the sole indexed-access method. Indexing is also limited in that an index can be created only on table columns whose data types are understood by the access methods and an indexed scan of a table can exploit only those predicates that are understood by the access methods. For example, when a B-tree is the sole indexed access method, only columns of built-in types can be indexed and only relational operators can be exploited during an indexed scan of a table.

This chapter presents a high-level framework of indexing for user-defined types. Our framework allows users to concentrate on the semantics of applications and user-defined predicates without being concerned with low-level details of locking, recovery, buffer management, or balanced search-tree updates. It is tightly integrated with the database engine and enhances the value of the underlying access methods, built-in or user-defined, in a database system by supporting indexing on new data types and indexed scans using new predicates.

In addition, the enhanced flexibility of providing user-defined methods for generating index entries and search ranges makes our high-level user-defined indexing support a very attractive solution for coupling object-relational databases with external, content-specific search engines that need to continue to store and maintain content-specific indexes outside the database. Using our approach, the content-specific indexing mechanisms of search engines, such as full-text retrieval engines, can be exploited without having to extend the database engine with new access methods or having to break up the search engine to map its indexing scheme to database index structures.

The proposed framework has been implemented in the IBM DB2 Universal Database (Chamberlin 1998). Its generality, ease of use, and performance advantage have been demonstrated in several different domains of applications including, among others, spatial databases (Wang et al. 1998), indexing (Chow et al. 1999) on structured XML (Extensible Markup Language) documents (XML 97), and coupling DB2 with an external full-text search engine.

The rest of this chapter is organized as follows. Section 4.2 revisits the implicit assumptions that are hard-wired in existing database systems that make them inadequate for indexing on user-defined objects. Section 4.3 presents our high-level framework for direct user control over the indexing of user-defined types. Section 4.4 demonstrates its application in two distinct domains. Section 4.5 focuses on using our high-level indexing framework for integrating external search engines. Section 4.6 reports on performance experiences, and Section 4.7 discusses related work and concludes the chapter.

4.2   Hard-Wired Indexing

B-trees are arguably the most popular indexed access method in relational databases (Bayer & McCreight 1972; Comer 1979). Existing database systems are heavily hard-wired to support only B-tree indexing on primitive data with relational operators. This section reviews the implicit assumptions that have been made and examines the resulting limitations for the indexing of user-defined types.

With B-trees as the built-in indexed access method, most database systems only support primitive indexing that is limited by the B-tree indexed access method. Indices are defined by specifying the table name, the set of index columns, the sort order, and the unique constraint of an index:

```
CREATE TABLE employee
    (empno Char(6), name Char(20), title Char(20),
    salary Integer);

CREATE INDEX salary_index on employee (salary ASC);
```

A B-tree index is a balanced tree where each node contains a set of sort range–pointer pairs. Sort ranges are identified by an index key value and are used to determine the path of the B-tree traversal. Pointers are used to go from one level of the B-tree to another. For intermediate nodes, they point to the child nodes where the corresponding sort range is further divided. For leaf nodes, the pointers point to tuples stored in the table.

When a tuple is inserted into a table, the values of all index columns are concatenated to form the index key that is used to traverse the B-tree for the insertion of the new index entry. Similarly, when a tuple is deleted, the index key is used to identify the index entry for deletion. Once an index is created for a table, subsequent queries can take advantage of the indexed access path provided by the index:

```
SELECT name, salary FROM employee WHERE salary > 50000;
```

Existing database systems make several implicit assumptions in their indexing support due to the use of B-trees as the built-in, indexed access method. First, an index is created on the values of table columns directly. The index key is the concatenation of the values of the index columns. Clearly this is not acceptable for user-defined objects, which can be large binary objects or text documents that are not appropriate as index-key values. Even if all the index columns have built-in types, users may want to create an index on some values derived from the values of the index columns, for example, compensation level based on the salary or keywords in the title of a book (Lynch & Stonebraker 1988).

Second, a total order is assumed over the domain of index-key values. An indexing search is restricted by a single range of index-key values. For example, the predicate `salary > 50000` maps trivially to the range (50,000, ∞). This is not sufficient for a user-defined predicate that may bound a search in more than one dimension, for example, within a certain distance from a specific location.

Third, for index exploitation, which exploits any available indexes for efficient query execution, only simple predicates of relational operators are considered by query optimizers. User-defined predicates, however, may contain external functions. In a spatial database, a predicate such as `distance(location, point(10,10))` ≤ 5 may limit the search space of `location` within the circle centered at (10, 10) and with radius 5. Query compilers need to be able to recognize user-defined predicates and know how to derive the corresponding search space in order to exploit any index of user-defined types for efficient query execution.

4.3   High-Level Indexing of User-Defined Types

As identified in Section 4.2, built-in indexed access methods such as B-trees show a number of restrictions, making them unsuitable for user-defined types and predicates. Our framework of high-level indexing of user-defined types sits on top of the underlying access methods in a database system and eliminates these restrictions by providing direct user control over index maintenance, search key generation for user-defined predicates, and efficient predicate execution through filtering. This approach, which is illustrated in Figure 4.1, opens up the hard-wired index maintenance and exploitation logic used for traditional data types and provides the capability to plug in user-defined index components that precisely define the support for user-defined types and predicates, based on the underlying conventional access method(s), such as B-trees.

Figure 4.1 | **High-level indexing of user-defined types.**

Traditional data types	User-defined data types
Hard-wired: Index maintenance Search/lookup	**High-level indexing:** Index maintenance
Conventional acess methods	

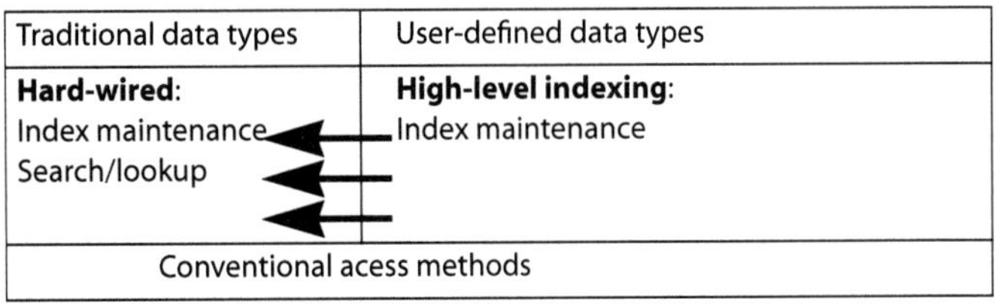

This section describes the main components of the framework and its implementation in IBM DB2 (Chamberlin 1998). To simplify the discussion, we consider indexing on a single column of a possibly user-defined type. This is not a restriction because indexing on multiple columns can be carried out in the same way, as if a new type were defined that contains one attribute for each index column.

4.3.1   Index Maintenance

Index maintenance deals with the update of an index when tuples are inserted, deleted, or updated in a table. Existing database systems often treat the value of an index column directly as its index key (i.e., the mapping from values of an index column to index keys is the trivial identity mapping). To untie index keys from the values of an index column, we allow a user-defined key transform. Given the value of an index column, the key transform returns one or more index key values. Therefore a key transform is, in general, a function that returns a set as its result and can be implemented as a table function in an object-relational DBMS. Each row in the result table forms an index key.

The introduction of key transforms brings several fundamental benefits. First of all, the domain of index keys is logically separated from the domain of values for an index column. Because an index column can be of any user-defined type, its values may be large objects (LOBs) or structurally rich text documents, among other things. It is impossible to store them directly in an index. Nevertheless, an index can still be created on them using index keys derived by the key transform.

Second, even if the values of an index column are all of built-in types, using index keys derived by a key transform can have some nice properties that are not satisfied by indexing on the index column values directly. For example, a high-dimensional space can be mapped to a linear-ordered space such that multidimensional clustering is preserved and reflected in the one-dimensional clustering (Bayer 1996; Jagadish 1990). Distance-preserving transformations have been successfully used to index high-dimensional data in many applications, such as time sequences (Faloutsos et al. 1994b) and images (Faloutsos et al. 1994a). In Berchthold et al. (1998), a new indexing method is proposed for high-dimensional data spaces that can be implemented through a mapping to a one-dimensional space. Key transforms allow the implementation of these new indexing methods on top of existing access methods such as B-trees.

Third, from an abstract interpretation point of view, index keys can be viewed as abstractions of the corresponding values of index columns and are simpler and/or occupy less space (Chow et al. 1999). For spatial applications, index keys often represent approximations of spatial objects, such as z-values in Orenstein & Manola (1988) or minimum bounding rectangles (MBRs) in R-trees (Guttman 1984). Depending on the abstraction defined by the key transform, the more information is stored in an index, the more filtering can be done by indexed search, thus offering a trade-off between indexing cost and search efficiency.

Fourth, a single value of an index column can be mapped to a number of index keys using a table function as a key transform. The relationship between values of an index column and index keys is no longer one to one, but many to many (e.g., z-transform, Orenstein & Manola 1988; and keywords in a book title, Lynch & Stonebraker 1988). Different values of an index column can have the same index key, and one value of an index column can have multiple index keys associated with it.

The idea of key transforms has been explored in Lynch & Stonebraker (1988) for keyword searching in textual databases. We are using the same idea as one of the building blocks for our framework of high-level indexing of user-defined types.

It should be mentioned that the idea of key transforms is not new (see Orenstein & Manola 1988). However, our framework allows users to define their own key transforms that will be managed automatically for index maintenance by the database system.

DEFINITION 1

Let S be a concrete domain and let I be a set of index keys. A key transform for S into I is a function K of type $S \rightarrow 2^I$. The key lookup for K is a function L from I to 2^S defined by $L(i) = \{s \mid i \in K(s)\}$. We call the quadruple (S, I, K, L) an index abstraction.

Notice that both K and L can be extended naturally to take a set of values and we will use the same symbol to denote such extensions.

EXAMPLE 1

The following are some examples of key transforms.
K_1: The identity function.
K_2: Maps a geographical object into a set of fixed-size grids.
K_3: Maps an XML document into a set of paths.
K_4: Maps a text document into a set of keywords.
The corresponding key lookup is the reverse mapping from index keys to user-defined objects. For example, the key lookup for K_4 maps a keyword into all documents containing the keyword.

In general, an index maintains the association between the indexed objects and their index keys. As far as users are concerned, an index provides a search function that, given an index key, returns the corresponding objects in the index. Because the set of objects that are indexed changes dynamically as tables are updated, the search function has to work correctly all the time. Definition 2 captures this notion of correctness more formally for the previously introduced concept of index abstractions.

DEFINITION 2 | Let $A = (S, I, K, L)$ be an index abstraction. An index with respect to A is a (search) function f from $2^S \times I$ to 2^S, where the first argument of f is a finite subset of S representing the set of objects that are currently in the index. An index f is sound (respectively, complete) if for every finite set $O \subseteq S$ (of indexed objects) and for every index key $i \in I$, $f(O, i) \subseteq O \cap L(i)$ (respectively, $f(O, i) \supseteq O \cap L(i)$).

The soundness of an index means that the search function will return only objects that have the given index key according to the key transform. The completeness of an index means that the search function will return all objects that have the given index key. In other words, given the set O of all objects that are currently indexed, the index-search function should compute exactly the restriction of the key lookup to O. For example, a textual index based on keywords should return exactly the set of indexed textual documents that contain a given keyword.

4.3.2 User-Defined Predicates and Search-Key Generation

Existing database systems support simple predicates of relational operators for which the corresponding search ranges can be easily determined based on the operators and the bound arguments. To provide extensible indexing over user-defined objects, two issues have to be tackled. First, a user-defined type may or may not support the standard relational comparisons. Even if it does, these relationships may not translate directly to search ranges over index keys. In addition, users may want to search based on application-specific predicates other than relational comparisons, such as `overlap` and `within` in spatial databases.

Second, a predicate or condition defined by a user can be an arbitrary condition representing some complicated relationship among different objects. When such a user-defined predicate is used to exploit any existing index for efficient query execution, the rich semantics of user-defined predicates requires the sophisticated computation of the corresponding search ranges to be used for the indexed scan of table. This is an efficiency issue because the complete range of index keys is always a logical candidate for search. Consider Example 2.

EXAMPLE 2 |
```
CREATE TABLE customer
    (name varchar(20), id integer, ..., xyloc location);

...

CREATE INDEX locationIdx on customer(xyloc);

...
```

```
SELECT * FROM customer WHERE within(xyloc, circle(...));
```

A straightforward representation is to use the x and y coordinates as the index key. An index key value is the concatenation of the x and y coordinates. Assuming that the concatenated keys are sorted first in the x coordinate and then in the y coordinate, then a single range over the index keys corresponds to a vertical slice in Figure 4.2. Thus, an implementation using B-trees for the SELECT statement can restrict the search only within the vertical slice. But the actual search region is the MBR containing the circle in the WHERE clause. This shows that a single range of index keys is insufficient to represent the search space accurately.

Figure 4.2 | **Search region for locating customers within a region.**

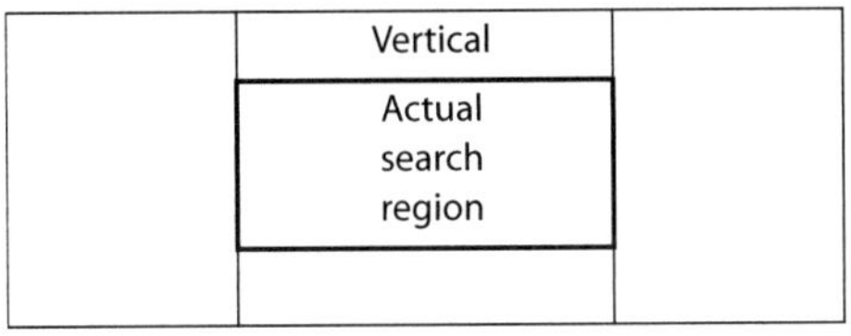

For extensible indexing with user-defined predicates, we want to represent the corresponding search region as closely as possible and introduce the concept of search methods. Each search method is a user-defined function that given a semantic relation over user-defined objects and one of its search patterns, returns a set of search keys.

DEFINITION 3 | Let $r(a_1, ..., a_n)$ be an n-ary relationship, where $n \geq 1$ and each a_i $(1 \leq i \leq n)$ is of some domain D_j. For each i $(1 \leq i \leq n)$, there is a corresponding search pattern of r for a_i in which a_i is the search target and every a_j $(j \neq i)$ is a search argument. Let A be an index abstraction of the form (D_j, I, K, L). A search method for the search pattern of r for a_i is a function of the search arguments, $g(a_1, ..., a_{i-1}, a_{i+1}, ..., a_n)$, that returns a subset of I. The search method $g(a_1, ..., a_{i-1}, a_{i+1}, ..., a_n)$ is sound with respect to relation r and index abstraction A if whenever $r(a_1, ..., a_n)$ holds, $a_i \in L[g(a_1, ..., a_{i-1}, a_{i+1}, ..., a_n)]$.

A search method computes the set of search keys over which the possible search targets can be found. For the query in Example 2, a search method can be defined for the semantic relationship within, where the first operand is the search target and the second operand is the search argument. Assuming that an index key is a fixed-size grid intersecting with an object, the search method can return the minimal set of grids that covers the circle given in the search argument.

A search method in general is only an approximation for the semantic relation r in the sense that every search target participating in the relation r with search arguments must have an index key among those returned by the search method. For instance, every geometric object that is `within` the circle given in the search argument must have a grid that is in the set of search keys generated by the search method.

However, a search method may not be exact, in the sense that some objects with an index key among those returned by the search method may not satisfy r with the search arguments. Therefore, it is necessary in general to evaluate r for every object that is found using the index keys from a search method.

4.3.3   Index Exploitation

Index exploitation is performed by query optimizers in order to use any index for efficient query execution. Traditionally, query optimizers have been able to exploit only simple relational operators for indexing because the corresponding search range can be easily determined. For index exploitation with user-defined predicates, the query compiler must be able to recognize them and find the relevant search methods to use. The definition of a user-defined function is extended to specify whether it can be used as a predicate and, if so, what search method to use when certain operands are search arguments. (See Section 4.3.4 for details of the syntax of predicate specifications.)

For the query in Example 2, suppose that `within` has been defined as a predicate that has an associated search method when the second operand is a search argument. The query compiler can choose an index scan over a table scan to retrieve records from the table `customer` for two reasons. One is that there is an index on `xyloc` attribute. The other is that the query compiler recognizes that the second operand of `within` is bound and `within` is a predicate with a search method when the second operand is a search argument. The index scan will use the corresponding search method to generate a set of search keys, which represents the minimal set of grids covering the circle in the second operand. The set of search keys will be used by the underlying access method to retrieve the relevant records from the table `customer`.

4.3.4   Implementation and Predicate Filtering

The high-level framework of indexing of user-defined types has been implemented in IBM DB2. In addition to index maintenance, user-defined predicates, and index exploitation, the implementation also provides user control over multistage evaluation of user-defined predicates through filtering. This avoids the potentially expensive evaluation of user-defined predicates and reduces both I/O and CPU costs.

Figure 4.3 shows the syntax for index extensions with the associated key transform and search methods. The semantic relation corresponding to a search method is not explicitly specified. The CREATE INDEX EXTENSION statement defines a parametric index extension. A parametric index extension is instantiated when an index is created on a table using CREATE INDEX statements. The parameters of an index extension can be used to specify, for example, the number of layers and the size of a grid in a multilayer grid index.

Figure 4.3 | Syntax for index extensions, where N^+ specifies one or more occurrences of N, with the separator ',' when appropriate.

```
<create index extension> ::=
    CREATE INDEX EXTENSION <header> <index maintenance>
    <index search>

<header> ::= <indexExtensionName> [ '(' {<parmName>
<parmType>}+ ')' ]

<index maintenance> ::=
    FROM SOURCE KEY '(' <colName> <colType> ')' /*
    index columns */
    GENERATE KEY USING  <key transform>

<index search> ::=
    WITH TARGET KEY '(' { <colName> <colType>}+ ')'
    SEARCH METHODS {<search method>}+

<search method> ::=
    WHEN <searchmethodName>  '('  {<colName>
    <colType>}+ ')' /* search arguments */
    RANGE THROUGH <search key producer>
    [ FILTER USING  <index filter> ]

<drop index extension> ::=
    DROP INDEX EXTENSION <indexExtensionName>

<create index> ::=
    CREATE INDEX <indexName> ON <tableName>
    '(' <colName> ')'
    USING <indexExtensionName> '(' {<constant>}+ ')'
```

The key aspects of an index extension include the key transform function (indicated by `<key transform invocation>`) and the associated search methods. Each search method contains a search-key producer function (indicated by `<search key producer>`) that computes the set of search keys given search arguments and an index-filter function (indicated by `<index filter>`) used inside the index component.

The user control over the index filter is a powerful concept. It provides early filtering using the index keys. This avoids the I/O cost of retrieving data that obviously do not satisfy the search criteria because data will not be retrieved from the disk using an index scan until the index keys are determined. This also makes it possible for users to combine multiple indexing mechanisms in a single search by plugging in an index filter that performs additional search (e.g., using an external search engine).

Figure 4.4 shows the syntax of user-defined functions that can serve as predicates. Each predicate specification indicates an optional filter function, and the associated search methods for various search patterns. The data filter aims to reduce the potentially expensive evaluation of the predicate by filtering out records that do not satisfy the predicate

Figure 4.4 | **Syntax for user-defined predicates and their associated search methods.**

```
<create function> ::=

    CREATE FUNCTION <functionName> '(' {[ <parmName}]

    <dataType>}+ ')'

    ...     /* additional options */

    [ PREDICATES '(' <predicate specification>+ ')' ]


<predicate specification> ::=

    WHEN  ( '=' | '<>' | '<' | '>' | '<=' | '>=' )

    ( <constant> | EXPRESSION AS <expr-name> )

    [ FILTER USING <data filter> ]

    <index exploitation>


<index exploitation> ::=

    SEARCH BY [ EXACT ] INDEX EXTENSION

    <indexExtensionName> <exploitation rule>+


<exploitation rule> ::=

    WHEN KEY '(' { <paramName> }+ ')'   /* search target */

    USE <searchmethodName> '(' { <paramName> }+ ')'
```

using simpler and cheaper operations. In `<exploitation rule>`, the parameters following `WHEN KEY` indicate the search argument.

The optional keyword `EXACT` following `SEARCH BY` requires a little explanation. When an index scan using a predicate is executed, the corresponding search method, which is a user-defined function, is invoked. It computes a set of search keys for the search target using the search arguments. The search keys are sent to the underlying access methods to retrieve the relevant records. The index filter associated with the search method is applied, if one exists, before the records are retrieved from the disk. The relational data manager then applies the data filter associated with the predicate specification. Finally, all records that pass through the data filter are evaluated using the predicate.

When the index lookup and the filters defined by an index extension provide only an approximation for the predicate (e.g., in spatial applications), the final step of predicate evaluation is still necessary. However, in other applications such as document search, the index lookup together with the (optional) index filter may compute the exact set of all answers that satisfy the predicate. The final step of data filter and predicate evaluation should not be carried out in this case. The keyword `EXACT` indicates such a situation.

Figure 4.5 shows the architecture of the implementation in DB2. It can leverage any underlying access methods that are available. The rectangular boxes represent places where user-defined functions can be plugged in to support user-defined search. The key transform is invoked in the index manager for index maintenance when tuples are

Figure 4.5 | **Implementation of high-level indexing of user-defined types.**

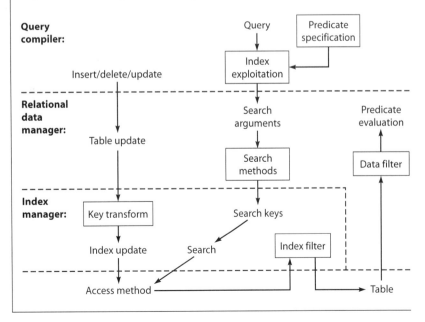

inserted, deleted, or updated in a table. The query compiler uses specifications of user-defined predicates for index exploitation. During a search based on a user-defined predicate, the corresponding search method is invoked by the relational data manager to generate a set of search keys.

For retrieval based on a user-defined predicate, two filters are included in the architecture. The purpose is to avoid the potentially expensive evaluation of user-defined predicates. Users can specify simpler and cheaper functions to be applied as filters before predicate evaluation. The index filter filters out records before they are retrieved from the disk into buffers inside the relational data manager. The data filter in the relational data manager presents another chance for cost-efficient filtering before expensive predicates are evaluated.

4.4　Applications

In this section, we illustrate how the generic framework for high-level indexing of user-defined types can be applied effectively in two widely different content domains: geographic information systems and XML document search. Note that the applicability of our framework is by no means limited to these areas.

4.4.1　Indexing for Geographical Information System Applications

In traditional geographical information systems (GISs), indexing on spatial data is provided through a set of proprietary APIs. When a query involves searching on spatial data, the spatial predicates are transformed for index exploitation, and the resulting query is then sent to the database for optimization and evaluation. The lack of integration of spatial indexing with the database engine leads to integrity issues and performance hits. Our framework of high-level indexing makes it possible to have spatial indexing in a database and still take advantage of the special search methods that have been developed in GISs.

EXAMPLE 3 | Suppose that the following user-defined types have been created.

```
CREATE TYPE envelop AS
     (xmin  int,
      ymin  int,
      xmax ç int,
      ymax  int);

CREATE TYPE shape AS
     (gtype varchar(20),
```

```
        mbr envelop,
        numpart sint,
        numpoint sint,
        geometry BLOB(1M))
NOT INSTANTIABLE;

CREATE TYPE point UNDER shape;

CREATE TYPE line UNDER shape;

CREATE TYPE polygon UNDER shape;
```

where `shape` serves as a supertype for various subtypes such as lines and polygons. Two tables have been defined in the database, one storing the information about schools and the other containing the information on households and their income information:

```
CREATE TABLE schools AS
    (name varchar(20),
     district varchar(20),
     address varchar(20),
     area shape,
     PRIMARY KEY (name, district));

CREATE TABLE households AS
    (address varchar(20),
     annualincome int,
     location shape);
```

The following query tries to compute the average annual income of all households inside the attendance area of a specific school:

```
SELECT  avg(h.annualincome)
  FROM  households h, schools s
 WHERE  s.name = 'Armstrong Elementary'
        AND s.district = 'Highland Park'
        AND within(h.location, s.area);
```

To allow the efficient execution of this query, we need to (a) create an index extension incorporating user-defined key transform and search methods for `shape`, (b) create an index on table `households` using the index extension, and (c) specify predicates for `within` and the associated search methods. The following statement defines an index extension over type `shape`. It uses a multilayer grid index for shapes.

```
CREATE INDEX EXTENSION gridshape(levels varchar(20)
FOR BIT DATA)
FROM SOURCE KEY (sh shape)
GENERATE KEY USING gridkeys(levels,
    sh..mbr..xmin, sh..mbr..ymin, sh..mbr..xmax,
    sh..mbr..ymax)
WITH TARGET KEY (level int, gx int, gy int,
    xmin int, ymin int, xmax int, ymax int)
SEARCH METHODS
    WHEN search_within(area shape)
    RANGE THROUGH gridrange(levels,
        area..mbr..xmin, area..mbr..ymin,
        area..mbr..xmax, area..mbr..ymax)
    FILTER USING checkduplicate(
        level, gx, gy, xmin, ymin, xmax, ymax,
        levels, area..mbr..xmin, area..mbr..ymin,
        area..mbr..xmax, area..mbr..ymax)
    WHEN search_contain(loc shape)
    RANGE THROUGH gridrange(levels,
        loc..mbr..xmin, loc..mbr..ymin,
        loc..mbr..xmax, loc..mbr..ymax)
    FILTER USING mbroverlap(xmin, ymin, xmax, ymax,
        loc..mbr..xmin, loc..mbr..ymin,
        loc..mbr..xmax, loc..mbr..ymax);
```

(DB2 uses the double-dot notation for accessing attributes of objects of user-defined types.) The index extension definition specifies the function for key transform, `gridkeys` and two search methods: one for searching within a specific area and the other for finding shapes that contain a specific location. Both search methods use the same function, `gridrange`, to generate a set of index keys for potential search targets. Each search method has its own filtering function. All the functions that are mentioned may be user-defined functions, whose definitions are omitted here.

We are now ready to create an index on the `location` column of table `households`:

```
CREATE INDEX houselocIDX ON households(location)
USING gridshape('10 100 1000');
```

The parameter indicates three levels of grid sizes.

For index exploitation, we need to define the predicates and their associated search methods. The following specification indicates that `within` should be viewed as a predicate.

```
CREATE FUNCTION within(s1 shape, s2 shape) RETURNS int
LANGUAGE C ... EXTERNAL NAME '/lib/spatial/
gislib!within'
PREDICATES (
    WHEN = 1
    FILTER USING mbrwithin(s1..mbr..xmin, s1..mbr..ymin,
        s1..mbr..xmax, s1..mbr..ymax,
        s2..mbr..xmin, s2..mbr..ymin,
        s2..mbr..xmax, s2..mbr..ymax)
    SEARCH BY INDEX EXTENSION gridshape
        WHEN KEY (s1) USE search_within(s2)
        WHEN KEY (s2) USE search_contain(s1));
```

The last three lines indicate that searching based on predicates of `within` will be done using an index extension `gridshape`. When the first argument `s1` is the search target, use search method `search_within` with `s2` as the search argument. When the second argument `s2` is the search target, use search method `search_contain`, with `s1` as the search argument. The query compiler is able to generate a plan that takes advantage of the access path provided by the index on `location` of table `households`. The key transform, search-key producer, and filtering functions will be called automatically at appropriate places.

4.4.2   Indexing on XML Documents

The high-level framework of indexing of user-defined types has also been applied to structured documents, such as XML documents (XML 1997). These documents are organized by nested tags with application-defined semantics. Searching for XML documents often requires a structured search, where queried words are matched only within particular structures. These structures are specified by a path expression consisting of a sequence of tags. For example, if a user wants to search for documents whose chapters contain the word "Data," the user may invoke a user-defined function `structSearch(content, 'book. toc.chapter', 'Data')`, where the argument `book.toc.chapter` specifies the path leading to chapters. If an XML document is stored as an attribute in a relational table, an immediate question is how to search these documents efficiently, or more specifically, how to create an index for a structured search that does not require scanning source documents at query-execution time.

Supporting a structured search requires a tight integration of searching on structures (matching path expressions) and searching on content (matching the keyword list) (Baeza-Yates & Navarro 1996; Consens & Milo 1994; McHugh et al. 1997). The challenge comes from the facts that indexing for a structured search is not readily available and that indexing for content search often relies on an external full-text index. With the high-level framework of indexing of user-defined types, we are able to achieve the necessary tight integration. The structure index is implemented inside DB2 and, at the same time, interacts with the external full-text index outside DB2.

EXAMPLE 4

The following shows the declaration of an index extension for a structured search.

```
CREATE INDEX EXTENSION xml_structure
FROM SOURCE KEY (xml db2xml)
GENERATE KEY USING pathGenerator(xml..doc)
WITH TARGET KEY (path varchar(100),
    doc varchar(100), position int)
SEARCH METHODS
    WHEN structure (path varchar(100), word varchar(20))
        RANGE THROUGH pathRange(path)
        FILTER USING checkFullText(path, doc,
                                    position, word);
```

where `db2xml` is a user-defined type for XML documents. The key transform is a user-defined function `pathGenerator`. It generates a set of paths from a document `docid` and results in a set of index keys of the form `(path, docid, position)`. There is only one search method in this index extension, `structure` with two arguments. The user-defined function `pathRange(path)` produces a set of search keys given a path, which is filtered inside the index manager by the user-defined function `checkFullText(path, docid, position, word)`. The filter actually invokes an external full-text index for content search, thus achieving an integration of a structured search with an external full-text content search.

The following shows an example of a table using the index extension and a user-defined predicate for index exploitation.

```
CREATE TABLE designdb(docid integer, author char(20),
                        notes db2xml);

...

CREATE INDEX docIdx on designdb(notes) using xml_structure;
```

```
. . .
CREATE FUNCTION searchStruct(xml db2xml, path varchar(100),
      word varchar(20)) RETURNS integer
LANGUAGE C . . .
EXTERNAL NAME '/home/chowjh/xml/xmllib!searchStructure'
PREDICATES (
    WHEN = 1
    SEARCH BY EXACT INDEX EXTENSION xml_structure
        WHEN KEY (xml) USE structure(path, word));

. . .

SELECT  *
  FROM  designdb
  WHERE  searchStruct(notes, 'book.toc.chapter', 'SQLJ');
```

For this query, the optimizer may generate a query plan that uses the index scan. Because the search target is the first argument of the predicate searchStruct, the search method structure is used. During query execution, the structured index of path expressions is first searched using the search argument 'book.toc.chapter'. All index keys that are found are then filtered by calling checkFullText, which returns only those index keys for which the word 'SQLJ' occurs at the corresponding position in the corresponding document. Only those XML documents that satisfy both criteria are retrieved from the table designdb. It should be mentioned that the integration of a structured search using path expressions with a content search using keywords occurs inside the index manager, thus avoiding unnecessary data retrieval from the disk.

Without our framework of high-level indexing, it is rather difficult for users to explore the integrated search of XML documents using both path expressions and keywords. For example, an alternative to Example 4 might be to have two separate user-defined predicates, one for exploring the structured index only and one for exploring the external full-text keyword index only:

```
SELECT  *
  FROM  designdb
  WHERE  searchpath(notes, 'book.toc.chapter') AND
         searchword(notes, 'SQLJ')
```

However, this is not really a viable alternative, in terms of neither semantics nor performance. The new query does not support the intended semantics where the keyword 'SQLJ' is searched for only within the structure indicated by the path expression. Instead it will search the entire document for the keyword. In terms of efficiency, only one predicate will be used for index exploitation and the other predicate will serve as a filter after the corresponding documents are retrieved from the disk.

4.5 Loose Integration of External Search Engines

The previous section showed the use of our high-level indexing approach for tightly integrating new search capabilities into the DB engine, storing the complete index data for content search inside the database itself. While this is, in general, the preferred approach, it may not always be feasible because it may require the mapping of highly tuned content-specific index data structures and the processing model of existing content-specific search and indexing engines to the indexing approach of the database system. This can very often be too costly or result in limitations. For example, consider the integration of full-text retrieval into the database. Following the standard approach of supporting full-text queries through inverted word lists, we can easily realize an index extension for text whose key-transform function produces a table of all the words that appear in an indexed document and stores each row of the table as a separate entry in the underlying B-tree. However, in order to process a proximity search on text, such as find all documents where the word "database" appears in the same sentence as "object-relational," a sophisticated full-text retrieval engine needs to also store positional information in the text index and needs to efficiently aggregate and combine index lookups for individual words with one another to determine the result of the text query. If we wanted to store the text index information in DB2 indexes completely, this would require the means to combine the outcomes of the index lookup operations for each word (i.e., "database" and "object-relational") using a join operation based on the document identifier (id) and sentence number. This goes beyond the capabilities offered by our extensible indexing approach. However, extensible indexing provides effective support for solving this problem through a loosely coupled approach for integrating external search engines, which we explore using the DB2 Text Extender.

4.5.1 DB2 Text Extender Overview

The DB2 Text Extender, a plug-in component developed for IBM's DB2 Universal Database product (Chamberlin 1998), employs DB2's object-relational features to provide user-defined types and user-defined functions for integrating text search into DB2 by using an IBM stand-alone text-search engine called SearchManager.

EXAMPLE 5

Using Text Extender, a user can define a table with a full-text document column in the following way to create a table with information about projects.

```
CREATE TABLE projects (
    proj_no         integer,
    title           varchar(50),
    budget          integer,
    description     CHARACTER LARGE OBJECT,
    description_id  db2texth)
```

Text content is stored in the table using the traditional data types available for character data, such as variable-length character data types or character LOBs. Each text column is accompanied by an additional column of type db2texth, which is a user-defined type introduced by Text Extender. The values of these columns (also called text handles) serve, among other things, to uniquely identify the text documents in the text column for the search engine.

When issuing text-search queries, the accompanying handle column has to be used instead of the text column itself, as illustrated in the following query.

```
SELECT  proj_no, title
  FROM  compschema.projects
 WHERE  contains(description_id,
          ' "database" IN SAME SENTENCE AS
          "object-relational" ') = 1
```

This query would return all projects with a textual description that contains the word "database" in the same sentence as "object-relational." The contains function involved in this query is used to perform the text search and has two arguments (a value of type db2texth and a search pattern string).

Figure 4.6 illustrates the basic architecture of the Text Extender in terms of the interaction of the database engine with the text-search engine and helps to clarify how the query in Example 5 would be evaluated. Please note that the architecture depicted in the figure is so far incomplete; it illustrates only aspects related to text-search user-defined functions (UDFs). Additional functionality and components of Text Extender, such as client components and administrative APIs, are not described. The query is submitted via a DB2 client to the DB2 server engine. For each row in the projects table, the engine calls the contains function with the contents of the description_id column and the search pattern as arguments. The contains function is a user-defined

Figure 4.6 | **Interaction of database and text-search engine in Text Extender.**

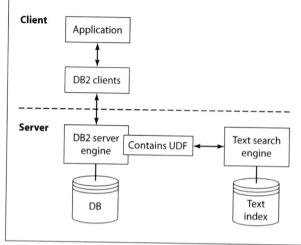

function written in a 3GL (C). It again calls the text-search engine (realized as a set of C functions in a shared library), passing it the search pattern as well as the name of the index covering the text documents stored in the `description` column of the `Projects` table.[1] The text-search engine returns the result of the text search to the contains UDF body in form of a list of document identifiers (i.e., values of the type `db2texth`). The UDF checks whether the identifier that has been supplied by the database engine is actually contained in the result list returned by the text-search engine and returns the appropriate result (1 for true, or 0 for false) to the database engine. Based on the result of the `contains` function call, the database engine will construct the query result. It is possible for the `contains` UDF to keep the results returned by the text-search engine across invocations inside of a query by using a special scratchpad memory area supplied by the engine. Therefore, the actual text search using the external text-search engine has to be performed only once, during the first invocation of the contains UDF inside of a query.

There are several issues related to this type of coupling that we address here very briefly.

- Text-index creation is initiated using a separate Text Extender API implemented on top of DB2. It used DB2-stored procedures to have the text engine build the index, which consists of a set of files stored outside DB2 in an index directory on the server system.

- Meta-information relevant for the text search, such as the names of database columns enabled for the text search and the names of the external text indexes covering a certain database column are stored

---

[1] This information is stored in Text Extender system catalogue tables in the database.

in additional catalogue tables. The catalogue table is a regular DB2 table whose contents are manipulated by the Text Extender administrative functions, but can be read by the end user using standard SQL.

- To construct the external text index, a separate process is initiated that accesses the text catalogue table and determines the text column containing the text data, as well as the associated handle column. It then reads the text data plus the handle on a per-document basis and analyzes the text for constructing the index entries, storing the text handle value as a unique identifier of the document inside the index.

- DB2 triggers, which may also call UDFs in the conditions and trigger bodies, are used to reflect updates performed on text columns correctly in the corresponding text indexes.

- The `contains` UDF for text search runs in the same process and address space as the database engine. This extremely minimizes UDF overhead by eliminating expensive interprocess communication.[2]

For a detailed description, the reader is referred to (IBM 1999).

4.5.2   Exploiting High-Level User-Defined Indexing

Although the described architecture permits the exploitation of an external text-search engine through its native APIs and usually limits the interaction to a single call (performed during the first call of the `contains` UDF), there is no way to avoid a full-table scan on the `Projects` table. In other words, although the text-search engine can provide the result in form of a set of identifiers in one call, the database engine will call the `contains` function for each row in the table. The main problem is therefore: How can the set of identifiers returned by a text index lookup (involving the API of the external text-search engine) be fed back into the database query-evaluation process in a way that is comparable to a traditional database index lookup to avoid the table scan.

In order to solve this problem, we use our user-defined indexing framework in a way that fundamentally differs from the use demonstrated in the previous sections. Instead of indexing on the text content itself (which is left under the control of the external text-search engine), we index only on the identifiers of the text documents. In other words, the index is built on the text handle of type `db2texth`, and the key-transform function only extracts the text document identifier that is stored as a part of that handle to populate the index entries in DB2. The search method of the index then passes the text-search

---

[2] In addition, DB2 supports a fenced execution mode for untrusted UDFs, in which the UDF runs in its own process, separate from the DB engine.

argument to its range-producer function, which uses the functionality of the text-search engine to perform the external index lookup for the text search. The list of text document identifiers returned by the search engine is then returned as a set of document identifier ranges as the result of the range-producer function of our new index type.

The following statement creates the index extension for our Text Extender.

```
CREATE INDEX EXTENSION TextIdx(protHd VARCHAR(60) FOR BIT
DATA)
FROM SOURCE KEY (handle-id db2texth)
    GENERATE KEY USING TXGetKey(handle-id)
WITH TARGET KEY (x_key VARCHAR(18) FOR BIT DATA)
SEARCH METHODS
    WHEN containSearch (s_arg LONG VARCHAR)
        RANGE THROUGH TXGetHandleSet(protHd, s_arg);
```

Additional index metadata can be provided at index creation time using the protHd (prototype handle) index parameter and is then available to the range-producer function. This includes information such as the name of the external text index, which has to be provided as an input parameter to the text search engine during text search.[3]

EXAMPLE 6   Let us illustrate index creation using the TextIdx index extension.

```
CREATE INDEX Desc_idx ON Projects(description_h)
USING TextIdx('...IX1234...')
```

This statement, whose effects are illustrated in Figure 4.7 on page 130, creates an index on the description_h column of the Projects table, providing the name of the external index IX1234 as a property of the newly created index. During index creation (and during further insert, update, or delete operations on the Projects table), the key-transform function TxGetKey is invoked and extracts the document identifiers from the text handles. These identifiers are stored in the DB2 index Desc_idx (together with the internal row identifiers used by DB2).

In order to be able to use the TextIdx index extension during a text search, we have to define the contains UDF as a user-defined predicate.

---

[3] Note that this data definition language (DDL) statement would be issued by the Text Extender administration component as part of enabling a column for text search. An end user would not need to know about the detailed meta-information.

```
CREATE FUNCTION contains(TextHd db2texth,
                         s_arg LONG VARCHAR)

   RETURNS INTEGER

      ...

PREDICATES (
   WHEN = 1
   SEARCH BY EXACT INDEX EXTENSION TextIDX
      WHEN KEY(TextHd) USE containSearch(s_arg));
```

Details of the index exploitation during text search are illustrated in Figure 4.8. When processing the example's SELECT statement, the optimizer realizes that contains is a user-defined predicate that is supported by an index extension, and determines that the existing index Desc_idx can be exploited to process the query. If an index access is indicated based on the cost information available to the optimizer, then the containSearch search method is used for the index lookup, based on the information provided in the CREATE FUNCTION statement. The text-search argument provided in the invocation of the contains function will be passed to the search method and, in turn, to the range producer function TxGetHandleSet. Together with the index meta-information, the search argument is then used by the range producer function to query the external index IX1234 using the text-search engine. The result of the text search, which is a list of identifiers, is then turned into a set of identifier ranges (in this case, with identical start-stop key values), which is then passed back to the index manager to do the lookup on the DB2 index Desc_Idx to locate the actual rows that match the text document identifiers. Because the text index itself gives back the exact results for the text search (instead of an approximate result that only provides a filtering capability), no further evaluation of the original contains UDF is required in the processing of the query.

4.5.3 Generalization for Arbitrary Predicates

The approach in Example 6 supports the rewrite of user-defined functions that return a Boolean value. What if a function returns other (numeric or non-numeric) values and appears as an operand of an arbitrary SQL predicate?

Assume the following definition for the UDF rank,

```
CREATE FUNCTION rank (id db2texth, arg LONG VARCHAR)
RETURNS DOUBLE PRECISION;
```

Figure 4.7 | **Creating an index of type TextIdx.**

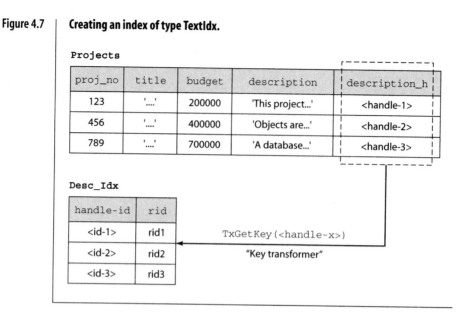

Figure 4.8

Exploitation of TextIdx index extension during search.

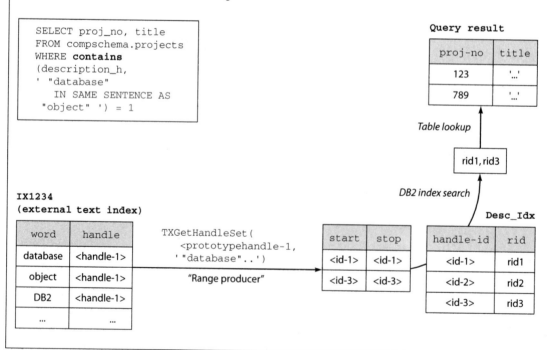

This function behaves like the `contains` function, but returns a rank value instead of a Boolean value, describing how well a document meets the text-search criteria. For example, the query

```
SELECT  proj_no, title
  FROM  projects
 WHERE  rank (description,
             '"database" IN SAME SENTENCE AS
             "object-relational"')
        >0.5
```

would retrieve all text information for documents that matches the given search argument with a rank value > 0.5 (all rank values range between 0 and 1). Instead of evaluating the rank UDF for each of the rows in the `projects` table, it is very desirable for performance reasons to be able to push down the rank value limit (0.5) into the index lookup, if the text-search engine supports the computation of the rank value as a part of the text index lookup or if its APIs allow the specification of a rank-value threshold for full-text retrieval.

Our approach of using the extensible indexing framework can be easily applied to solve this problem as well. The first step is to provide another search method as part of the text index extension that accepts a rank-value threshold.

```
CREATE INDEX EXTENSION TextIdx(protHd VARCHAR(60) FOR
BIT DATA)
FROM SOURCE KEY (handle-id db2texth)
    GENERATE KEY USING TXGetKey(handle-id)
WITH TARGET KEY (x_key VARCHAR(18) FOR BIT DATA)
SEARCH METHODS
    WHEN containSearch (s_arg LONG VARCHAR)
        RANGE THROUGH TXGetHandleSet(protHd, s_arg)
        WHEN rankSearch (s_arg LONG VARCHAR,
                      limit DOUBLE PRECISION)
        RANGE THROUGH TXGetRankHandleSet(protHd, s_arg,
                                                limit);
```

In addition, the definition of the `rank` UDF would have to reflect the potential exploitation of the text index extension in the following way.

```
CREATE FUNCTION rank(TextHd db2texth, s_arg LONG VARCHAR)
    RETURNS DOUBLE PRECISION

        . . .

PREDICATES (
    WHEN > EXPRESSION AS limit
```

```
SEARCH BY EXACT INDEX EXTENSION TextIDX
    WHEN KEY(TextHd) USE rankSearch(s_arg, limit));
```

The clause EXPRESSION AS limit and the use of limit as an additional argument in USE clause defines that the limit used as the second operand of the > predicate will be provided as an additional argument to the rankSearch search method if the DB2 optimizer chooses to exploit the index extension. Given our example, this would finally result in the following invocation of the range-producer function for the rankSearch search method.

```
TXGetRankHandleSet(

    '...IX1234...',

    '"database" IN SAME SENTENCE AS "object-relational"',

    0.5)
```

4.6   Performance

Our framework of high-level indexing of user-defined types extends the expressive power and integrated optimization of SQL queries to user-defined types. This section presents some preliminary performance measurements for GIS applications using the existing GIS architecture and our integrated approach, introduced in Section 4.4.1 and also implemented in the DB2 Spatial Extender.

The existing GIS architecture is represented by Spatial Database Engine, SDE 3.0.2 on DB2 UDB Version 5 from ESRI (ESRI 2000), which uses a spatial data engine external to the database for optimization of spatial queries. Given a table with business data and a column of spatial attributes, SDE introduces a new feature table to represent spatial data and a new index to process spatial queries. The feature table contains an id column as the primary key and all the spatial attributes and the geometric shapes. The spatial column in the original table (called business table) is replaced by an id column that is a foreign key for the feature table.

In addition to the feature table, SDE maintains a spatial index table, which uses a three-level grid-based index method in our example. The spatial index table contains the feature id (which is a foreign key for the feature table) and the indexing information such as the location of the lower-left grid cell and the feature's MBR.

When processing a spatial search query, SDE uses the spatial index table and the feature table to compute a list of (ids of) candidate shapes that satisfy the spatial predicate. The computed list of candidate shapes is then used to retrieve data from the business table by applying the remaining predicates in the WHERE clause of the spatial search query.

Currently SDE handles the join between the business table and the feature table itself by executing different queries.

EXAMPLE 7

We use the census block data for the state of Kentucky, which has 137,173 polygons, with an average of 31 points per polygon. The table `kentuckyBlocks` has a column `boundary` of spatial type `POLYGON`, in addition to other attributes such as the name and the total population. Each polygon represents an area, containing as few as 4 points and as many as 3416 points.

```
CREATE TABLE kentuckyBlocks
    (name varchar(20), ..., boundary POLYGON)
```

The following queries represent some typical operations in GIS applications.

- Loading: Includes raw-data loading through a sequence of SQL insert statements and the maintenance of spatial indexes.
- Region queries: For three predefined regions in different locations, with the sizes of the answer sets being 3155, 2387, and 1457.
- Point queries: One hundred random point searches, simulating users pointing at a polygon during spatial browsing.
- Region queries with attributes: Same as region queries except that nonspatial attributes such as the name and the total population are also fetched in addition to the spatial data.
- Fetch all: Measures how fast data can be pumped out of a database.

All queries were run on the IBM RS6000/J40 server and during off-hours to minimize variations due to other users and processes. The GIS client programs are run on the same machine as the server. The measurements of query execution time (rounded to seconds) are shown in Table 4.1. Data loading was run once, while the rest of the queries were run three times (the averages are shown).

Table 4.1 **Performance measurements of spatial queries.**

Queries	Loading	Region Queries			Region Queries with Attributes			Point Queries	Fetch All
		R1	R2	R3	R1	R2	R3		
GIS	3012	19	13.66	8	20	14.66	9	9.66	731
Integrated	706	8	5	3.33	7.66	4.66	3	8	169.67

In both loading and fetch all, we process the entire table and the integrated approach is about four times faster. In the case of loading, an insert statement for a row in the integrated approach becomes three insert statements in the GIS approach, one for the business table, one for the feature table, and one for the spatial index table. In the case of fetch all, because the GIS approach handles the join between the business table and the feature table by itself, it executes a separate query against the feature table repeatedly, once for each set of data retrieved from the business table.

For region queries without nonspatial attributes, the integrated approach is approximately two and one-half times faster than the GIS approach, but is about three times faster for region queries with nonspatial data. The difference is that the second case involves the access of the business table.

The GIS approach performs very well for point queries. Overall, the results show that our integrated approach of high-level indexing of spatial data has a much better performance. This shows the value of enhancing the database engine for the extensible indexing of complex data.

4.7   Related Work and Conclusion

Universal applications involving both complex queries and complex data demand strong and flexible support for nontraditional data such as geographical information and structured documents. Indexing of user-defined types with user-defined predicates is crucial to meeting the demands of component database applications. Therefore, component DBMSs have to support the concept of plug-in components, not only for data type and functions, but also at the index management level to allow for the definition of new data access methods for user-defined types.

Several approaches have been investigated to provide extensibility in data access and indexing. One approach is to support extensible indexing through query rewriting. Normally a separate entity manages the special access methods and indexing on complex data of which the database engine is unaware. A user query involving predicates on complex data is transformed into a different query by taking into consideration the access methods and indexing specific to complex data. The indexes may be stored in a relational database or in external files. For example, in a typical GIS such as ESRI's SDE (ESRI 2000), a spatial data engine supplies a set of proprietary spatial functions and predicates and uses a relational database to store both user tables and side tables representing the spatial indexes. Spatial predicates in a user query are converted by the spatial data engine into joins with and predicates on the side tables. The resulting query is then given to the relational database for optimization and execution.

The query-rewriting approach does not require modifications to the database engine and is therefore the only option for an application developer if the underlying DBMS does not support indexing on complex data. The query-rewriting approach offers an excellent solution to the problem of building advanced spatial applications with decent performance. However, its lack of integration with the database engine raises integrity, usability, and performance issues. For data integrity, the indexes on complex data must be kept consistent with other business data, which is now the responsibility of the application developer or the database administrator (e.g., by using triggers to achieve consistency). In general, usability suffers from the fact that the application programmer more or less has to be aware of the index model and structure, which is now exposed as part of the overall data model unless there is an additional API layer that hides the database completely. From a performance perspective, because the database engine is unaware of special indexes for complex data, it may fail to generate the most efficient query-execution plan.

One can also implement application-specific access methods. There is no shortage of special access methods for spatial or multidimensional data (Gaede & Günther 1998). Unfortunately, only B-trees (Bayer & McCreight 1972; Comer 1979) and R-trees (Guttman 1984) have found their way into commercial database systems. One of the reasons is that an implementation of a new access method or a generic search tree is a huge undertaking because it interacts closely with low-level components of the database engine such as concurrency control, lock manager, and buffer manager. Reliability is of paramount importance for a mature database product, which often discourages extensive changes to low-level components of the database engine. In addition, applications now require new data types and more advanced searches, such as nearest neighbor for spatial data (Roussopoulos et al. 1995) or regular path expressions for semistructured data (Goldman & Widom 1997). It is expected that the access methods supported by a database system will not always match the growing needs of applications.

A better approach to extensible access and indexing is through user-defined access methods and user-defined indexing that are tightly integrated with the database engine. Stonebraker (1986) and Stonebraker et al. (1999) introduced user-defined access methods by describing an interface for implementing a new access method. Users specify functions for opening a scan of an index, getting the next record in a scan, inserting a record, deleting a record, replacing a record, and closing a scan. These functions are called by the database engine at appropriate places when executing a query plan.

User-defined access methods have a performance advantage because they are tightly integrated with the database engine. However, experience has shown that it is extremely difficult for application developers to define a new access method. The reason is that a new access method has to interface with several low-level components of a database engine, including the lock manager for locking of index objects, log manager for recovery, and buffer manager for page management. Few nondatabase-engine developers possess such an intimate knowledge of the internals of a database engine as to be able to write an access method effectively. Extensive changes to low-level components of a database engine are always a risky proposition that is not taken lightly in the context of real-world applications of a mature database product.

Researchers have also extended the concept of search in a user-defined access method in the form of generalized search trees (Hellerstein et al. 1995). The notion of a search key is generalized to a user-defined predicate that holds for every datum below the key in a search tree. Users define six key methods that are invoked during the top-down search and insertion or deletion of generalized search trees. This has been further extended in Aoki (1998) to allow more powerful searches such as nearest-neighbor and ranked search.

Indexing aims to provide the efficient search and querying of data using some underlying indexed access method. The purpose of user-defined indexing is to extend indexing capabilities to data types and predicates that may not be directly supported by the underlying indexed access methods. Stonebraker (1986) introduced a mechanism (called extended secondary indexes in Lynch & Stonebraker 1988) that allows users to apply existing access methods such as B-trees to new data types. In the case of B-trees, an operator class can be defined that provides a list of user-defined operators and specifies the correspondence between the user-defined operators and the standard relational operators for B-trees. Users can specify an operator class when creating an index on a table column of a new data type.

The mechanism of extended secondary indexes in Stonebraker (1986) is generalized in Lynch & Stonebraker (1988) so that predicates that cannot be mapped neatly to comparison operators can also be used for an indexed scan of a table. For instance, one may want to index on keywords occurring in the titles of books. Their idea is to introduce another operator that is applied to values of a column to generate index-key values (e.g., an operator that returns a list of keywords occurring in a given string). The result of the operator can be a list of values that can be compared. The introduction of this operator essentially provides a logical separation between values of a table column to be indexed (e.g., the `title` of a book in a table `books`) and the corresponding index keys (e.g., keywords occurring in the title of a book).

Our framework of high-level indexing of user-defined types generalizes the extended secondary indexes in Stonebraker (1986) and Lynch & Stonebraker (1988) in two important ways. First, we provide user control over search in indexing that maps a predicate with a search argument into search ranges used by an underlying access method for an indexed scan of a table. Such mapping is no longer limited to a single search range based on a relational operator. For a user-defined predicate, users can provide their own method of generating possibly multiple search ranges based on the search arguments of the predicate. Second, we provide user control over the execution of possibly expensive user-defined predicates using a multistage procedure for filtering with approximate predicates (Shivakumar et al. 1998).

The framework is tightly integrated with the database engine, especially with the index manager and query optimizer. It is orthogonal to the underlying access methods and can take advantage of any special access methods whenever they are available. Our main contribution is not in developing a new access method or a special search algorithm, but rather in providing a framework in which users have direct control over index maintenance, exploitation, index filtering, and predicate evaluation.

More specifically, users can define their own key transforms. The idea of key transforms is not new; examples are transforming a geometric object into an MBR for R-trees (Guttman 1984) or into a set of z-values (Orenstein & Manola 1988). Following Stonebraker (1986) and Lynch & Stonebraker (1988), we give the power to users to decide what abstractions or approximations to use as index keys for a user-defined type.

Users can define their own search-key producers for search patterns of arbitrary predicates. Although search key producers are not sufficient by themselves to support advanced searches such as ranked and nearest neighbor (which require direct support from the underlying access methods), they bridge the semantic gap between user-defined predicates and the limited access methods that are available.

Users can define their own filters to avoid expensive predicate evaluation. Multistage predicate evaluation has been explored in Brinkhoff et al. (1993, 1994). Researchers have also investigated query optimization issues with expensive predicates (Chaudhuri & Shim 1996; Hellerstein & Stonebraker 1993) and with filtering using approximate predicates (Shivakumar et al. 1998). Our contribution is in integrating multistage evaluation of predicates with the database engine, especially the index manager, thus providing an implementation framework where approximate predicates can be used effectively for efficient query execution. As we have shown, the index filter is a powerful technique that makes it possible to avoid the I/O cost of retrieving useless data into the memory buffer. Furthermore, it offers an interesting mechanism to combine multiple indexing mechanisms in a single search (e.g., structured search with external full-text indexing).

As we have shown, our framework for high-level indexing can also be effectively used to integrate external search engines in situations where the content-specific index data need to reside outside the database system in a proprietary format. This is especially important for a vendor that is specialized in search technology for specific types of content and would like to implement a database plug-in component for an existing object-relational component DBMS. Here, a tight integration that stores the index in the database system may not be feasible because it requires the mapping of highly tuned content-specific index data structures and the processing model of the indexing engine to the indexing approach of the database system, which can very often be too costly or result in limitations. Loosely integrated approaches, based on logical query rewrite, that solve this problem have been explored in Chaudhuri & Shim (1993) and Deßloch & Mattos (1997). However, because logical query rewrite usually precedes cost-based optimization in the overall process of query evaluation and may not be tightly integrated with the optimizer, decisions on whether to exploit an index may happen prematurely and have a negative effect on the quality of the query-execution plan. In comparison, our approach uses extensibility at the index level, which consequently gives our cost-based optimizer complete control over index exploitation.

The tight integration with the database engine means that it is possible for the query compiler to exploit user-defined predicates in the standard framework of query optimization. This means that the full querying capabilities of SQL, including multiple predicates in a WHERE clause, aggregate functions, subqueries, and recursion, are now available for universal applications through DB2.

5

Enabling Component Databases with OLE DB

José A. Blakeley
Michael J. Pizzo
Microsoft Corp.

5.1 Introduction

Today's data-intensive applications bring a challenging collection of requirements to data management. These requirements include

- Accessing data from heterogeneous data sources. Data are stored not only in traditional database management systems (DBMSs), but also in simple files, index-sequential files, desktop databases, spreadsheets, project management tools, electronic mail, directory services, and spatial and multimedia data stores. Recently, the explosive growth of the World Wide Web (WWW) has transformed this medium into a vast repository of information and knowledge. All these data are usually heterogeneous in their native forms.

- Specialized data management. Given that heterogeneous data sources are the norm, each data source tends to have different strengths and weaknesses in the areas of data model, query language, transaction, and indexing support. Applications want to access data directly from their source of origin and exploit their data stores' native capabilities. For example, messaging data stores have a tree-structured name space and manage collections of heterogeneous objects such as messages, appointment, and contacts. Spatial and image data stores require support for geometric data types, indexes, and query language.

- Different data navigation models. The environments where the application runs may have different requirements for the way data are navigated. For example, an application running in a middle tier may operate on a small subset of data cached entirely within the application space and provide bidirectional or positional access to data. An application running in the database usually works on large data sets and tends to navigate data by reading records sequentially in a forward-only direction.

It is possible to consider a solution to all these requirements using a single DBMS. Indeed, several database companies have pursued a traditional database-centric approach, which this chapter refers to as the *universal database*. In this approach, the database vendor extends the database engine and programming interface to support new data types, including text, files, spatial, video, and audio. The vendor requires customers to move all data needed by the application, which can be distributed in diverse sources across a corporation, into the vendor's database system. An advantage of this approach is that many DBMS services such as queries, transactions, and utilities can be generalized to manage all these heterogeneous data in a uniform way. A disadvantage is that moving data from their source of origin into the database may be very laborious and expensive. An even greater problem arises when there are other tools that work with the data in their native format outside of the database, such as a map-drawing program or email application.

An alternative approach, which we call *universal data access* (UDA), is based on the premise that heterogeneity of data and sources is the norm and will stay so. UDA allows applications to efficiently access data where they reside without replication, transformation, or conversion. Common abstractions and interfaces allow connectivity among all data sources. Independent services provide for distributed queries, caching, updating, data marshaling, distributed transactions, and content indexing among sources. UDA can be implemented as a complementary approach and used in combination with the universal database approach.

Microsoft developed OLE DB and ActiveX Data Objects (ADO) in support of the UDA approach. OLE DB is a fairly detailed, system-level interface used by system developers to encapsulate component database functionality. OLE DB interfaces are the key enabler of UDA's component architecture. Early in the design of OLE DB, it became clear that this was not an interface appropriate for business-application developers. Therefore, Microsoft developed ADO as a set of application-level interfaces designed to simplify access to data and provide a more natural data access experience for programmers from multiple languages. Together, OLE DB and ADO enable applications to have uniform access to data stored in DBMS and non-DBMS sources. Microsoft released OLE DB 1.0 in August 1996 as part of a data-access Systems Developer's Kit. To date, the OLE DB architecture has been used by applications that access data from multiple heterogeneous data sources, as a component interface to build services that augment the data store's native functionality, as a way to build custom solutions on top of commercial data stores, and as a component interface inside a DBMS.

In the remainder of this chapter, we identify some of the aspects of the architecture that contribute to OLE DB's inherent component nature. Then, after looking at the base objects that comprise the abstractions for connecting and representing data, we show how those base abstractions have been extended to support particular types of data. Finally, we take a look at some of the generic services that have been built using OLE DB's component nature to augment the functionality of existing data providers, how custom solutions have been built on top of existing data stores, and how OLE DB has been used in several component database scenarios. But first, let us take a look at how OLE DB enables the componentization of Microsoft's UDA Architecture.

5.2   Universal Data Access

UDA is a component database architecture built as a collection of data management components and services, whose behavior is defined by a set of interfaces. OLE DB, based on the Microsoft Component Object Model (COM) (Box 1998), defines the system-level programming interfaces that encapsulate various DBMS components. ADO, based on Automation (Microsoft 1997a), defines an application-level data-access model that allows enterprise programmers to write applications over OLE DB data from any language including Visual Basic, Java, VBScript, JavaScript, C, and C++. Figure 5.1 illustrates the UDA architecture. There are three general kinds of database components: data providers, services, and consumers.

- Data providers are components that represent data sources such as SQL databases, index-sequential files, and spreadsheets.

- Services are components that add functionality to existing OLE DB data. Services can be combined with other components because they consume and produce data using the same set of interfaces. For example, a cursor engine is a service component that consumes data from a sequential, forward-only data source to produce scrollable data. A relational query engine is an example of a service over OLE DB data that produces rowsets satisfying a Boolean predicate.

- Consumers are components that consume OLE DB data. The best example of a consumer is ADO, which provides a high-level data-access programming model over OLE DB services and data providers to enable business applications to be written in languages such as Visual Basic, C++, or Java.

All interactions among components in Figure 5.1 (indicated by bidirectional arrows) may occur across process and machine boundaries

Figure 5.1 | **Universal Data Access (UDA Architecture).**

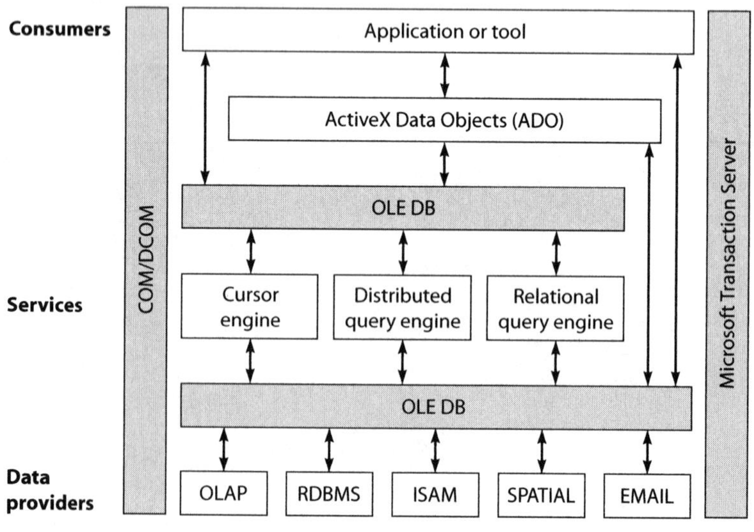

through network protocols such as Distributed COM (DCOM) (Eddon & Eddon 1998) or Hypertext Transfer Protocol (HTTP) (HTTP 1997). Transacted interactions among components are possible via a distributed transaction coordination service such as the one included in Microsoft Transaction Server (Homer & Sussmann 1998).

5.3   OLE DB: A Component Data Model

This section describes how OLE DB provides a component architecture for accessing and managing data. This is not intended to be an exhaustive reference for the interface, but rather a high-level overview of the basic abstractions defined in OLE DB and some of the extensions built with, and on top of, those abstractions to extend the model with domain-specific functionality. In particular, we will emphasize those aspects of OLE DB that contribute to its inherent extensibility and compositional nature. A complete interface reference is documented in Microsoft (1998a).

5.3.1   The Microsoft Component Object Model

OLE DB is designed as a Microsoft COM interface. COM provides the foundation for OLE DB's compositional nature. In order to understand how OLE DB is used to build component solutions, it is necessary to understand a bit about COM. The following section provides an overview of the COM concepts of interface factoring, inheritance, interface navigation, and object reference counting, encapsulation, and aggregation. A complete reference to COM can be found in Box (1998).

Interface Factoring. In COM, a single object exposes one or more interfaces. Each interface exposed by the object represents a fixed set of functionality, such that the total functionality of the object is factored among the various interfaces.

The full set of functionality defined in the OLE DB specification is factored into multiple discrete interfaces that group related levels of functionality for each object. This interface factoring is what makes OLE DB so accessible to simple data stores. Rather than forcing every data store to implement a full relational engine in order to be accessible through common tools, the data store implements an object comprising only those interfaces that represent native functionality for that data store. At a minimum, this includes core interfaces that provide a simple forward-only, read-only view of the data.

In this chapter interfaces are denoted by the interface name in **boldface**, prefixed with the letter **I**, for example, **IUnknown** or **IRowset**. Methods specific to an interface are denoted by the interface name, followed by the method name, separated by double-colons and followed by parentheses, for example, **IUnknown::QueryInterface()**. Where unambiguous, the interface name is omitted, as in **QueryInterface()**.

Interface Inheritance. Interface inheritance refers to the ability to define a new interface that extends the functionality of an existing interface. Inheriting from an existing interface means that the new interface is designed to automatically support all of the methods defined in the inherited interface. When implementing the new interface, the object automatically supports the inherited interface and consumers can call inherited methods through either interface. Multiple interfaces may inherit from the same base interface, in which case all such interfaces support the same subset of methods. COM only allows an interface to inherit from a single parent, although the parent interface may itself inherit from another interface, and such nesting is allowed to go arbitrarily deep. In this chapter we indicate interface inheritance as the name of the inheriting interface followed by the name of the inherited interface, separated by a single colon, as in **IRowset:IUnknown**.

Interface Navigation and Object Reference Counting. Each interface instance in COM inherits directly or indirectly from a common interface implemented on each COM object called **IUnknown**, such that the **IUnknown** interface is the super-parent of every other interface supported by the object. **IUnknown** contains **AddRef()** and **Release()** methods, which control the lifetime of the object through reference counting, and a **QueryInterface()** method for navigating between the different interfaces on the object. Figure 5.2 shows a single COM object that implements two interfaces, **IRowset** and **IRowsetFind**, in addition to **IUnknown**.

Encapsulation. Because the interface definition defines the contract with the consumer, the details of how that interface is implemented are hidden from the consumer. Oftentimes a COM object may implement some or all of its functionality by calling other COM objects internally. These internal COM objects are hidden from the consumer, and all calls

Figure 5.2 | **Factoring of functionality between interfaces.**

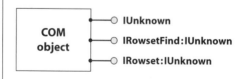

go through the outer object. Only those methods and interfaces implemented by the outer object are exposed to the consumer. This is called encapsulation.

Figure 5.3 shows how one COM object (object A) may call another COM object (object B) internally through encapsulation. Note that the consumer calls both **IRowset** and **IRowsetFind** as implemented directly on object A. Object B exposes its own **IUnknown** interface (labeled **IUnknown′**), and object B's **IRowset** inherits from object B's **IUnknown′**. Object B's interfaces are not available to the consumer and are called only by object A in order to provide object A's exposed functionality. This looks like a single object (object A) to the consumer, which has no knowledge of object B.

COM Aggregation. Another way a COM object can be written to take advantage of a separate object's existing functionality is through aggregation. Aggregation is a lot like encapsulation, except that in aggregation the consumer can call interfaces on the inner object directly, including interfaces that the outer object does not know about. Exposing functionality that is unknown to the outer object is called blind aggregation.

In aggregation, when the inner COM object (object B) is created, it is provided with the **IUnknown** interface of the outer COM object (object A). In this case, each interface exposed by the newly created object B inherits from object A's **IUnknown** implementation. This controlling **IUnknown** then manages the navigation between sets of functionality supported by interfaces implemented on object A and sets of functionality supported by interfaces on object B. Object B's **IUnknown** interface is only exposed to object A and is used by object A to navigate between object B's interfaces.

Figure 5.4 shows a COM object (object B) that supports the **IRowset** interface, and a controlling object (object A) that implements the **IRowsetFind** interface. When the consumer calls methods in **IRowset**, it is calling the method implemented on object B directly. When the consumer calls methods in **IRowsetFind**, it is calling the method implemented on object A, which may in turn use object B's **IRowset** interface under the covers. The **QueryInterface()**,

Figure 5.3 | **Object A encapsulates object B.**

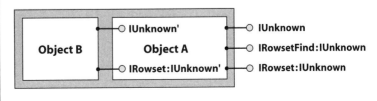

Figure 5.4 | **Object A aggregates object B.**

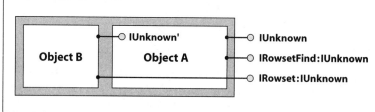

AddRef(), and **Release()** methods of the **IUnknown** interface implemented by object A are used, whether the methods are called from the **IUnknown** interface directly or through either the **IRowset** or **IRowsetFind** interface. This controlling unknown navigates between the interfaces supported by the two objects. To the application, this appears as a single object that implements both **IRowset** and **IRowsetFind** (in addition to **IUnknown**).

5.3.2   Introspection via Properties

For a consumer to use a generic data provider, it must be able to determine the characteristics, functionality, and behavior of that provider. The ability to determine these characteristics at runtime is referred to as introspection.

OLE DB provides a rich property model for data stores to expose provider-specific options and behavior, and for requesting extended functionality. Using properties the consumer can

- Determine data provider information. Properties provide a way for the consumer to determine information about the data provider; for example, the data provider's name and version, level of SQL supported (if any), case sensitivity, and maximum row size. Data-source informational properties also allow the consumer to determine the data provider's behavior, for example, the effect of committing or aborting a transaction on any prepared statements or how null concatenation is treated.

- Specify connection information. Properties provide a way for the consumer to determine what connection information (server, user-name, password, etc.) is required by the data provider in order to connect to a data source and to specify the required information.

- Request extended functionality. Properties provide a way for the consumer to request that an object support certain functionality above and beyond the minimal base functionality. For example, the consumer may specify that a set of results should be updatable and support scrolling. In this way, the consumer can specify exactly the level of functionality it requires, and the data provider is free to make optimizations by not supporting any extended functionality not requested by the consumer.

Properties are divided into property sets, identified by a globally unique identifier (GUID). There are predefined GUIDs for each group of OLE DB–defined properties, and consumers can define their own GUIDs for provider-specific properties. Consumers can request specific properties or request all properties of a given type, for example, all initialization properties used to connect to a data source. The provider returns information about all of the OLE DB–defined properties it supports, as well as any provider-specific properties. This information includes a name for the property, its type, whether it is required or optional, and possible values for enumerated properties. Thus, a general consumer (one not tied to a particular data source) can present these properties to a user, along with the necessary information needed by the user to set them to appropriate values, without knowing the properties ahead of time.

5.3.3   Common Abstractions

OLE DB is built on a small set of common abstractions, along with a set of common extensions for exposing additional functionality of diverse types of data stores. By building on a set of common abstractions, OLE DB enables generic components to operate on those abstractions as individual entities, without needing to know how the entities were generated or the details of what they represent.

OLE DB defines three core object classes common to any data provider; the data source object (DSO) provides a common abstraction for connecting to a data store, the session object provides a transactional scope for multiple concurrent units of work, and the rowset object provides a common abstraction for representing data in a tabular fashion, as shown in Figure 5.5. All of the extensions, built on OLE DB, extend this basic object hierarchy.

Figure 5.5 shows the use of the **CoCreateInstance()** function to create an instance of a particular DSO. The DSO supports an **IDBCreateSession** interface, whose method **CreateSession()** returns an instance of a session object. The **IOpenRowset** interface on the session object, in turn, returns a rowset object that supports, at minimum, the **IRowset** interface.

Connection Abstraction. The OLE DB connection model defines how data providers are located and activated. The DSO and the session object are the basis for the OLE DB connection model. To access a data provider, a consumer must first instantiate a DSO. Windows provides a registry for COM objects, and each data provider's DSO is identified by a unique class identifier (CLSID) in this registry. A particular data

Figure 5.5 | **Hierarchy of data source, session, and rowset objects.**

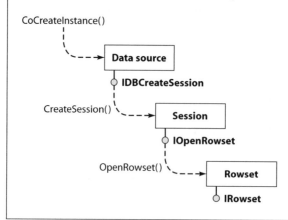

provider's DSO is instantiated by calling the OLE **CoCreateInstance** function, which creates an instance of the object through the object's class factory. The DSO exposes the **IDBProperties** interface, which consumers use to provide basic authentication information such as the user ID and password (for cases when the data source does not exist in an authenticated environment) and the name of the data source (computer, file, and database name) containing the data to be accessed. Once these properties have been specified, consumers use **IDBInitialize** to establish a connection with the data store.

Once a DSO has been successfully initialized, it exposes data source information properties through which a consumer can query the capabilities of a provider. These capabilities include the interfaces, rowset properties (e.g., scrollability), transaction properties (e.g., isolation levels), SQL dialects, command operations (e.g., left outer joins, text-search operators), and security options a provider supports. From the initialized data source, the consumer calls **CreateSession** in order to create a session object. The session object exposes, at a minimum, **IOpenRowset**, a simple interface through which providers expose their data as rowsets.

The Rowset: A Common Data Representation. A rowset is a unifying abstraction that enables OLE DB data providers to expose data in tabular form. Conceptually, a rowset is a multiset of rows where each row has columns of data. Base table providers present their data in the form of rowsets. Query processors present the results of queries in the form of rowsets. This way it is possible to layer components that consume or produce data through the same abstraction. Rowsets are also used to return metadata, such as database schemata, supported datatype information, and extended column information.

The most basic rowset object exposes three interfaces: **IRowset**, which contains methods for navigating through its rows sequentially;

Figure 5.6 | **Rowset object.**

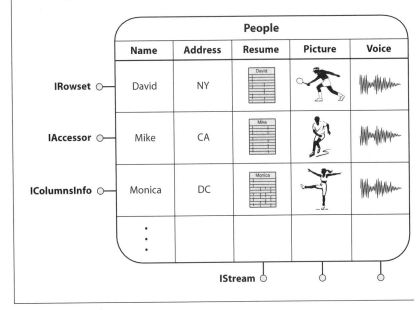

IAccessor, which permits the definition of groups of column bindings describing the way in which data are bound to consuming components; and **IColumnsInfo**, which describes the columns of the rowset and their types. Using **IRowset**, data may be traversed sequentially or in a bidirectional manner, depending on the properties of the rowset. Figure 5.6 illustrates a typical rowset object representing a collection of people. Other rowset interfaces capture rowset properties a provider may support. For example, rowsets that support updatability may expose interfaces to insert, delete, or update rows. In addition, there are rowset interfaces that expose richer row navigation models, such as direct row access and scrollability.

5.3.4 Common Extensions

In order to be suitable as a primary interface to a variety of data stores, OLE DB defines a set of common extensions on top of the base abstractions. On page 150 we show how the base abstractions have been extended to provide support for issuing a query, navigating an index, navigating hierarchical data, representing heterogeneous data, and navigating multidimensional information in a natural manner. By building these extensions on the common defined abstractions, generic consumers can view all data through the common abstractions while special-purpose consumers can access the domain-specific functionality through common extensions.

Query Syntax Support. The first extension to the basic hierarchy exposes the ability to issue a textual command to a data store through a command object. The command object encapsulates the functions that enable a consumer to invoke the execution of data definition or data manipulation commands such as queries over a relational database. The command object is obtained from the session object by calling the **CreateCommand** method on the **IDBCreateCommand** interface. Once a command object is created, the consumer sets the command text to be executed through the **SetCommandText** method on the **ICommand** interface, and then calls the **Execute** method on the same interface. When the command represents a query, the **Execute** method returns the results in a rowset object, as shown in Figure 5.7. The consumer can specify required or optional properties to be supported on the resulting rowset by setting those properties prior to executing the command. Because OLE DB is designed to work with any query-capable provider, it does not mandate a specific syntax or semantics for queries. It is entirely up to the provider to define the language for formulating queries. For example, currently there are OLE DB providers for relational DBMSs, full-text-search engines, OLAP engines, directory services, email stores, and spatial stores. Each of these query-capable data stores exposes a different query language. Table 5.1 lists some of the query languages supported by various OLE DB providers. A command object may be built to consume one or more rowsets, such as a rowset exposed by a simple tabular data provider, and expose the results of the query evaluation as a rowset to the user.

ISAM Navigation. Many types of data stores do not support the ability to query data through textual commands, but do support basic indexing functionality. This functionality allows services such as query processors to efficiently access contiguous rows of data within a range of keys.

Table 5.1   **Query languages supported by various OLE DB providers.**

Type of Data Source	Product	Query Language
Relational	Microsoft SQL Server 7.0	SQL
Full-text indexing	Microsoft Index Server	Index Server Query Language[a]
OLAP	Microsoft OLAP Services	MDX[b]
Email	Microsoft Exchange	SQL with hierarchical query extensions
Directory services	Microsoft Active Directory	LDAP

[a] Swank and Kittel (1997).
[b] Thomsen et al. (1999).

Figure 5.7 | **Executing a command.**

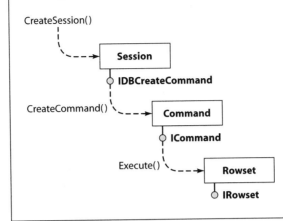

The index object abstracts the functionality of B-trees or index-sequential files by exposing a rowset with extended functionality (Figure 5.8). Indexes are traversed using the **IRowset** interface, information about the index entries is obtained via the **IColumnsInfo** interface, and insertions and deletions are performed through the **IRowsetChange** interface. By building on the common rowset abstraction, developers can apply much of the same logic, tools, and even code for manipulating an index as they would use for any other rowset.

Hierarchical Navigation. In order to support a simple, efficient mechanism for navigating homogeneous one-to-many relationships, such as a master-detail relationship between departments and employees, OLE DB defines hierarchical rowsets. In a hierarchical rowset there is one rowset per level of hierarchy representing all data instances at a given level. In other words, each rowset in the hierarchy captures an entire

Figure 5.8 | **Rowset object representing an index.**

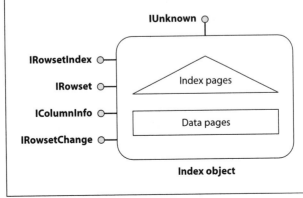

relationship between two entities. The rowsets at each level in the hierarchy support the basic rowset abstraction discussed earlier. The rowsets are linked together via chapters, which are a mechanism to identify groups of related children rows. Chapters behave as separate collections with a beginning and an end, but also share the facilities (such as accessors and notifications) of the rowset to which they belong.

EXAMPLE 1

To illustrate hierarchical result sets, consider first a SQL statement producing a flat collection of rows:

```
SELECT   d.name, e.name, e.phone
  FROM   Department d LEFT OUTER JOIN Employee e
         ON d.dno = e.dno
  ORDER  BY d.name
```

The execution of this statement produces a single rowset containing the employee names and their phone numbers per department in an organization. The department name is repeated for each employee working in that department.

This statement can be reformulated to produce a two-level hierarchy where the department name occurs only once and each department is associated with its corresponding set of employees:

```
SELECT   d.name, SET (e.name, e.phone) as emps
  FROM   Department d LEFT OUTER JOIN Employee e
         ON d.dno = e.dno
  GROUP  BY d.name
```

The result of executing the second statement is a hierarchy of two rowsets, one containing department and the other containing employee information. Each rowset represents a complete hierarchy level in the result. The root rowset—the rowset returned from **ICommand::Execute** —contains the department name (name), and a chapter column (emps). Each chapter value in emps references a (possibly empty) set of rows in the second rowset containing information about employees.

Each grouping of a detail set of rows, such as the employees working for a particular department, is treated as a collection with a beginning and end. A chapter identifies this detail group. A chapter can be implemented as a partial key to the details or as a parameterized query. Because it is partial, it might lead to a set rather than a single row. The functions that take a chapter as a parameter use the beginning, membership, and end implied by the chapter to limit the rows that the request may return.

Although a chapter value may be held in a column of a table, that value is not the same thing as the physical instantiation of the chapter. The chapter may be instantiated when a command is executed or on demand when the chapter value is used. In any case, the actual chapter belongs not to the parent rowset that had the chapter value, but to the rowset containing the rows the chapter references. Hence, the lifetime of chapter instances is controlled by the rowset containing the detail rows.

Heterogeneous Data and Containment Relationships. Rowsets are well suited for representing homogeneous results—results that have the same set of columns from one row to the next. This works well for structured data, such as the results of a query, but becomes a limitation when dealing with collections of dissimilar rows. For example, an email inbox is a collection of items. Each item can be of a different type, such as an email message, a calendar entry, a journal entry, or a folder. They may share a common set of attributes, such as name, date, or size, but each also has its own specific attributes that are not relevant to the other items. Because rowsets expose a common set of columns for each row, representing all of these items in a single rowset would require exposing a column in each row of the rowset for each possible attribute of any item within the rowset.

In order to simplify support for heterogeneous collections, in which some columns may vary from one row to another, OLE DB defines a row object. Each row object represents an individual row instance, which can be a member of a rowset or a single result value such as the result of a singleton SELECT statement in SQL. Consumers can navigate through a set of rows viewing the common set of columns through the rowset abstraction and then obtain a row object for a particular row in order to view row-specific columns.

In addition to heterogeneous collections, hierarchies of row and rowset objects can be used to model containment relationships common in tree-structured data sources, such as all files within a directory in a file system or all messages within a folder in an email system. These hierarchies can be used not only to navigate through the data, but also to manipulate the underlying tree and its contents. Row objects have their own metadata and can contain rowset-valued columns. Row objects contain their own interfaces to add or remove columns and to create new row objects. In addition, row objects can be augmented to support specialized interfaces that implement operations whose semantics scope all dependent objects (rows and rowsets) in the containment hierarchy rooted at the row. Just as an OLE DB consumer can change the rows in a rowset and transmit those changes to the underlying data store, it can also create new objects in a tree-structured name space, such as directories and email folders. Or it can move, copy, or delete entire subtrees through various scoped operations on the appropriate row objects.

OLAP Data. Online Analytical Processing (OLAP) provides a way to consolidate raw data into a multidimensional view. For example, an OLAP report might show the number of computer sales by region, broken down by salesperson.

In order to provide support for OLAP, OLE DB defines a multidimensional expression language (MDX) (Thomsen et al. 1999). Multidimensional queries written in MDX may be submitted to OLAP data providers through the standard OLE DB command object. A special GUID, MDGUID_MDX, is defined for the MDX dialect so that providers that can support both SQL and MDX queries can distinguish between the two.

General consumers can view the results of an MDX query through the standard rowset abstraction. In this view, the results of the query are flattened into a tabular view.

OLAP consumers, however, are often designed to navigate and manipulate the results of an MDX query along its multiple dimensions. For these types of consumers, it is convenient to expose a multidimensional data object. OLE DB defines such an object, called the dataset, which exposes interfaces for navigating and accessing the results of an MDX query in multiple dimensions.

Other than the specification of the MDX query language and addition of the dataset object for manipulating data in multiple dimensions, OLE DB required little in the way of extensions to support OLAP data. The same connection model, commands, and rowsets continue to apply to OLAP data providers. Although OLE DB defines additional metadata schema for cubes, measures, dimensions, hierarchies, levels, properties, and members, these metadata are accessed through the **IDBSchema-Rowset** interfaces on the session object, just as are any other metadata. By requesting that the results of an MDX query be returned as a flattened rowset, generic consumers can talk to OLAP data providers in the same manner as a relational or other command-based provider.

5.4   Services

The previous section describes how OLE DB defines a small set of common abstractions and builds on that base level of functionality by defining common extensions that reuse those abstractions where appropriate. This section discusses how OLE DB facilitates building services that can be composed in order to provide a component-based solution for accessing and managing data. In each case, the service described illustrates how common components are implemented in order to extend existing data providers with discrete sets of functionality—namely, connection facilities, resource pooling, and rich client-cursor functionality.

5.4.1 Adding Generic Connection Facilities through Data Link

A good example of a component that makes use of OLE DB's extensible property model for introspection is the Microsoft Data Link Component, shipped as part of the Microsoft Data Access Components (MDAC) version 2.0 (Microsoft 1999a).

Prior to the Data Link Component, OLE DB applications had to implement their own logic for determining and specifying connection information. This information could vary from one provider to another. In addition, consumers wanted an easy way to persist, load, and exchange connection information, preferably in the form of a string.

The Data Link Component provides a common connection property editor. This component queries the individual data provider for a list of its initialization (connection) properties and exposes these to the consumer through a simple common interface. The property names and datatypes are determined from the provider, along with possible values for enumerated types. The Data Link Component uses the property's option values to enable the consumer to distinguish between required and optional properties.

Applications can call this component directly in order to provide a common interface for specifying connection properties. The component returns a DSO for the selected provider with the specified properties set.

Once the initialization properties have been set on a provider, the consumer can obtain a ConnectionString representation of those properties that can be used internally or written to a universal data link (udl) file. The ConnectionString is built in the form of property name–value pairs, where the name of the property is again obtained from the property information obtained from the provider. In this way, the Microsoft Data Link Component can build and parse connection strings with no a priori knowledge of the provider's set of valid properties. There is also a stand-alone utility for creating or modifying .udl files.

5.4.2 Adding Common Resource-Pooling Facilities

The introduction of a common component for specifying connection information also gave Microsoft the ability to implement logic for pooling connections and providing automatic transaction enlistment in an Microsoft Transaction Server (MTS) environment.

By connecting through this common component, with or without exposing the connection dialog to the user, OLE DB Service Components are able to aggregate (as described in Section 5.3.1) the data provider's DSO in order to examine the connection information. If this is the first such connection, a pool is created to hold similar connections, and a connection is created from within that pool. OLE DB Service Components then check to see whether or not the calling thread is in a transactional context and, if so, create an OLE DB session and enlist it in the global transaction. This session is held as long as the data source is connected, so that when the application calls CreateSession, the Service Component that aggregates the DSO intercepts the call and returns this held session. If the consumer requests a second session without releasing the first, a new session is created and enlisted in the global transaction, but is not held if the consumer releases it.

When the consumer releases the DSO, OLE DB Services again intercept the release and return the connected data source (and its session object) to the pool. If another request with the same connection information (including security and transactional context) comes within a specified amount of time (default, 60 seconds), the existing connection is returned directly to the user, without undergoing an expensive reconnect and possible reenlistment, to the server. If the data source is not used within the specified period of time, the object is released and the connection freed.

Because these resource-pooling facilities are implemented through COM aggregation, the functionality can be implemented on top of existing data providers, without requiring special code in the provider; data providers built according to the original OLE DB specification simply work without changes.

This ability to pool database connections and transaction enlistment increased the scalability and performance of ADO and OLE DB components in web applications by several orders of magnitude.

5.4.3 Providing a Rich Client-Cursor Service

Relational databases were initially designed to provide a forward-only cursor over data. In fact, scrolled cursors were not introduced until SQL-92. Even then, scrolled cursors are not required for SQL-92's minimum entry-level conformance and not required to support updating until the highest full-conformance level. As a result, many database systems support cursor semantics no richer than a forward-only traversal of data. Even for those databases that do support richer scrolling models, keeping a cursor open on the server for each user and incurring a network round trip each time the user scrolls may not be practical for many types of multitier distributed applications.

Still, many types of applications, particularly those that interact with users, require the ability to scroll back and forth through results. Having to write code within the application to cache results, scroll through the cache, and synchronize the cache with the database is not only onerous for the typical client application, but means that the application cannot take advantage of native cursor functionality in the data source where it is appropriate and supported by the data provider.

In order to allow applications to rely on rich cursor functionality over any data provider, Microsoft implemented a cursor service that provides client-side cursoring functionality on behalf of any OLE DB provider.

As with resource pooling, the cursor service is invoked when needed by OLE DB Service Components. A component manager aggregates the session and command objects, and intercepts the properties set by the consumer that specify the desired functionality of a rowset to be created. If the consumer requests properties that can be supported by the cursor service, including rich scrolling functionality, client-side filtering, sorting, or finding values within a result, the component manager passes those properties to the underlying provider as optional. If the data provider is able to satisfy all of the requested properties and the consumer has not explicitly requested client-side cursoring, the data provider's rowset is returned to the user without invoking the cursor service. On the other hand, if the data provider cannot provide all of the requested functionality or the customer specifically asks for client cursors, the component manager hands the underlying data provider's rowset to the cursor service, and the cursor service returns a rich cursor on top of that underlying rowset by caching results (synchronously or asynchronously) and allowing the user to manipulate data within the cached results. Changes to the results are synchronized with the data source through update, insert, and delete SQL statements generated from the rowset's metadata and the affected rows by the cursor service.

5.5   Custom Data Providers

In addition to building services that augment the functionality of data providers, OLE DB allows developers to build custom data providers that reuse existing data providers as the underlying component of a more-vertical solution.

In many cases, developers want to expose a customized view of data in an existing data store. For example, they may want to expose custom methods that return fixed sets of data or custom queries over a subset of the tables in a data store. OLE DB allows these types of developers to expose custom semantics by building custom data providers on top of existing data providers.

Custom data providers may be hard-coded to a specific underlying data provider or may work with a variety of data providers. Developers of custom data providers may expose as much or as little of the underlying data source's functionality as they want. Custom data providers generally aggregate or encapsulate the underlying data provider. In this manner, they can intercept calls that they want to customize and let the others flow through unchanged.

For example, a developer may want to expose a custom data provider for a management system that connects to an Oracle database based on the user's `EmployeeID`. Once the user specifies his or her

EmployeeID, the custom provider can connect to the database using a hidden username and password. Once connected, the custom provider may expose a natural-language query syntax that allows the user to ask for a list of employees, their projects, or their past reviews. A simple parser takes that request and translates it into an Oracle query, using parameters to limit the information based on the EmployeeID specified during connection. The custom provider can then return the data provider's rowset directly to the consumer if the developer does not want to add any semantics on top of the data. Users can select their choice of ADO- or OLE DB–enabled products to access this custom provider; regardless of which they select, they will always see the same customized view of the data.

An example of an actual custom data provider is the MSShape Provider, shipped as part of the Microsoft Data Access Components 2.0. This custom provider appears as any other provider to the consumer. When the consumer connects to the provider, it specifies the name of the underlying data source it wants to connect to and valid connection information for that source. The Shape Provider implements its own command object that supports a custom syntax for building hierarchical results by relating multiple rowsets. The syntax for specifying the individual rowsets is particular to the underlying data provider; the Shape Provider simply passes that portion of the query through and obtains rowsets from the underlying data source. The data from those rowsets are then read into a local cache (the same local cache used for client cursors), and the Shape Provider relates rows from the rowsets according to relations specified in the shape command. The user can then navigate from rows in the parent rowset to rows in the child rowset through chapter columns built by the Shape Provider. The Shape Provider also supports custom aggregates and other calculated columns.

5.6 Component Database Scenarios

We have seen three ways that OLE DB's component nature lends itself to reuse and extension. Having a common way to represent data, be it raw data, metadata, or other types of information, and defining common extensions from that foundation builds on developer knowledge and encourages code and development tool reuse. Factoring the full set of functionality into discrete interfaces and building on COM's component model allows common services to be introduced to augment the functionality of existing data providers. And through encapsulation, existing providers can be used as component building blocks, allowing developers to expose custom views of data and functionality without rewriting the entire data store or access methods. In this section we see a fourth way that products can take advantage of OLE DB's inherent component nature by describing five component database scenarios in the context of a commercial RDBMS.

5.6.1   Database Server

The database server of Microsoft SQL Server 7.0 has two main parts: the relational engine and the storage engine. The architecture of SQL Server 7.0 clearly separates the relational and storage engine components in the server and uses OLE DB interfaces to allow them to communicate with one another (Figure 5.9). The processing for a SELECT statement that references only tables in local databases can be briefly described as follows. The relational engine compiles the SELECT statement into an optimized execution plan. The execution plan defines a series of operations against simple rowsets from the individual tables or indexes referenced in the SELECT statement. The rowsets requested by the relational engine return the amount of data needed from a table or index to perform the operations needed to build the SELECT result set.

EXAMPLE 2

The following query computes the result from two indexes.

```
SELECT   CompanyName, OrderID, ShippedDate
   FROM   Customers AS Cst JOIN Orders AS Ord
                              ON (Cst.CustomerID
                                 = Ord.CustomerID)
```

The relational engine requests two rowsets, one for the clustered index on Customers and the other on a nonclustered index in Orders. The relational engine then uses the OLE DB interfaces to request that the storage engine open rowsets on these indexes. As the relational engine works through the steps of the execution plan and needs data, it uses OLE DB to fetch the individual rows from the rowsets. The storage engine transfers the data from its data buffers to the execution operators of the query, which is executing in the relational engine. The relational engine combines the data from the storage engine rowsets into the final result set transmitted to the user.

This clear communication between the relational engine and the storage engine via OLE DB interfaces enables the relational engine to process queries against any data source that exposes such interfaces. Such data sources can be other SQL Server DBMSs (distributed queries), and other relational or nonrelational OLE DB data providers (heterogeneous queries).

Figure 5.9 | **OLE DB as an internal DBMS interface.**

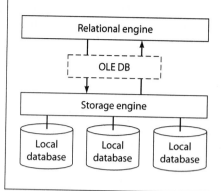

5.6.2 Distributed and Heterogeneous Query Processing

Microsoft SQL Server 7.0 represents an implementation of the UDA (see Section 5.2) approach to integrating heterogeneous data. Its distributed heterogeneous query capability allows transactional queries and updates against a variety of relational and nonrelational OLE DB data providers running in one or more computers.

SQL Server 7.0 supports two methods for referencing heterogeneous OLE DB data sources in Transact-SQL statements. The linked-server-names method uses the system-stored procedures `sp_addlinkedsrv` and `sp_addlinkedserverlogin` to associate a server name with an OLE DB data source. Objects in these linked servers can be referenced in Transact-SQL statements using the four-part name convention described here.

EXAMPLE 3

If a linked server name of `DeptSQLSrvr` is defined against another copy of SQL Server 7.0, the following statement references a table on that server:

```
SELECT  *
   FROM  DeptSQLSrvr.Northwind.dbo.Employees
```

An OLE DB data source is registered in SQL Server as a linked server. Once a linked server is defined, its data can be accessed using the four-part name `<linked-server>.<catalog>.<schema>.<object>`.

EXAMPLE 4

The following establishes a linked server to an Oracle server via an OLE DB provider for Oracle.

```
EXEC sp_addlinkedserver OraSvr, 'Oracle 7.3', 'MSDAORA',
                         'OracleServer'
```

A query against this linked server is expressed as

```
SELECT   *
   FROM   OraSvr.CORP.ADMIN.SALES
```

In addition, the SQL Server supports built-in, parameterized table-valued functions called `OpenRowset` and `OpenQuery`, which allow sending uninterpreted queries to a provider or linked server, respectively, in the dialect supported by the provider.

EXAMPLE 5

The following query combines information stored in Oracle and index server-linked servers. It lists all documents containing the words "Data" and "Access" and their authors, ordered by the author's department and name.

```
SELECT   e.dept, f.DocAuthor, f.FileName
   FROM   OraSvr.Corp.Admin.Employee e,
          OPENQUERY(EmpFiles, 'SELECT DocAuthor, FileName
                                 FROM scope("c:\EmpDocs")
                                 WHERE contains("Data" near()
                                 "Access")>0') f

   WHERE   e.name = f.DocAutor
   ORDER   BY e.dept, f.DocAuthor
```

The linked server name can also be specified in an `OPENQUERY` statement to open a rowset from the OLE DB data source. This rowset can then be referenced like a table in Transact-SQL statements. The ad-hoc-connector-names method is used for infrequent references to a data source. This method uses a table-valued function called `OPENROWSET` where the information needed to connect to the data sources is provided as arguments to the function. The rowset can then be referenced the same way a table is referenced in SQL statements.

EXAMPLE 6

The following query accesses the `Employee` table stored in the Northwind database in a Microsoft Access data provider. Note that unlike the linked-server-name approach described earlier, which encapsulates all information needed to connect to a data source, the ad-hoc-connector-names approach requires a user to specify the name of the data provider (`Microsoft.Jet.OLE DB.4.0`), the complete path name of the data file, the user identifier, the password, and the name of the table being accessed.

```
SELECT   *
   FROM   OPENROWSET('Microsoft.Jet.OLE DB.4.0',
                       'c:\MSOffice\Access\Samples
                       \Northwind.mdb'; 'Admin';
                       ''; Employees)
```

The relational engine uses the OLE DB interfaces to open the rowsets on linked servers, to fetch the rows, and to manage transactions. For each OLE DB data source accessed as a linked server, an OLE DB provider must be present on the server running SQL Server. The set of Transact-SQL operations that can be used against a specific OLE DB data source depends on the capabilities of the OLE DB provider. Whenever possible, SQL Server pushes relational operations such as joins, restrictions, projections, sorts, and group by operations to the OLE DB data source.

SQL Server uses Microsoft Distributed Transaction Coordinator and the OLE DB transaction interfaces of the provider to ensure atomicity of transactions spanning multiple data sources. Here is a typical scenario for using distributed queries. Consider a large insurance company that has subsidiaries in several countries. Each regional office selects the product that stores its sales data. The United Kingdom subsidiary stores its data in Oracle; the Australian subsidiary stores its data in Microsoft Access; the Spanish subsidiary stores data in Microsoft Excel; and the United States subsidiary stores its data in SQL Server. A worldwide sales executive wants a report that lists, on a quarterly basis for the last 3 years, the insurance policies, the subsidiaries, and the sales representatives with the highest quarterly sales figures. Each of these three queries can be accomplished by using a single distributed query, running on SQL Server.

5.6.3 Full-Text Queries on Relational Data

The full-text capability in Microsoft SQL Server supports the creation and maintenance of full-text indexes on character string and image columns stored inside SQL Server tables as well as full-text searches based on these indexes. The full-text capability is implemented by the Microsoft search service, originally developed independently of SQL Server to enable full-text searches over file-system data. The first step toward the integration of the search service with SQL Server was to transform the search service into an OLE DB provider. This step immediately enabled applications to be written in mainstream languages such as Visual Basic and C++ against data stored in the file system using ADO, and the full-text provider to be plugged into SQL Server as a heterogeneous data source enabling heterogeneous queries spanning related but disjoint data stored in relational tables inside the SQL Server and data stored in the file system. The second step involved a loosely coupled integration between SQL Server and the search service to enable full-text indexing of table content. This integration is loosely coupled in the sense that full-text indexes are stored in the file system outside the database. Figure 5.10 illustrates the general architecture of this integration.

Figure 5.10 | **Integration of a full-text component with a relational DBMS via OLE DB.**

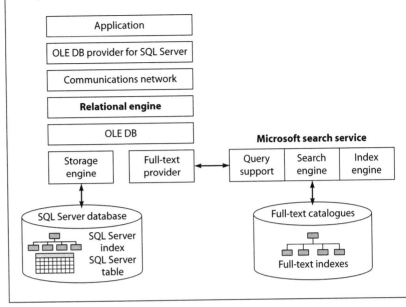

There are two aspects to full-text support: index creation and maintenance, and query support. Indexing support involves creation, update, and administration of full-text catalogues and indexes defined for a table or tables in a database. Query support involves the processing of full-text-search queries. Given a full-text predicate, the search service determines which entries in the index meet the full-text selection criteria. For each entry that meets the selection criteria, the query component of the search service returns an OLE DB rowset containing the identity of the row whose columns match the search criteria and a ranking value. This rowset is used as input to the query being processed by the SQL relational engine just like any other rowset originating from tables or indexes inside the server. The relational engine joins this rowset with the base table on the row identity and, along with other predicates in the query, evaluates the execution plan that yields the final result set. The types of full-text queries supported include searching for words or phrases, words in close proximity to each other, and inflectional forms of verbs and nouns. The full-text catalogues and indexes are not stored in a SQL Server database. They are stored in separate files managed by the Microsoft search service. The full-text catalogue files are not recovered during SQL Server recovery activity, and cannot be backed up and restored using the BACKUP and RESTORE statements. The full-text catalogues must be resynchronized separately after a recovery or restore operation.

The following is the sequence of steps involved in processing a full-text query:

1. An application programmed in a mainstream language such as Visual Basic or C++ sends SQL Server a SQL statement with a full-text construct via the OLE DB provider for SQL Server.

2. The SQL Server relational engine processes this request. First, it validates the full-text construct by querying the system tables to determine if the column reference is covered by a full-text index. After query optimization, the relational engine reduces the SQL statement to a query-execution plan that references rowsets at the leaves of the query plan. The relational engine uses OLE DB to pass the operations to the underlying storage engine and full-text provider. The relational engine transforms any full-text construct into a command request for a rowset from the full-text provider instead of the storage engine. The rowset returned by the full-text provider contains two columns: the set of keys satisfying the search condition and a ranking indicating how well the data for each key met the search condition criteria. The command request to the full-text provider includes the full-text search condition.

3. The full-text provider validates the command request and changes the search conditions to a form used by the querying support component of the Microsoft search service. The request is sent to the search service.

4. The querying support component uses its search engine component to extract the requested data from the full-text index. These data are passed back to the full-text provider in the form of a rowset.

5. The full-text provider returns the rowset to the relational engine, which combines all the rowsets it receives from the storage engine and the full-text provider to build the final result set sent back to the client application.

While OLE DB and UDA facilitated the integration of the full-text search service with SQL Server, the integration was not entirely plug-and-play. Several aspects of the integration such as extending the SQL compiler and optimizer to properly process new full-text predicates, adding mechanisms to maintain full-text indexes reasonably up to date with table updates, managing integrated security, and adding full-text index administrative tasks were done in a specialized manner.

5.6.4 Distributed Transformation Services

Data warehousing is an approach to managing data in which heterogeneous data sources (typically from multiple online transaction processing, OLTP, databases) are migrated to a separate homogenous database. Data warehouses provide several benefits to business intelligence users: Data are organized to facilitate analytical queries rather than transaction processing; differences among data structures across multiple heterogeneous databases can be resolved; data transformation rules can be applied to validate and consolidate data when data are moved from the operational OLTP database into the data warehouse; and security and performance issues can be resolved without requiring changes in the production systems. Data Transformation Services (DTS) provide the functionality to import, export, and transform data among multiple heterogeneous data sources interactively or automatically on a regularly scheduled basis. All data sources are accessed uniformly via OLE DB providers. Scripts perform transformations tasks between source and destination sources. The extraction, transformation, and load process involves data validation in the operational systems, data migration, data normalization to a common domain (i.e., data scrubbing), and data transformations to map or summarize values.

A DTS activity is organized in a package that includes three components. Connection objects define each source or destination OLE DB data source. Task objects define the specific actions to be performed. Step objects define the sequence in which tasks are to be performed. Steps also define whether the execution of one task is dependent on the results of a prior task.

The DTS Data Pump is a multithreaded OLE DB service component that provides the infrastructure to import, export, and transform data between heterogeneous OLE DB data sources. DTS Data Pump tasks allow the invocation of user programs that perform complex mappings between the source and destination columns while the data are transferred. The processing done by a DTS Data Pump task (Figure 5.11) includes connecting to the source and destination connection objects; determining the properties of the source rowset, which is built from the

Figure 5.11 | **Data Transformation Services (DTS) access diverse data sources through OLE DB.**

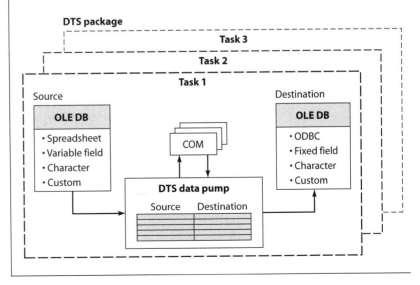

column formats of either the source table or the result of executing a query; and passing this information and a definition of all the specified transformations to the DTS Data Pump. During execution, the DTS Data Pump fetches rows from the data source, and the source columns are copied to the destination column as defined in the transformation mappings encapsulated in as COM scripts. Each transformed source row is pushed into the OLE DB destination data source.

5.6.5   Online Analytical Processing Services

Another area where the UDA architecture proved to be effective was the creation of the OLAP services in SQL Server. The OLAP services organize data from a data warehouse into multidimensional cubes with precomputed summary information to provide efficient answers to complex analytical queries. The primary OLAP object is the cube, a multidimensional representation of detail and summary data (see Section 5.3.4). A cube consists of a data source, dimensions, measures, and partitions. A data warehouse can support many different cubes, such as a SalesCube, an InventoryCube, and so on. Multidimensional queries against cubes return dataset objects.

OLAP services provide server and client capabilities to create and manage multidimensional OLAP data (Figure 5.12). Server operations include creating multidimensional data cubes from relational data

Figure 5.12 | **Integration of an OLAP server and a relational DBMS via OLE DB.**

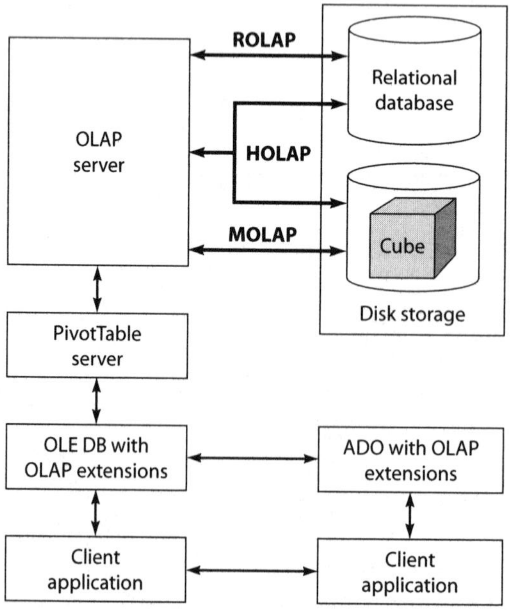

warehouse databases and storing cubes in multidimensional cube structures, in relational databases, and in combinations of both. Metadata for multidimensional cube structures are stored in a repository in a relational database. Client operations, provided by the PivotTable service is an OLE DB provider that supports the OLE DB for OLAP interface extensions. The PivotTable service is an in-process desktop OLAP server designed to provide online and offline data analysis and online access to OLAP data. The PivotTable service functions as a client of the OLAP Services.

PivotTable-service functionality includes data analysis, cube construction, and cache management PivotTable service functions as a service provider for relational data sources to implement multidimensional functionality and expose the OLE DB interfaces with OLAP extensions; a tabular data provider by supporting a subset of SQL; and a multidimensional data provider by processing MDX expressions. PivotTable service can store data locally on the client computer for offline analysis and offers connectivity to the multidimensional data managed by OLAP services, other OLE DB–compliant providers, and to non-OLAP relational data sources.

5.7   Microsoft Data Access Software Developer's Kit

In addition to publishing the complete technical specification for OLE DB, Microsoft makes available a Software Developer's Kit (SDK) to assist developers in writing OLE DB data providers or consumers. Version 2.0 of this SDK accompanies the *OLE DB 2.0 Programmer's Reference* (Microsoft 1998a), and version 2.5 (described here) is available through the Microsoft MSDN web site (Microsoft 1999b).

5.7.1   Documentation

The Microsoft Data Access SDK contains extensive online documentation for the Microsoft Data Access technologies, including:

- Programmer's references. The complete ADO and OLE DB programmer's references are available online as part of the SDK, including the core programming model, the extensions for heterogeneous and multidimensional data, and the MDX grammar. Also included is the programmer's reference for Microsoft's Open DataBase Connectivity (ODBC) technology.

- Whitepapers. A rich set of over 30 technical articles are included on subjects such as selecting the right data-access technology for your needs, improving the performance of your data-access application, mapping ADO methods to OLE DB interfaces, moving from

Microsoft Data Access Objects (DAO) to ADO, and an overview of OLE DB targeted at developers familiar with ODBC.

5.7.2 ActiveX Data Objects (ADO)

OLE DB is a low-level C and C++ interface that makes extensive use of language constructs such as pointers and arrays of structures to minimize calls, optimize performance, and give the programmer full control over processes such as memory allocation and reuse. This low-level control is necessary for building components that integrate together with no loss of performance, but exposes more granularity than is typically required at the application level. In addition, it prohibits OLE DB from being called directly from other languages that do not support these constructs.

In order to make OLE DB more approachable for the consuming application and callable from languages such as Visual Basic, Java, VBScript, and JavaScript, Microsoft provides an implementation of a ADO, user-friendly OLE Automation (Microsoft 1997a) interface.

ADO sits on top of any OLE DB data provider and exposes high-level objects for connecting to a data source, executing a command, and describing and retrieving returned data. It also exposes simple methods for querying database metadata and executing Data Definition Language (DDL) commands such as defining tables and columns or administering users and privileges. ADO supports the OLE DB extensions for heterogeneous data, and supports the OLE DB for OLAP extensions through an extension called ADO Multi-Dimensional (ADO MD).

ADO does not expose all of the functionality of the OLE DB provider, but instead a significant subset that is required for application programmers. For accessing low-level or data provider-specific functionality, ADO provides methods to get to the underlying OLE DB objects. Because the OLE DB objects are designed to be shared, consumers of the services include the following components.

- Data Links. The Data Link Component (Section 5.4.1) provides a common tool for creating and persisting information for connection to OLE DB providers. In addition to a stand-alone configuration utility for connections, Data Link provides the application programmers the ability to expose a standard user interface for collecting connection information from the user at runtime and services for converting connection information to and from a persistable string. Finally, it provides a common entry point for other services such as resource pooling, transaction enlistment, and cursoring services.

- Resource pooling. Resource pooling (Section 5.4.2) provides the ability to reuse connections and enlisted transactions across multiple method invocations without tearing down and recreating the connection to the data source each time. This is invaluable in building the type of high-performance, scalable applications demanded by today's Internet marketplace. With the Internet, database interactions are generally frequent and short in duration with no client state, such as connections held between client interactions. A single component may connect, check an account balance, and disconnect, while a second component transfers money by doing a transacted set of credit-debit operations. The overhead of making a connection and enlisting in a transaction for each of these steps may be many times the expense of the operation itself. By connecting through components provided in the Microsoft Data Access SDK, applications written to either ADO or OLE DB obtain the benefits of resource pooling without changing their programming model.

- Transaction enlistment. In order to provide atomicity across work done by multiple individual specialized components, that work must be scoped by a single, possibly distributed transaction. Microsoft Transaction Services (MTS) (Homer & Sussmann 1998) makes assembling applications out of these individual components simpler by providing a transactional context for such components. When operating in an MTS context, the core services provided as part of the Microsoft Data Access SDK automatically enlist OLE DB sessions in a distributed transaction to guarantee this atomicity of work across individual components.

- Cursor service. A cursor service (Section 5.4.3) is included in the Microsoft Data Access SDK and provides rich client-side cursoring capabilities, such as the ability to scroll through results, find a row by value, or update rows in the result using query-based searched updates. This service can be explicitly invoked by the OLE DB or ADO consumer by setting a property when opening the rowset, or it can be automatically invoked in order to provide requested functionality where not supported by the underlying OLE DB data provider.

- Data Conversion Component. OLE DB defines a set of required and optional conversions between data types. A common Data Conversion Component is provided in the Microsoft Data Access SDK to ease the burden on data-provider writers and to provide consistency across providers. This common Data Conversion Component is not generally exposed to the consumer but is called directly by the data provider in order to provide the conversions requested by the consumer through the standard OLE DB interface.

- Root Enumerator. The Root Enumerator gives programmers who don't want to go through the standard Data Link facility the ability to directly enumerate the set of data providers registered on a Windows machine. The application can then provide its own user interface or application logic for consuming those data providers.

- Root Binder. The Root Binder is a common component that resolves URL bindings for data providers that register to support specific uniform resource locator (URL) prefixes, such as the Microsoft OLE DB Provider for Internet Publishing.

5.7.3   OLE DB Data Providers

Also part of the MDAC set of components is a standard set of OLE DB data providers. These include providers for Microsoft ODBC, Microsoft SQL Server, Oracle, Microsoft Access, Shape Provider, and Microsoft OLE DB Provider for Internet Publishing.

The Microsoft OLE DB data provider for ODBC drivers ensures that applications written using ADO or OLE DB are able to access the wealth of data currently available through Microsoft's ODBC specification. This highly tuned data provider delivers equivalent performance and scalability when accessing ODBC data sources through either ODBC or OLE DB.

The Microsoft SQL Server OLE DB data provider is a native data provider that is written to directly consume Microsoft SQL Server's Tabular Data Stream (TDS) protocol off the wire. Performance gains are realized by working with the network packets directly, rather than through an intermediate layer.

Microsoft's OLE DB data provider for Oracle is written over Oracle's public Oracle Call Interface (OCI) layer. This data provider exposes an efficient, forward-only cursor over Oracle data which, combined with the cursor service (see Section 5.4.3), can be used to obtain a robust scrollable and updatable result.

The Microsoft Access OLE DB data provider gives OLE DB and ADO programmers direct access to Microsoft Access (.mdb) database files.

The Microsoft Shape Provider is a custom data provider (see Section 5.5). It is able to sit on top of any other data provider and build hierarchical results by relating multiple rowsets from the underlying provider according to relations defined by the consumer. It also supports the addition of custom aggregates and other calculated columns to rowsets generated by the underlying provider.

The Microsoft OLE DB Provider for Internet Publishing is an OLE DB 2.5 data provider that allows developers to access documents that reside on HTTP servers supporting the FrontPage Web Extender Client (WEC) or extensions for Web Distributed Authoring and Versioning (WEBDAV) protocol (Goland et al. 1999).

5.7.4   Simple Provider Toolkit

The OLE DB Simple Provider (OSP) Toolkit allows developers in any automation language, including Visual Basic, Java, C, or C++, to expose a simple in-memory array of data as an OLE DB provider. Developers in any of these languages expose a few simple methods for returning data indexed by row and column, allowing that data to be consumed by any OLE DB or ADO consumer.

5.7.5 Test Tools

The Microsoft Data Access SDK also includes a comprehensive set of tests for validating an OLE DB data provider against the specification. Included is a conformance test in the form of source code for testing all of the required objects, interfaces, and properties defined in the OLE DB specification. Along with the source code are a test harness for running compiled tests called Local Test Manager (LTM) and additional tests written in ADO for validating that an OLE DB data provider will work with ADO.

5.7.6 Samples

The Microsoft Data Access SDK includes a wide range of samples, including ADO samples written in C++, Visual Basic, and Java, OLE DB samples, and an online catalogue and order placement sample application.

5.8 Summary

It has been slightly more than 3 years since Microsoft released version 1.0 of OLE DB on August 28, 1996. Although the adoption of OLE DB and ADO continues to increase, and we continue to learn how people are using this technology in the process, there are certain conclusions we can draw about its success as component architecture from its introduction and use to date.

The first lesson is that with extensibility comes complexity. The property mechanism in OLE DB, in striving to be both extensible and efficient, is also somewhat complex. Because multiple properties can be specified in a single call, from both provider-specific and OLE DB–defined property sets, and the consumer has the ability to request a property as either optional or required, validation and error reporting for partial success cases are difficult.

COM aggregation, while incredibly powerful, is not well documented, and certain erroneous assumptions about how things should be implemented can lead to failure. When we released the Service Component architecture in OLE DB 2.0 that relied on COM aggregation, we only exposed services for providers that were enabled through a registry entry after the provider's implementation of aggregation had been verified.

This complexity is nicely hidden from the ADO consumer, but the complexity slowed initial adoption somewhat for provider writers. Fortunately, Microsoft Visual C++ provides templates to hide much of this complexity and make it significantly easier to build providers that conform to the specification and work well with generic consumers.

Because there is no common implementation on either the provider or the consumer side of the interface, compatibility is provided solely through the specification. As a result, the OLE DB specification is excruciatingly detailed, both in terms of syntax and semantics. Providers must follow the specification exactly in order to be interoperable, and Microsoft has had to write and make available as part of the SDK, extensive tests to validate conformance to the specification. Without this level of specification detail and without such comprehensive tests, interoperability would not be possible. Again, the OLE DB provider templates go a long way toward helping C++ developers write conforming data providers.

Still, the simple base abstractions defined in OLE DB have proven to be incredibly extensible. Microsoft, with the input of key players in the OLAP community, was able to build on the core connection, command, schema, and rowset model, and introduce a single new dataset object, in order to provide a compelling interface for working with OLAP data. Microsoft was further able to extend OLE DB to work with heterogeneous data, such as file systems and message stores, through the addition of a row object and URL binding. And by simply adding a few domain-specific schema rowsets, the Open GIS community enabled OLE DB to be an accepted standard for accessing spatial data. All of these extensions were entirely additive to the original base specification; providers of OLAP, heterogeneous, or spatial data conform to the original OLE DB 1.0 specification and can be consumed by OLE DB 1.0 consumers.

In addition, OLE DB's component model and inherent extensibility has enabled Microsoft to build core services, including connection management, pooling, and advanced cursor components that improve the performance, scalability, and functionality of existing providers for all types of applications. Existing providers can be leveraged as building blocks by building custom providers that surface a specific functionality set and view over an existing provider's underlying data. And component databases can be built by leveraging OLE DB internally—as the interface between a relational engine and a storage engine, as a heterogeneous interface to a distributed query processor, or to extend a database with full-text, data warehousing and OLAP functionality.

OLE DB was designed to be suitable as a native interface to any data store. Thus, it was a requirement that it expose all of the data store's native functionality, behavior, and semantics. As a result, developers can get the utmost functionality and performance when writing to any one data store and can reuse a great deal of common tools, knowledge, and code when writing similar applications to different data providers. However, writing a generic application that attempts to take advantage of extended functionality across multiple providers still requires extra work, unless services exist to implement that functionality on behalf of less capable data providers.

In summary, there really is no magic in creating a component architecture. Providing an extensible component infrastructure such as OLE DB is just part of the solution. Vertical solutions can be developed relatively easily by plugging components into this infrastructure that are designed and tested to work together. Building generic components is somewhat harder and requires strict adherence to an extremely detailed specification, with a rich set of common tests to validate that conformance. Finally, higher-level abstractions such as ADO are useful in that they hide the low-level complexity, but must be carefully designed in order not to sacrifice performance or hide useful functionality from the consumer.

6

An Architecture for Transparent Access to Diverse Data Sources

Mary Tork Roth
Propel.com

Peter Schwarz
Laura Haas
Almaden Research Center, IBM Corp.

6.1　Introduction

Most large organizations have collected a considerable amount of data and have invested heavily in systems and applications to manage and access that data. Even within a single organization, these legacy data management systems typically vary widely, ranging from simple text files with little or no support for queries or other database functionality to complex database management systems with sophisticated query engines. In many cases, specialized indexing technology and query engines have been developed to facilitate efficient searching of particular kinds of data, for example, for finding compounds with a certain substructure in chemical databases, for finding overlapping regions in a geographic database, or for finding images with similar color or texture in an image archive. It is increasingly clear that powerful applications can be created by combining information stored in these historically separate data sources. For example, a medical system that integrates patient histories, EKG readings, lab results and MRI scans will greatly reduce the amount of time required for a doctor to retrieve and compare these pieces of information before making a diagnosis. Likewise, a pharmaceutical application that can combine a chemical compound-similarity search with the results of biological assays will be a powerful tool for discovering new drugs.

There are several approaches to providing such an integrated view of heterogeneous data. One is to move the data en masse to a new integrated database system that is tailored to provide a unified view of data of different types. For example, object-relational systems can store image, video, and text and provide some query support for these non-traditional data types (Stonebraker et al. 1999). Many relational database vendors have extended their systems to do the same (Carey et al. 1999). The drawback of this universal server approach is that the data are often already adequately managed by the legacy systems and existing applications written against those systems' interfaces must be rewritten to work with the new database. Thus, migration to an entirely new system is often not a practical solution. Furthermore, the special functionality associated with these data types must be reproduced in the database engine itself.

An alternative approach is to access such data through a CDBMS (component database management system) middleware system that provides an integrated view of heterogeneous legacy data without changing how or where the data are stored. Such a system can leverage the storage and data management facilities provided by the legacy systems and provide a unified schema and common interface for advanced new applications without disturbing existing applications. Freed from the responsibilities of storage and data management, the CDBMS can focus on providing powerful high-level query services for heterogeneous data.

The CDBMS relies on a particular kind of component, namely wrappers (Tork Roth & Schwarz 1997; Kapitskaia et al. 1997; Papakonstantinou et al. 1995a), to encapsulate the underlying data and mediate between the data source and the middleware. The wrapper architecture and interfaces are crucial because wrappers are the focal point for managing the diversity of data sources. Below a wrapper, each data source, or repository, has its own data model, schema, programming interface, and query capability. The data model may be relational, object-oriented, or specialized for a particular domain. The schema may be fixed or vary over time. Some repositories support a query language, while others are accessed using a class library or other programmatic interface. Most critically, repositories vary widely in their support for queries. At one end of the spectrum are repositories that only support simple scans over their contents (e.g., files of records). Somewhat more sophisticated repositories may allow a record ordering to be specified or be able to apply certain predicates to limit the amount of data retrieved. At the other end of the spectrum are repositories such as relational databases that support complex operations such as joins or aggregation. Repositories can also be quite idiosyncratic, allowing, for example, only certain forms of predicates on certain attributes or joins between certain collections.

The wide variance in repository query capability means that a wrapper interface that required a standard level of query support from each repository would be impractical. If the level chosen were low, the middleware system would be unable to take full advantage of the native query power of sophisticated repositories, resulting in performance far below what it could be. If the level chosen were high, the complexity of producing a wrapper for a simple data source would be unacceptable. The wrapper architecture of Garlic (Carey et al. 1995), an object-oriented middleware system, addresses the challenge of diversity by standardizing how information in data sources is described and accessed, while taking an approach to query planning in which the wrapper and the middleware dynamically negotiate the wrapper's role in answering a query.

This chapter describes the Garlic wrapper component architecture and summarizes our experience building wrappers for 10 data sources with widely varying data models and degrees of support for querying. The next section gives a brief overview of the system and is followed by a section that summarizes the goals of the wrapper architecture. Section 6.4 describes in detail how a wrapper is built, and Section 6.5 summarizes the implementation details of wrappers for a set of diverse data sources. Section 6.6 briefly summarizes related work. Section 6.7 concludes the chapter and presents some opportunities for future research.

6.2   System Overview

Garlic applications see heterogeneous legacy data stored in a variety of data sources as instances of objects in a unified schema. Rather than invent yet another object-oriented data model, Garlic's data model and programming interface are based closely on the Object Database Management Group (ODMG) standard (Cattell & Barry 1997). Garlic's query language is an extension of SQL that adds support for path expressions, nested collections, and methods. Object-oriented data models are a good choice for middleware because they are general enough to support complex nested structures, allow relationships among entities to be modeled as references, and allow methods to be associated with data. The last is of particular importance to Garlic, because it provides a convenient and natural way to model the specialized search and data manipulation facilities of nontraditional data sources. For example, the ability of a text server to rank documents by relevance to some subject is easily modeled as a method that takes the subject as a parameter and returns a numeric score for the document. By extending SQL to allow invocations of such methods in queries, Garlic provides a single straightforward language extension that can support many different kinds of specialized search.

The overall architecture of Garlic is depicted in Figure 6.1. Associated with each repository is a wrapper component. In addition to the repositories containing legacy data, Garlic provides its own repository for Garlic complex objects, which users can create to bind together existing objects from the other repositories. Garlic also maintains global metadata that describe the unified schema. Garlic objects can be accessed both via a C++ programming interface and through Garlic's query language. The heart of the Garlic middleware is the query-

Figure 6.1 | **The Garlic architecture.**

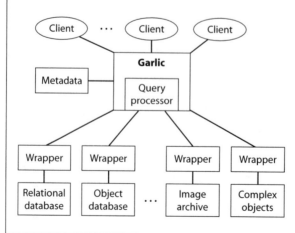

processing component. The query processor develops plans to efficiently decompose queries that span one or more repositories into pieces that the individual repositories can handle. The query execution engine controls the execution of such a query plan by assembling the results from the repositories and performing any additional processing required to produce the answer to the query.

6.3   Goals for the Wrapper Component Architecture

Our experience in building wrappers for Garlic confirms that the wrapper component architecture should be designed with the following four goals in mind to ensure that the middleware system is well suited to integrate a diverse set of data sources.

First, the startup cost to write a wrapper should be small. We expect a typical application to combine data from several traditional sources (e.g., relational database systems from various vendors) with data from a variety of nontraditional systems, such as image servers and searchable web sites, and from one-of-a-kind sources, such as a home-grown chemical-structures database. Although the middleware system may ship with a set of wrappers for popular data sources, we must rely on third-party vendors and customer data administrators to provide wrappers for more specialized data sources. To make wrapper authoring as simple as possible, the Garlic wrapper component architecture requires only a small set of key services from a wrapper and ensures that a wrapper can be written with very little knowledge of Garlic's internal structure. In our experience, a wrapper that provides a base level of service for a new repository can be written in a matter of hours. Even such a basic wrapper permits a significant amount of the repository's data and functionality to be exposed through the Garlic interface.

Second, wrappers should be able to evolve. Our standard methodology in building wrappers has been to start with an initial version that models the repository's content as objects and allows Garlic to retrieve their attributes. We then incrementally improve the wrapper to exploit more of the repository's native query-processing capabilities, which should lead to better query performance.

Third, the architecture should be flexible and allow for graceful growth. The Garlic wrapper component architecture requires only that a data source have some form of programmatic interface and makes no assumptions about its data model or query-processing capabilities. Wrappers for new data sources can be integrated into existing Garlic databases without disturbing legacy applications, other wrappers, or existing Garlic applications. We have successfully built wrappers for a diverse set of data sources. These include two relational database systems (DB2 and Oracle), a patent server stored in Lotus Notes, searchable sites on the World Wide Web (including a database of business listings and a hotel guide), and specialized search engines for collections of images, chemical structures, and text. In addition, we implemented the repository for complex objects by writing a wrapper for an object-oriented database system.

Fourth, the architecture should readily lend itself to query optimization. The author of a wrapper need not code to a standard query interface that may be too high level or too low level for the underlying data source. Instead, a wrapper is a full participant in query planning and may use whatever knowledge it has about a repository's query capabilities and specialized search facilities to dynamically determine how much of a query the repository is capable of handling. This approach allows us to build wrappers for simple data sources quickly and still exploit the unique query-processing capabilities of unusual data sources such as search engines for chemical structures and images.

6.4   Building a Wrapper

As shown in Figure 6.2, the Garlic wrapper component architecture requires a wrapper to provide four major services. First, a wrapper models the contents of its repository as objects and allows Garlic to retrieve references to these objects. Second, a wrapper allows Garlic to invoke methods on objects and retrieve their attributes. This mechanism is important, because it provides a means by which Garlic can get data out of a repository, even if the repository has almost no support for querying. Third, a wrapper participates in query planning when a Garlic query ranges over objects in its repository. The Garlic metadata do not include information about the query-processing capabilities of individual repositories, so the Garlic query processor has no a priori knowledge about what predicates and projections can be handled by a given repository. Instead, the query processor identifies portions of a query relevant to a repository and allows the repository's wrapper to determine how much of the work it is willing to handle and at what cost. The final service provided by a wrapper is query execution. During query execution, the wrapper completes the work it reported it could do in the query-planning phase. A wrapper may take advantage of whatever specialized search facilities the repository provides in order to return the relevant data to Garlic. In the sections that follow, we describe each of these services in greater detail, and provide an example of how to build wrappers for a simple travel agency application.

6.4.1   Modeling Data as Objects

The first service that a wrapper provides is to turn the data of the underlying repository into objects accessible by Garlic. Each Garlic object has an interface that abstractly describes the object's behavior and an imple-

Figure 6.2

Services provided by a wrapper.

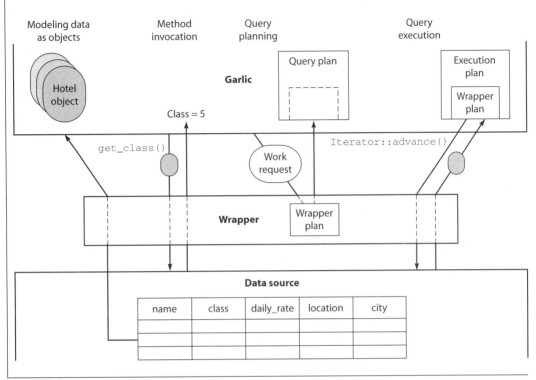

mentation that provides a concrete realization of the interface. The Garlic data model permits any number of implementations for a given interface. For example, two relational database repositories that contain information about disjoint sets of employees may each export distinct implementations of a common `Employee` interface.

During an initial registration step, wrappers provide a description of the content of their repositories using the Garlic Data Language (GDL). GDL is a variant of the ODMG's Object Description Language (ODMG-ODL). The interfaces that describe the behavior of objects in a repository are known collectively as the repository schema. Repositories are registered as parts of a Garlic database and their individual repository schemata are merged into the global schema that is presented to Garlic users.

A wrapper also cooperates with Garlic in assigning identity to individual objects so that they can be referenced from Garlic and from Garlic applications. A Garlic object identifier (OID) has two parts. The first part is the implementation identifier (IID). It is assigned by Garlic and identifies which implementation is responsible for the object, which in turn identifies the interface that the object supports and the repository in which it is stored. The second part of the OID, the key, is uninterpreted by Garlic. It is provided by the wrapper and identifies an object within a repository. It is the combined responsibility of the wrapper and repository to generate an OID when a reference to an object is needed, to ensure that no two objects with the same implementation have the same key, and to ensure that the combination of IID and key is sufficient to locate the object's data in the repository.

Specific objects, usually collections, can be designated as database roots. Root objects are identified by name, as well as by OID, and as such can serve as starting points for navigation or querying (e.g., root collection objects can be used in the from clause of a query).

As an example of how data are modeled as objects in Garlic, consider a simple application for a hypothetical travel agency. The agency stores information about the countries and cities for which it arranges tours as tables in a relational database. It also has access to a web site that provides booking information for hotels throughout the world and to an image server in which it stores images of travel destinations.

EXAMPLE 1

These sources are easily described in GDL and integrated as a Garlic database. First, consider the relational database. The database contains two relations, Countries and Cities. The Countries relation contains general information about the countries that the travel agency serves, and its primary key is the country name. The Cities relation contains information about cities that can serve as travel destinations, including a column named country that contains the country name. The country name and the city name together form the primary key for the Cities relation, and the country name also serves as a foreign key to the Countries relation. Both relations have a scene column that stores the name of an image file containing a representative scene of the location.

The wrapper for the relational database exports two interfaces, one for the Countries relation and one for the Cities relation. Their description in GDL is shown in Figure 6.3 (a). The attributes of each interface correspond to the columns of each relation. Note that the wrapper exposes the foreign key country on the Cities relation as a typed Garlic object reference, rather than as a string, which is its internal representation in the relational database. Similarly, the scene attribute on each relation is exposed as a Garlic reference to an instance of the Image interface, which is described later. For each relation, the wrapper also exports an implementation of the corresponding interface. Each implementation maps the tuples of a relation into Garlic objects. The primary-key value of a tuple serves as the key portion of the Garlic OID. Last, the wrapper exports a collection corresponding to each relation. Cities is registered as a root collection of City objects and Countries as a root collection of Country objects.

EXAMPLE 2

Next, consider the web site, which provides information about daily rates, class ratings, location, and so on, for hotels throughout the world. Garlic's web wrapper models this source as a repository that exports a single interface, `Hotel`, and a single root collection of `Hotel` objects. The GDL for the `Hotel` interface is shown in Figure 6.3(b).[1] Because the web site does not support updates, the attributes are marked read-only. The web site provides unique identifiers on the HTML (Hypertext Markup Language) page for the hotel listings it returns, and these identifiers serve as the key portion of `Hotel` OIDs.

EXAMPLE 3

Last, consider the image server. We have built a wrapper for an image server based on the QBIC (Query by Image Content) image search engine (Niblack et al. 1997). It manages collections of images stored in files, and allows these images to be retrieved and ordered according to features such as color, shape, and color position within an image. As shown in Figure 6.3(c), the wrapper for the image server exports an interface definition for `Image` objects. Each object has a single read-only attribute, the name of the file in which the image is stored. The image file name also serves as the key portion of an `Image` OID. The image server's search capability is expressed in GDL as a `matches()` method, which takes as input the name of a file containing the description of an image feature and returns as output a score that indicates how well a particular image matches the feature. An additional method, `display()`, models the server's ability to output an image on a specified device. The image server wrapper exports two collections of `Image` objects—one that contains scenes of countries and one that contains scenes of cities. The `scene` attributes of the relational wrapper's `Country` and `City` interfaces are references to objects in these collections.

6.4.2 Method Invocation

The second service a wrapper provides is a means to invoke methods on the objects in its repository. Method invocations can be generated by Garlic's query-execution engine (see Section 6.4.3), or by a Garlic application that has obtained a reference to an object (either as the result of a query or by looking up a root object by name).

---

[1] Note that we have chosen to model the `city` attribute of `Hotel` objects as a string attribute, not as a reference to an object that supports the `City` interface. This choice seems appropriate for this example because the web site is outside the travel agency's control and has information about cities around the world, whereas the relational database containing `City` tuples was developed by the travel agency and is constrained to cities that the travel agency serves. If necessary, Garlic complex objects or views could be used to link hotels with cities, or cities with sets of hotels. See Carey et al. (1995) for further discussion of Garlic complex objects and views.

Figure 6.3

Travel agency application schema: (a) relational repository, (b) web repository, (c) image server repository.

```
Relational repository schema          Web repository schema
interface Country {                   interface Hotel {
   attribute string name;                attribute readonly string name;
   attribute string airlines_served;     attribute readonly short class;
   attribute boolean visa_required;      attribute readonly double daily_rate;
   attribute Image scene;                attribute readonly string location;
}                                        attribute readonly string city;
                                      }
interface City {
   attribute string name;             Image server repository schema
   attribute long population;         interface Image {
   attribute boolean airport;            attribute readonly string file_name;
   attribute Country country;            double matches (in string file_name);
   attribute Image scene;                void display (in string device_name);
}                                     }
```

EXAMPLE 4

Consider the C++ application code fragment in Figure 6.4 The application uses the `oql()` function to submit a query that retrieves the `scene` attribute for countries in the travel agency database that are served by American Airlines. The value of the `scene` attribute is a reference to an `Image` object, and, for each `Image` reference retrieved, an invocation of the `display()` method is used to render the image on the user's screen.

Figure 6.4

A Garlic application fragment.

```
Iterator<GStruct> *result_iter;
GStruct result_tuple;
...
oql(db, result_iter,
    "select C.scene from Countries C where C.airlines_served LIKE '%American%'");
while (result_iter->next(result_tuple)) {
  Image *i = result_tuple[0].get_reference();
  i->display(myScreen);
}
```

In addition to explicitly defined methods such as `display()`, two types of accessor methods are implicitly defined for retrieving and updating an object's attributes—a get method for each attribute in the interface and a set method for attributes that are not read-only. For instance, a `get_file_name()` method would be implicitly defined for the read-only `file_name` attribute of the `Image` interface.

Garlic uses the IID portion of a target object's OID to route a method invocation to the object's implementation. The implementation must be able to invoke each method in the corresponding interface, as well as the implicitly defined accessor methods. Unlike interfaces, which can be described by GDL, an implementation typically consists of code that maps Garlic method invocations into appropriate operations provided by the underlying repository. To accommodate the widest possible range of repositories, Garlic provides two variants of the method invocation interface. The first variant, stub dispatch, is a natural choice for repositories whose native programming interface is a class library. A wrapper that uses stub dispatch provides a stub routine for each method of an implementation. The stub routine converts method arguments from a standard form specified by Garlic into the form expected by the repository, invokes the corresponding method from the repository's class library, and performs a similar translation on the method's return value. When a wrapper using stub dispatch is initialized, it exports a table that contains the entry point addresses of these stub routines.

The image server is an example of a repository for which stub dispatch is appropriate. For the `display()` method, for example, the image server wrapper provides a short routine that first extracts the file name of the target image from the key field of the OID and unpacks the display device name from the argument list supplied by Garlic. To display the image on the screen, the routine calls the appropriate display function from the image server's class library, providing the image file name and display name as arguments. (If the display function has a return value, upon return the stub routine will package the value into the standard form expected by Garlic.) Other repositories for which stub dispatch is appropriate include those that store data as persistent programming language objects, for example, those implemented using object-oriented databases such as ObjectStore (Lamb et al. 1991) or O_2 (Deux 1990).

The second variant of the method invocation interface, generic dispatch, is useful for repositories that themselves support a generic method invocation mechanism or for repositories that do not directly support objects and methods. A wrapper that supports generic dispatch exports a single method invocation entry point. The method name is given as a parameter, and its arguments are supplied in a standard form as previously described. An important advantage of generic dispatch is that it is schema independent. A single copy of the generic dispatch code can be shared by repositories that have a common programming interface but different schemas.

The relational wrapper is well-suited for generic method dispatch. This wrapper supports only the implicitly defined accessor methods, and each method invocation translates directly to a query over the relation that corresponds to the implementation.

EXAMPLE 5

Consider an invocation of the `get_population()` method on a `City` object. Garlic sends the name of the method and the OID of the object to the relational wrapper. The wrapper maps the method name into a column name, maps the IID portion of the object's OID into a relation name, and extracts the primary key value from the OID. It uses these values to construct the following query.

```
select population
from Cities
where name = <OID key value for name>
    and country = <OID key value for country>
```

Our web wrapper also uses generic dispatch. Since the attributes of its `Hotel` objects are read-only, the web wrapper supports only get methods. A method invocation is translated into a search uniform resource locator (URL) for the web site. The wrapper extracts the hotel listing key from the object's OID and forms the URL to retrieve the HTML page. Once the page is loaded, it parses the retrieved HTML page to find the hotel listing that corresponds to the `Hotel` object, and returns the required attribute to Garlic.

6.4.3 Query Planning

A wrapper's third obligation is to participate in query planning. The goal of query planning is to develop alternative plans for answering a query and then to choose the most efficient one. The Garlic query optimizer (Haas et al. 1997) is a cost-based optimizer modeled on Lohman's grammar-like rule approach (Lohman 1988). STARs (Strategy Alternative Rules) are used by the optimizer to describe possible execution plans for a query. The optimizer uses dynamic programming to build query plans bottom-up. First, single-collection access plans are generated, followed by a phase in which two-way join plans are considered, followed by three-way joins, and so on, until a complete plan for the query has been generated. Garlic extends the STAR approach by introducing wrappers as full-fledged participants during plan enumeration. During each query-planning phase, the Garlic optimizer identifies the largest possible query fragment that involves a particular repository and sends it to the repository's wrapper. The wrapper returns zero or more plans that implement some or all of the work represented by the query fragment. The wrapper associates a set of properties and cost information with each of these plans. This information allows the optimizer to incorporate the wrapper's plans into the set of plans it is considering to produce the results of the entire query, adding operators to perform in Garlic any portion of the query fragment that the wrapper did not agree to handle.

As noted previously, repositories vary greatly in their query-processing capabilities. Furthermore, each repository has its own unique set of restrictions on the operations it will perform. These capabilities and restrictions may be difficult or impossible to express declaratively. For example, relational databases often have limits on the number of tables involved in a join, the maximum length of a query string, the maximum value of a constant in a query, and so forth. These limits vary for different relational products and even for different versions of the same product. As another example, our web wrapper is able to handle SQL LIKE predicates, but is sensitive to the exact placement of wild-card characters. A key advantage to our approach is that the optimizer does not need to track the minute details of the capabilities and restrictions of the underlying data sources. Instead, the wrapper encapsulates this knowledge and ensures that the plans it produces can actually be executed by the repository.

Our approach allows a wrapper to model as little or as much of the repository's capabilities as makes sense. If a repository has limited query-processing power, then the amount of code necessary to support the query-planning interface is small. On the other hand, if a repository does have specialized search facilities and access methods that Garlic can exploit, the interface is flexible enough for a wrapper to encapsulate as much of these capabilities as possible. Even if a repository can do no more than return the OIDs of objects in a collection, Garlic can evaluate an arbitrary SQL query by retrieving data from the repository via method invocation (as described in Section 6.4.2) and processing it in Garlic.

Query-Planning Overview. A wrapper's participation in query planning is controlled by a set of methods that the optimizer may invoke during plan enumeration. The `plan_access()` method is used to generate single-collection access plans, and the `plan_join()` method is used to generate multiway join plans. Joins may arise from queries expressed in standard SQL, or joins may be generated by Garlic for queries that contain path expressions, a feature of Garlic's extended SQL. The `plan_bind()` method is used to generate a specific kind of plan that can serve as the inner stream of a bind join. Additional planning methods such as `plan_group_by()` are provided to handle other SQL operations. Each method takes as input a work request, which is a description of the query fragment to be processed. The return value is a set of plans, each of which includes a list of properties that describe how much of the work request the plan implements and cost information that describes how much the plan will cost to execute. The plans are represented by instances of a wrapper-specific specialization of the `Wrapper_Plan` class. In addition to the property list, they encapsulate any repository-specific information a wrapper needs to actually perform the work described by the properties list.

A wrapper author only needs to provide implementations of the planning methods that make sense for a given repository. For example, if a repository is unable to process joins, the wrapper does not need to implement the `plan_join()` method. A default implementation supplied by Garlic will return an empty set of plans, and, as a result, joins over collections in that repository will be handled by the Garlic execution engine. Note, however, that if a wrapper does not provide at least a minimal `plan_access()` method, there is no way for the Garlic execution engine to iterate over the objects in the repository's collections. As a result, objects in such a repository can be accessed in a Garlic query only if references to them can be found in other repositories. The execution engine will have to use method invocation to retrieve the objects' attributes.

The data structure that describes the work request is designed to be as lightweight as possible. Wrappers can use a simple request-response protocol to quickly obtain the pieces of the work request that they care about. Predicates and projection expressions are described by simple parse trees, and a class library is provided for common operations such as moving projection-list elements and predicates from the work request to the plan and the properties list. To help wrappers quickly filter out complicated expressions that they can't handle, methods are provided to help analyze expressions at a high level. For example, a wrapper may invoke the methods `refers_to_method()` and `refers_to_OID()` to determine whether or not an expression refers to a method or an object id without actually having to traverse the entire expression tree.

As described in Tork Roth et al. (1999), the properties list and the cost information are used by the optimizer to incorporate the work performed by the wrapper into the set of plans it is considering to produce the results of the entire query. Wrapper plans show up as leaves of the query plan tree, and, as a result, the following three estimates are sufficient for the optimizer to incorporate the wrapper plan costs into the cost of the entire query: total cost (the cost in seconds to execute the wrapper's plan and get a complete set of results), reexecution cost (the cost in seconds to execute the plan a second time), and cardinality (the estimated result cardinality of the plan). The difference between the total and reexecution cost is the cost of any initialization that may need to be performed the first time the wrapper's plan is executed. These three estimates provide an intuitive level of abstraction for wrappers to provide cost information about their operators to the optimizer. Total cost, reexecution cost, and result cardinality can be computed without having to comprehend the complex details of the optimizer's internal cost equations. Yet, these estimates give the optimizer enough information to integrate the cost of a wrapper's plan into the cost of the global query plan without having to modify any of its cost equations or understand anything about the execution strategy of the external data source.

In addition to wrapper-plan costs, the Garlic optimizer will also need other information to compute the costs of its own operators in the global query plan. For example, because Garlic clients are allowed to invoke methods in their queries and the Garlic execution engine itself may need to invoke methods, the Garlic optimizer also asks a wrapper to provide the following cost estimates for its methods: total method cost (the cost to execute the method once) and reexecution method cost (the cost to execute the method a second time). As another example, in order to correctly compute the cost and cardinality of a FILTER operator applied to a wrapper plan, the optimizer must compute the selectivity of the predicates applied as part of the filter operation. Optimizers typically rely on statistics about the base data in order to compute such selectivity estimates. As a result, wrappers are asked to provide uniform distribution statistics about the attributes of their objects, such as the number of distinct values, the second-highest value, and the second-lowest value.

To help wrappers provide cost information, the wrapper architecture includes a default cost model to compute the cost estimates needed by the optimizer and makes routines available to compute cardinality estimates using the optimizer's selectivity formulas. A wrapper's plan corresponds to an executable iterator (see Section 6.4.4), and the default cost model is based on the execution model of an iterator. The work of an iterator can be divided into two basic tasks: reset, the work performed to initialize an iterator for execution, and advance, the work required to retrieve the next set of results. Thus, the total cost of a wrapper's plan can be computed as a combination of the reset and advance costs of the corresponding iterator. The default model exploits this observation to estimate the total and reexecution costs of a wrapper plan. Wrappers may use this model without modification, and experiments have shown that the default model is sufficient for many simple data sources (Tork Roth et al. 1999). If the default implementation is not sufficient, wrappers for more complex sources build on the facilities provided to produce more accurate information.

The wrapper architecture also includes facilities to help wrappers generate statistics and compute method costs required by the optimizer, as well as to generate any new statistics used in its own costs computations. The statistics facility allows a wrapper to execute a workload of queries against a repository, and use the results of these queries to compute various statistics and method costs, which can then be stored in the Garlic metadata. Again, wrappers may use these facilities without modification or tailor them to a repository as appropriate.

Single-Collection Access Plans. The `plan_access()` method is the interface by which the Garlic query optimizer asks a wrapper for plans that return data from a single collection. It is invoked for each collection to which a Garlic query refers. The work request for a single-collection access includes predicates to apply, attributes to project, and methods to invoke. Because the Garlic optimizer does not know which (if any) of the predicates a wrapper will be able to apply, the projection list in a work request contains all relevant attributes and methods mentioned in the query, including those that only appear in predicates. This gives the wrapper an opportunity to supply values for attributes that the Garlic execution engine will need in order to apply predicates that the wrapper chooses not to handle. As a worst-case fallback, the projection list also always includes the OID, even if the user's original query makes no mention of it. The execution engine uses the OID and the method-invocation interface to retrieve the values of any attributes it needs that are not directly supplied by the wrapper.

It is completely up to the wrapper to decide how much of the request it can handle. The decision depends on the general query-processing capabilities of the repository, on the amount of effort that has gone into writing the wrapper, and on any limitations of the data source's programmatic interface (e.g., limits on query-string length or the number of predicates that can be applied). If necessary, the wrapper may consult with the repository about any restrictions specific to individual queries. Note, however, that during planning a process boundary will never be crossed unless the wrapper chooses to consult with the underlying data source in this manner, and in any event none of the data referenced by the query will be transferred during planning.

A wrapper for a simple repository that only supports iteration over collections of objects, or an initial implementation of a wrapper for a more sophisticated repository, need not apply any predicates or projections. If the wrapper just returns a plan for the query `select OID from <collection>`, the optimizer will append to the wrapper's plan the operators necessary for the Garlic execution engine to complete the work request. The wrapper for a more sophisticated repository, such as a relational database, may perform more detailed analysis and consume as many predicates and projections as it can. However, even a relational database may refuse to handle some expressions, such as those involving method invocations.

EXAMPLE 6

Figure 6.5 shows the first phase of query planning for a simple single-collection query against our travel agency database. Suppose a Garlic user submits a query to find five-star hotels with beach-front property. The Garlic query optimizer analyzes the user's query and identifies the fragment that involves the `Hotels` collection. Because the `Hotels` collection is managed by the web wrapper, it invokes the web wrapper's `plan_access()` method with a description of the work to be done. This description contains the list of predicates to apply and attributes to project, including the OID.

Figure 6.5

Construction of a wrapper access plan.

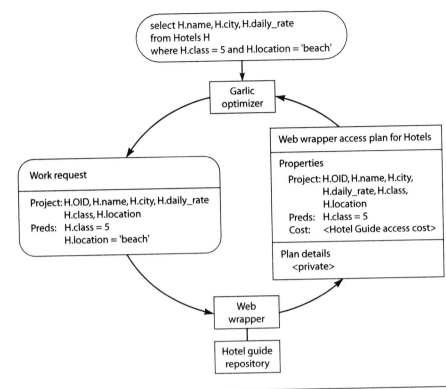

During the execution of plan_access(), the web wrapper looks at the work request to determine how much of the query it can handle. In general, our web wrapper will accept predicates of the form <attr> <op> <const>, where <op> is either = or the SQL keyword LIKE.[2] However, the web wrapper cannot handle equality predicates on strings because the web site does not adhere to SQL semantics for string equality. The web site treats the predicate location = 'beach' as location LIKE '%beach%', which provides a superset of the results of the equality predicate. This difference in semantics means that the web wrapper cannot report to the optimizer that it can apply a string equality predicate. Nevertheless, when string equality is requested, it is still

[2] Indeed, the web wrapper insists that the work request contain at least one predicate because the web site imposes this requirement. This restriction means that some Garlic queries that are syntactically correct are not answerable. For example, although the Garlic query select name, class from Hotels is syntactically correct, the web wrapper will not return an access plan for it because no predicate was specified. Without a wrapper plan, Garlic has no way of generating a plan to scan the collection, and therefore the query cannot be executed.

beneficial for the wrapper to apply the less restrictive LIKE predicate in order to reduce the amount of data returned to Garlic. The wrapper therefore creates a plan that will perform the predicate location LIKE '%beach%', while reporting through the plan's properties that the equality predicate will not be applied.

In Example 6 (Figure 6.5), the wrapper analyzes the work request and creates a Wrapper_Plan containing the information it will need in order to execute the plan (including application of a LIKE predicate on location). The plan's property list indicates that the plan will apply the predicate on class, but omits the predicate on location. The HTML pages returned by the web site contain all of the information for a hotel listing, so the wrapper agrees to handle the entire projection list: OID, name, city, daily_rate, class, and location. Note that since the wrapper agreed to apply the predicate on class, it really does not need to return the value of class to Garlic. However, the query optimizer could not predict ahead of time that the wrapper would handle this predicate. It conservatively requested that the wrapper return the class attribute so the engine would not have to get it via a get_class() method invocation in order to apply the predicate. Last, the wrapper assigns the plan an estimated cost, including the expected cardinality of the plan. These estimates were computed using the default cost model and statistics obtained by using the statistics facility provided by the wrapper interface.

This access plan is returned to the optimizer. If it is chosen to be part of the global plan for the user's query, the optimizer will need to add the necessary FILTER operator to apply the predicate on location, although it would be applied to a far smaller set of objects than if the wrapper had not (covertly) applied the LIKE predicate.

Join Plans. The optimizer uses the access plans generated in the first phase of optimization as a starting point for join enumeration. If the optimizer recognizes that two collections reside in the same repository, it invokes the wrapper's plan_join() method (if one is implemented) to try to push the join down to that repository. The work request includes the join predicates as well as the single-collection access plans that the wrapper had previously generated for the collections being joined. In the plan_join() method, the wrapper can reexamine these plans and consider the effect of adding join predicates. As in the plan_access() case, the wrapper can produce zero or more plans and agree to handle any subset of the original projections and predicates, and/or the join predicates, as long as the property lists for the new plans are properly filled out. The optimizer will add the new wrapper plans to the set it has under consideration. During the next phase of join enumeration, the optimizer will follow a similar procedure for three-way joins of collections that reside in the same repository, and so on.

EXAMPLE 7

Let's return to our travel agency. Suppose that a user submits a query to find the names of cities in Greece with a small population. This query involves two collections, `Countries` and `Cities`, both managed by the relational wrapper. Because relational databases handle joins, our relational wrapper implements the `plan_join()` method. The wrapper will accept all predicates and projection requests that can be directly translated into SQL for the relational database. Join predicates may be on any attribute described in the interface or an equality predicate on OID. The wrapper maps a Garlic work request to an SQL query against the underlying database, and stores the elements of the `select`, `from`, and `where` clauses of the query in the private section of its plan.

Figure 6.6 shows how the relational wrapper provides a plan for the join between `Countries` and `Cities`. In the first phase of optimization (omitted from the picture), the optimizer requests access plans for `Cities` and `Countries`. The relational wrapper returns a plan for each and agrees to handle the simple predicates and projections on those collections. During join enumeration, the optimizer invokes the relational wrapper's `plan_join()` method and passes in the join predicate as well as the two access plans previously created. The wrapper agrees to perform all of the work from its original access plans and to accept the join predicate, and creates a new plan for the join. The new plan's properties are made up of the properties from the input plans and the new join predicate. The relational wrapper uses selectivity cost formulas provided by the query-planning interface to predict the result cardinality of the join, and its own cost model based on a simplified model of relational query processing to predict the cost of the join.

Bind Plans. During the join-enumeration phase, the optimizer also considers a particular kind of join called a bind join, similar to the fetch-matches join methods of Mackert & Lohman (1988) and Lu & Carey (1985). In a bind join, values produced by the outer node of the join are passed by Garlic to the inner node, and the inner node uses these values to evaluate some subset of the join predicates. A bind join is attractive if the amount of data transferred from the outer node to the inner node is small and the bind join predicates are selective enough to significantly reduce the amount of data returned by the inner node to Garlic. Not all wrappers can or need to serve as the inner node of a bind join. A wrapper is well suited to serve as the inner node of a bind join if the programming interface of its underlying data source provides some mechanism for posing parameterized queries. As an example, Open DataBase Connectivity (ODBC) (Microsoft 1997b) and the call-level interfaces of most relational database systems contain such support.

Figure 6.6

Construction of a wrapper join plan.

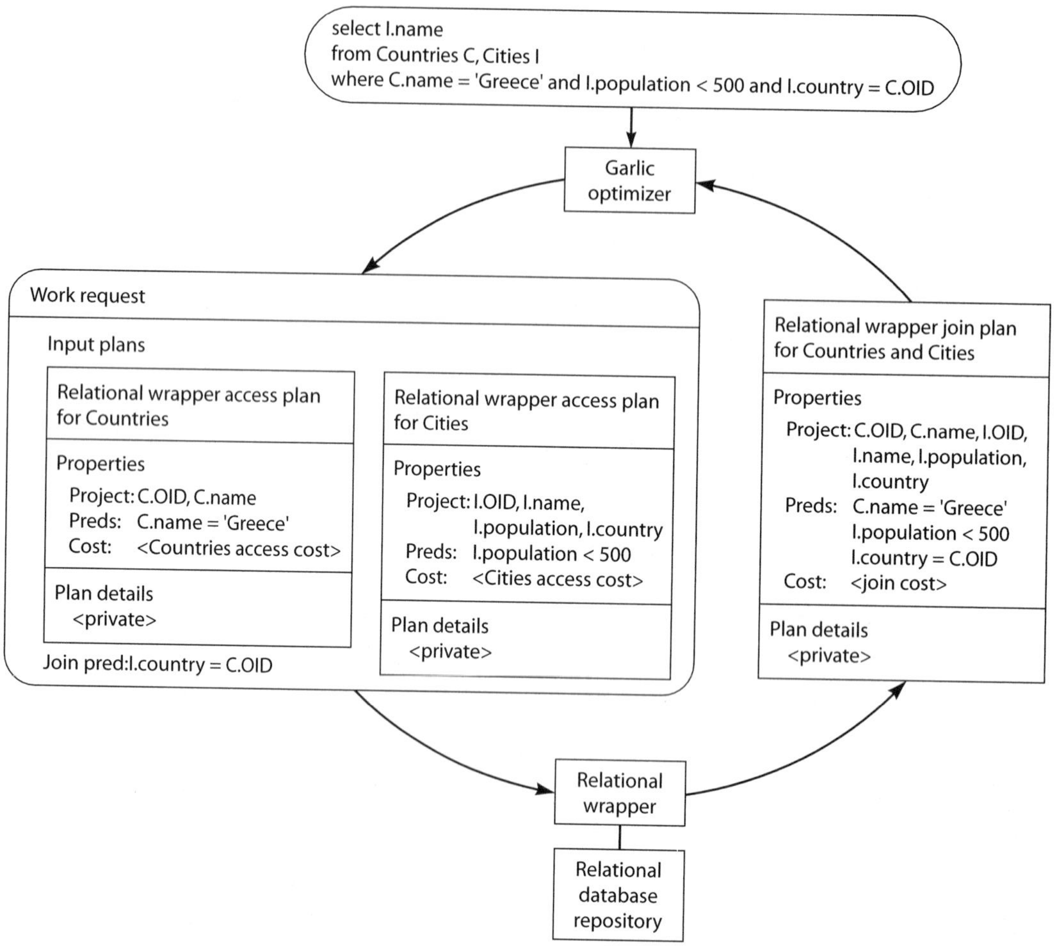

Suppose our travel agency user is interested in finding five-star hotels on beaches in small towns in Greece. This query involves the `Countries` and `Cities` collections managed by the relational wrapper, and the `Hotels` collection managed by the web wrapper. The web wrapper does not support the `plan_bind()` method, but the relational wrapper does. Figure 6.7 shows how a bind plan for this query is created. During the first phase of optimization, the optimizer has requested and received an access plan from the web wrapper for the `Hotels` collection as described in the section "Single-Collection Access Plans." It has also requested and received access plans for the `Countries` and `Cities` collections from the relational wrapper. While considering two-way joins, the optimizer has received a join plan for `Countries` and

`Cities` from the relational wrapper, as described in the previous section.

Next, the optimizer develops a plan to join all three collections. The optimizer recognizes that a bind join is possible, with the web wrapper's access plan as the outer stream and the join plan provided by the relational wrapper as the inner stream. The optimizer invokes the relational wrapper's `plan_bind()` method, passing in a work request that consists of the join plan for `Countries` and `Cities` that the wrapper previously provided and the description of the bind join predicate between `Cities` and `Hotels`. In the bind join predicate, `$BIND_1` represents the name of a city where a hotel is located, as returned for each hotel by the access plan for the `Hotels` collection. The relational wrapper is able to handle the bind predicate and creates a new plan that handles the work of the original join plan plus the bind predicate. It uses the input plan's properties to fill in the new bind-plan properties, adds in the bind predicate, and adjusts the cost and cardinality estimates to include the effects of applying the new bind predicate.

Other Query-Planning Methods. In addition to the basic collection access and join-planning routines, the query-planning interface provides support for more complex query processing. For example, the `plan_group_by()` method provides a mechanism by which wrappers can generate plans to handle group by clauses and aggregates. As another example, the optimizer may recognize a large fragment of a query that could be handled by a single repository. Instead of planning such a fragment bottom-up (e.g., by repeated calls to `plan_access()`, `plan_join()`, and `plan_group_by()`), the optimizer may opt to call the method `plan_fragment()` to allow the wrapper to plan the entire fragment all at once. Again, a wrapper writer would implement these additional methods only if they make sense for a given repository.

6.4.4 Query Execution

A wrapper's final service is to participate in plan translation and query execution. A Garlic query plan is represented as a tree of operators, such as FILTER, PROJECT, and JOIN. Wrapper plans show up as the operators at the leaves of the plan tree. Figure 6.8 shows an example of a complete Garlic plan based on the bind-join plan for the query discussed in Example 8. The outer node of the bind join is the web wrapper's access plan for the `Hotels` collection (from Example 6), and the inner node is the relational wrapper's bind plan for `Countries` and `Cities` (from Example 8). Because the web wrapper reported that it only handled the predicate on `class`, the Garlic optimizer added a FILTER operator to handle the predicate on `location`. Finally, because the select clause of the user's query contained `name` and `daily_rate`, the optimizer added a PROJECT operator to project those fields out.

Figure 6.7 | **Construction of a wrapper bind plan.**

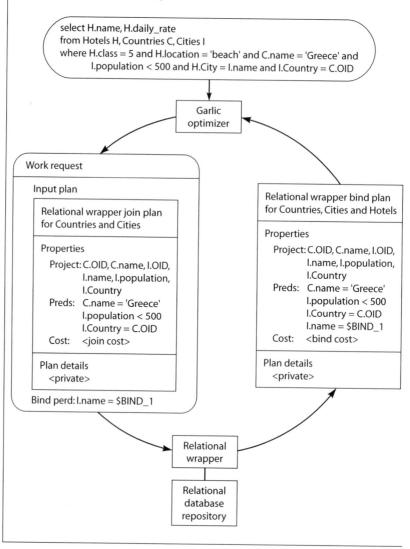

Translation. Once the optimizer has chosen a plan for a query, the plan must be translated into a form suitable for execution. As is common in demand-driven runtime systems (Graefe 1993), operators of the optimized plan are mapped into iterators, and each wrapper provides a specialized `Iterator` subclass that controls execution of the work described by one of its wrapper plans. The wrapper must also supply an implementation of `Wrapper_Plan::translate()`, a method that takes no arguments and returns an instance of the wrapper's `Iterator` subclass, as described in the next section. At plan translation time, the Garlic query processor walks the optimized query plan and creates a tree of

Figure 6.8 | **A plan for a Garlic query.**

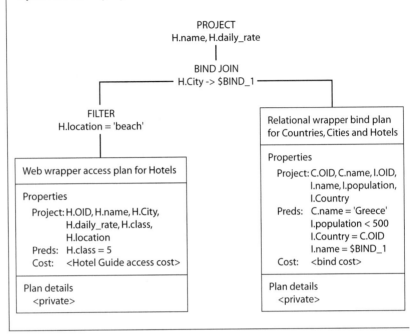

iterators. Whenever a wrapper's plan is encountered, it invokes the wrapper's `translate()` method.

For most wrappers, translation involves converting the information stored in the plan into a form that can be sent to the repository. For example, our relational wrapper stores the elements of the `select`, `from`, and `where` clauses of the query in the private section of its plan. At plan translation time, the wrapper extracts these elements, constructs the query string to be sent to the relational database, and stores it in an instance of its `Iterator` subclass. OIDs mentioned in the plan are converted into accesses to the appropriate relation's primary key fields. If the plan is a bind plan, question marks appear in the query string to represent the unbound values.

EXAMPLE 9

The query string that would be generated for the relational wrapper plan in Figure 6.8 is the following (recall that `name` is the primary key for the `Countries` relation, and `name, country` is the primary key for the `Cities` relation):

```
select C.name, I.name, I.country, I.population
from Countries C, Cities I
where C.name = 'Greece' and I.population < 500 and
                I.country = C.name and I.name = ?
```

Similarly, our web wrapper stores the list of attributes to project and the set of predicates to apply in the private data section of its plan in Figure 6.8. At plan translation time, the predicates are used to form a query URL that the web site will accept. In order to form a correct URL, the web wrapper will have to fill in default values for attributes that do not have predicates specified in the plan.

Execution. The Garlic execution engine is pipelined and employs a fixed set of methods on iterators at runtime to control the execution of a query. Default implementations for most of the methods exist, but for each operator, two methods in particular define the unique behavior of its iterator: `advance()` and `reset()`. The `advance()` method completes the work necessary to produce the next output value, and the `reset()` method resets an iterator so that it may be executed again. An additional `bind()` method is unique to wrapper iterators and provides the mechanism by which Garlic can transfer the next set of bindings to the inner node of a bind join. Only wrappers that provide bind plans need to implement this method.

Our relational wrapper uses standard ODBC calls to implement `reset()`, `advance()`, and `bind()`. `reset()` prepares a query at the underlying database, and `bind()` binds the parameters sent by Garlic to the unbound values (represented by question marks) in the query string. The `advance()` method fetches the next set of tuples from the database. For efficiency, the wrapper maintains a small buffer and fetches blocks of tuples at a time. The wrapper repackages the retrieved data before returning it to Garlic. For example, after executing the relational query described in Example 9, the wrapper repackages the primary key and foreign key values retrieved from the relational database into the OIDs that the query processor is expecting.

The web wrapper's `Iterator` subclass is very simple. The `reset()` method loads the HTML page that corresponds to the query URL generated at plan translation time. In the `advance()` method, the wrapper parses the HTML page to retrieve the next set of results. To manufacture OIDs for the plan in Figure 6.8, the wrapper uses the internal keys for hotel listings stored on the page. Several results may appear on a page, so as does the relational wrapper, the web wrapper maintains a small buffer. Thus, in subsequent calls to `advance()`, the wrapper retrieves results stored in its buffer. Each HTML page provides a link to the next page of results, so after all of the results in the buffer are returned to Garlic, the wrapper loads the next page and loads its buffer with the results stored on that page.

6.4.5 Wrapper Packaging

In previous sections, we describe the services that a wrapper provides to the Garlic middleware. Table 6.1 summarizes the tasks a wrapper

Table 6.1   **Tasks performed by a wrapper author.**

Service	Tasks
Modeling data as objects	Describe interface of objects using GDL, provide key portion for OIDs of objects in repository, and identify selected objects as roots
Method invocation	Implement accessor methods and methods explicitly defined in interfaces
Query planning	Provide `Wrapper_Plan` subclass and implement query planning methods that model as much of the repository's query processing and search facilities as desired
Query execution	Provide `Iterator` subclass to control execution of a query plan, and implement `Wrapper_Plan::translate()` to create an iterator instance from a plan

author performs in order to provide these services. The wrapper author's final task is to package these pieces as a complete wrapper module. A wrapper module may include three kinds of components:

1. Interface files, which contain one or more interface definitions written in GDL.

2. Libraries, which contain dynamically loadable code to implement schema registration, method invocation, and the query interfaces. These are further subdivided into core libraries, which contain common code shared among several similar repositories, and implementation libraries, which contain repository-specific implementations of one or more interfaces.

3. Environment files, which contain name-value pairs to encode repository-specific information for use by the wrapper. Garlic parses environment files and makes their contents available to the wrapper, but does not interpret them itself.

Packaging the code portion of wrapper modules as dynamically loadable libraries that reside in the same address space as the Garlic query processor keeps the cost of communicating with a wrapper as low as possible. This is important during query processing because a given wrapper may be consulted several times during the optimization of a query and nontrivial data structures (work requests and plans) are exchanged at each interaction. Furthermore, wrapper authors are not constrained to use a particular interprocess communication or remote-procedure-call protocol to communicate with Garlic. Very simple repositories can be accessed without crossing address space boundaries at all, and repositories that are divided into client and server components are easily accommodated by linking their wrapper with the repository's client-side library. This approach encapsulates the choice of a particular client-server protocol (e.g., CORBA-IIOP; ActiveX or DCOM; or ODBC) within the wrapper, allowing Garlic to integrate repositories regardless of the particular protocols they support.

Decomposing wrapper modules into interface files, libraries, and environment files gives the designer of a wrapper for a particular repository or family of repositories considerable flexibility. For example, different instances of our image server share the same schema and have the same query capabilities, but are contacted via different network addresses and export differently named collections of images. Therefore, this wrapper module is packaged as an interface file and core library that are shared among all image servers, plus environment files for each individual server. Our wrapper for relational database systems packages generic method dispatch, query-planning code, and query-execution code as a sharable core library. For each repository, an interface file describes the objects in the corresponding database, and an environment file encodes the name of the database to which the wrapper must connect, the names of the roots exported by the repository and the tables to which they are bound, the correspondence between attributes in interfaces and columns in tables, and so forth.

Implementation libraries are useful when a wrapper that employs stub dispatch is built for a data source whose schema can evolve over time. As new kinds of objects are added to the repository schema, additional implementation libraries can be registered with stubs for the new implementations.

6.5 Wrapper Implementations

To date, we have implemented wrappers for a diverse set of data sources. Table 6.2 describes some of the features of these wrappers. Wrappers such as the relational wrapper and the web wrapper have been fine-tuned and are fairly mature. Others are still in a state of evolution. For example, we have been investigating different database products to serve as Garlic's complex object repository, including object-oriented databases and object-relational systems. As a result, we modeled the wrapper as a simple repository so that we could quickly change the underlying data source. When we settle on the actual implementation of the complex object repository, we will enhance its wrapper appropriately.

Based on our experience writing these wrappers, we have identified three general categories of wrappers and provide a base class for each category. We also provide wrapper writers with a library of schema registration tools, query-plan-construction routines, a facility to gather and store statistics, an object cache to improve the performance of repeated method invocation (Haas et al. 1999), and other useful routines in order to automate the task of writing a wrapper as much as possible. To test our assertion that wrappers are easy to write, we asked developers out-

Table 6.2   **A description of existing wrappers.**

Data Source	Schema Description	Method Invocation	Query Capability	Cost Model
DB2, Oracle	Columns of a relation map to attributes of an interface; relations become collections of objects; primary key value of a tuple is key for OID	Accessor methods only; generic dispatch	General expression projections, all basic predicates, joins, bind joins, joins based on OID, ordering, aggregation	Provides formulas for plan costs; uses default method cost formulas; adds additional collection statistics
Searchable web sites: http://www.hotelguide.ch, a hotel guide; http://www.bigbook.com, a directory of U.S. business listings; http://us.imdb.com, an internet movie database	Each web site exports a single collection of listing objects; HTML page data fields map to attributes of an interface; unique key for a listing provided by web site is key for OID	Accessor methods only; generic dispatch	Attribute projection, equality predicates on attributes, `LIKE` predicates of the form `"%<value>%"`	Uses default model
Proprietary database for molecular similarity search	A single collection of molecule objects; interface has `contains_ substructure()` and `simliarity_to()` methods to model search capability of engine; molecule -number is key for OID	Stub dispatch	Attribute and method projection, predicates of the form `<attr><op> <const>` and `<method><op> <const>`, where `<op>` is a comparison operator	Uses default model
QBIC image server that orders images according to color, texture and shape features	Collections of image objects; interface contains `matches()` method to model ordering capability; image file name is key for OID	Stub dispatch	Ordering of image objects by image feature	Provides formulas for plan and methodized additional method statistics
Glimpse[a] text search engine that searches for specific patterns in text files	Collections of files; interface contains several methods to model text search capability and retrieve relevant text of a file; file name is key for OID	Stub dispatch	Projection of attributes and methods	Uses default model
Lotus Notes databases: Phone Directory database, Patent Server database	Notes database becomes a collection of note objects; interface defined by database form; note `NOTEID` is key for Garlic OID	Accessor methods only; generic dispatch	Attribute projection, predicates containing logical, comparison and arithmetic operators, `LIKE` predicates, tests for `NULL`.	Uses default model
Complex object wrapper	Collections of objects; interface corresponds to interface of objects in database; database OID is key for Garlic OID	Stub dispatch	Iteration	Uses default model

[a] Mamber et al. 2000.

side of the project to write several of the wrappers listed in Table 6.2. For example, a summer student wrote the text and image server wrappers over a period of a few weeks, and a chemist was able to write the molecular database wrapper during a two-day visit to our lab.

The relational wrapper is by far the most complex. We spent a considerable amount of effort on it because a substantial amount of legacy data resides in relational databases, and we intend to package Garlic with a relational wrapper. The wrapper can be quickly adapted to any relational database system with a call-level interface. A relational database can be integrated into a Garlic database in a matter of minutes, and we provide tools to automate the process. A database administrator (DBA) runs a tool that generates the GDL and environment files for the database by scanning the relational catalogues and then uses a utility to register the wrapper as part of a Garlic database. After the registration step, the database can immediately be accessed through the Garlic interface.

6.6   Related Work

Presenting a uniform interface to a diverse set of information sources has been the goal of a great deal of previous research, dating back to projects such as the CCA's (Computer Corporation of America's) Multibase (Rosenberg & Landers 1982). A common thread in most of this work has been an assumption that the underlying information sources are themselves database systems of one kind or another, and consequently provide relatively complete query-processing services. As a result, much of the research has been focused on topics such as the formalization of mappings between different data models and their associated query languages, strategies for concurrency control and recovery among databases with different transaction models, and the reconciliation of data semantics and representation when several databases contain information about the same real-world entities. Surveys of much of this work can be found in Bukhres & Elmagarmid (1996), Elmagarmid & Pu (1990), Kim (1995), and Ram (1991). The architectures of most earlier systems are built around a lingua franca for communicating with the underlying information sources. A query that requires access to multiple data sources goes first to a central query-decomposition facility, where it is broken into fragments that are expressed in a common language or by means of a common data structure. Each source provides a local query translator that maps fragments represented in this form into appropriate operations on the data source. In Pegasus (Ahmed et al. 1991), for example, fragments are represented in the Heterogeneous Object SQL (HOSQL) query language. MAKBIS (Elshiewy 1995) uses MAKBIS-QL and EDA/SQL (Stout 1995) uses iSQL. All of these systems assume that any data source, assisted by the translator, can readily execute any query fragment.

Recently, the proliferation both in number and kind of information sources on the World Wide Web and elsewhere has stimulated interest in systems, like Garlic, that attempt to integrate a wider variety of data sources. The assumption that all data sources provide general-purpose query-processing capabilities is much harder to justify in this context; hence, for these systems, accommodating a range of query-processing power has become an important area of research.

OLE DB (Blakeley 1996a) takes a step toward integrating heterogeneous data sources by defining a standardized construct, the rowset, to represent streams of values obtained from a data source. A simple tabular data source with no querying capability can easily expose its data as a rowset. More powerful data sources can accept commands (either as text or as a data structure) that specify query-processing operations peculiar to that data source and produce rowsets as a result. Thus, although OLE DB does not include a middleware query-processing component such as Garlic, it does define a protocol by which a middleware component and data sources can interact. This protocol differs from the Garlic wrapper interface in several ways. First, the format of an OLE DB command is defined entirely by the data source that accepts it, whereas Garlic query fragments are expressed in a standard form based on object-extended SQL. Second, an OLE DB data source must either accept or reject a command in its entirety, whereas a Garlic wrapper can agree to perform part of a work request and leave any parts it is unable to handle to be performed by the middleware.

A different set of techniques for integrating data sources with various levels of query support relies upon an a priori declarative specification of query capability for each data source. The Information Manifold (Levy et al. 1996) requires each data source to supply a set of capability records that describes its ability to retrieve and filter data. The capability record for each relation (or class of objects) specifies three sets of attributes. The first set lists input attributes. In a supported query, some minimum number of these (also specified in the capability record) must be bound to constant values. The second set lists output attributes. A supported query can request the values of up to some maximum number of these as output. The third set lists selection attributes. A supported query may contain range predicates that compare any or all of these attributes to a constant.

DISCO (Kapitskaia et al. 1997) defines a query-processing model based on an algebra of logical operators such as `select`, `project`, and `scan`, and imposes this model on the wrappers. At wrapper registration time, the wrapper describes the subset of the logical operators that are supported by the data source. The wrapper interface language contains some support for describing restrictions on supported operators, such as which operators can be applied to which collections or which predicates can be applied to which attributes. The language also provides some support for restricting the combination of operators that a data source supports.

In the TSIMMIS system (Papakonstantinou et al. 1995a), specifications of query power are expressed in the Query Description and Translation Language (QDTL) (Papakonstantinou et al. 1995b). A QDTL specification for a data source is a context-free grammar for generating supported queries. In its simplest form, a QDTL specification is a query template containing one or more placeholders, variables that will be bound to constant values in actual queries. A specification may also contain metapredicates, built-in or source-specific C functions that test the value bound to a placeholder. More complex QDTL specifications use nonterminal symbols and recursion to allow a large number of query templates to be expressed compactly. For example, we can describe a class of predicates and the attributes to which they can be applied without enumerating all possible combinations of predicates and attributes. A yacc-like wrapper-generation tool is provided to facilitate the translation of query fragments expressed in MSL (Mediator Specification Language), the system's query language. The tool allows a wrapper author to augment QDTL specifications with semantic actions that generate corresponding primitives understood by the data source. A more recent paper (Papakonstantinou et al. 1996) discusses the Relational Query Description Language (RQDL), an extension of QDTL that supports schema-independent specifications. For example, in RQDL, we can compactly specify a template that describes the ability to apply a certain kind of predicate to any attribute of any relation.

The idea of compact declarative specifications of query power is inherently attractive, but there are some practical problems with this approach. First, it is often the case that a data source cannot process a particular query, but can process a subsuming query whose answer set includes the answer set of the original query. In such cases, a good execution strategy is to send the subsuming query to the data source for evaluation and to subsequently apply a filter to obtain the answer to the original query. In general, finding minimal subsuming queries is computationally costly and choosing the optimal subsuming query may require detailed knowledge of the contents, semantics, and statistics of the underlying data source (Papakonstantinou et al. 1995b).

Second, in defining a common language to describe all possible repository capabilities, it is difficult to capture the unique restrictions associated with any individual repository. For example, as we note earlier, relational database systems often place limits on the query-string length, the maximum constant value that can appear in a query, and so forth. Likewise, our web wrapper can handle LIKE predicates, but only if the pattern is of a specific form. The molecular wrapper is sensitive to which attributes and methods appear together in the projection and predicate lists. A language to express these and other repository-specific restrictions would quickly become very cumbersome. Furthermore, in a strictly declarative approach such as DISCO, as new sources are integrated, the language would need to be extended to handle any unanticipated restrictions or capabilities introduced by the new sources.

As we show in Section 6.4.3, Garlic forgoes the declarative approach for one in which a wrapper dynamically examines a query fragment and presents the Garlic optimizer with one or more supported subsuming queries. Rather than solve the query-subsumption problem in general at the Garlic level, we ask wrapper authors to solve the simpler special-case problem for their own repositories, taking advantage of repository-specific semantic knowledge as they see fit. Because our approach is not limited by the expressive power of a query-specification language, it can accommodate the idiosyncrasies of almost any data source.

6.7 Conclusion

In this chapter, we have described the wrapper component architecture for Garlic, a middleware system designed to provide a unified view of heterogeneous legacy data sources. Our architecture is flexible enough to accommodate almost any kind of data source. We have developed wrappers for sources that represent a broad spectrum of data models and query capabilities, including standard data sources such as relational databases, searchable web sites, image servers, and text search engines, as well as specialized data sources such as a chemical-compound search engine. For sources with specialized query-processing capabilities, representing those capabilities as methods has proven to be viable and convenient.

The Garlic wrapper architecture makes the wrapper writer's job relatively simple, and, as a result, we have been able to produce wrappers for new data sources in a matter of days or hours instead of weeks or months. Wrapper authoring is especially simple for repositories with limited query power, but even for more powerful repositories, a basic wrapper can be written very quickly. This allows applications to access data from new sources as soon as possible, while subsequent enhancements to the wrapper can transparently improve performance by taking greater advantage of the repository's query capabilities.

Our design also allows the Garlic query optimizer to develop efficient query-execution strategies. Rather than requiring a wrapper to raise a repository's query-processing capabilities to a fixed level, or dumbing down the query-processing interface to the lowest common denominator, our architecture allows each wrapper to dynamically determine how much of a query its repository is capable of handling.

In the future, we will continue to refine the wrapper interfaces. We would like to investigate the possibility of introducing QDTL/RQDL-style templates to allow a wrapper to declare up-front a specification of the expressions it will support. With such information, the Garlic query processor could filter out expressions that a wrapper is unable to handle before the work request is generated. For example, a wrapper could use a template to indicate that it only supported comparisons of the form <attr> = <const>. Given this information, the query processor would never include predicates like <attr> > <const> in a work request for that wrapper. Such templates would be a step toward a hybrid system, combining Garlic's dynamic approach to query planning with the declarative approach of TSIMMIS and the Information Manifold; striking an appropriate balance between the two techniques is an interesting research opportunity.

7

Building Component Database Systems Using CORBA

M. Tamer Özsu
Bin Yao
University of Waterloo

7.1 Introduction

The componentization of database management system (DBMS) services is a topic of recent interest and discussion (Silberschatz & Zdonik 1996). The issue arises because of the divergent requirements imposed on DBMSs by the new application domains that the technology has started to penetrate. Applications such as computer-aided design (CAD) and computer-aided manufacturing (CAM), software development, office information systems, collaborative design, and multimedia information systems have widely varying requirements (e.g., see Özsu 1996 for a discussion of the requirements of multimedia information systems). Building general-purpose DBMSs that can address these varying demands requires either that the systems themselves be customizable or that more-open system architectures be developed that lend themselves to the integration of different DBMSs with different requirements. In either case, componentization is a necessity, even though the granularity of components is different. In the first case, each component provides one DBMS function, leading to a customizable DBMS with plug-and-play components; in the second case, each component is itself a DBMS, leading to an interoperable system.

Even though the first type of componentization has been discussed in literature, there are no known DBMS implementations that use componentization extensively (i.e., more than ordinary code modularization). However, there are many examples of interoperable DBMSs.

One of the fundamental requirements for building these systems is the availability of a proper infrastructure and a methodology. In this chapter, we start with the basic assumption that object technology provides the most promising methodology for building componentized DBMSs (of either type). Consequently, we argue that the distributed object platforms provide the necessary infrastructure for componentization. There are arguments that favor internet-based approaches to building large-scale interoperable systems. However, this is beyond the focus of this chapter.

There are two distributed object computing platforms: Object Management Architecture (OMA) from Object Management Group (OMG) and ActiveX from Microsoft. The former is now in its third iteration (commonly referred to as CORBA-3), and the latter started its life as Component Object Model (COM) and Distributed COM (DCOM) and has recently been renamed ActiveX. This chapter deals only with the Common Object Request Broker Architecture (CORBA).

The OMG was formed in 1989 as an industry consortium, with the aim of addressing the problems of developing interoperable, reusable, and portable distributed applications for heterogeneous systems, based on standard object-oriented interfaces. It addresses this problem by introducing an architectural framework with supporting detailed interface specifications. OMG's role is that of an interface and functionality specifier; it does not develop software itself. In this chapter, we discuss the overall architectural framework that OMG has proposed (Section 7.2), the fundamental interoperability infrastructure called CORBA (Section 7.3), and the specifications for the other components of OMG's platform (Sections 7.4 and 7.5). Finally, we discuss some experiences with using CORBA infrastructure for database interoperability.

7.2   Object Management Architecture

OMA (OMG 1997b) is the architectural environment defined by the OMG for facilitating interoperability. There are two related models in the OMA—the object model and the reference model—describing how distributed objects and the communications among them can be specified in platform-independent ways. The object model provides an organized description of objects distributed over a heterogeneous environment, while the reference model categorizes interactions among these distributed objects. The computational model supported by OMA is client-server, and implementing peer-to-peer computing in this environment, though possible, is not easy.

OMA's object model defines an object as an identifiable, encapsulated entity that provides services through well-defined encapsulating interfaces to clients, which are any entities capable of issuing requests to the object. The detailed implementations of services are transparent to clients. The object model describes not only basic object concepts such as object creation and identity, requests and operations, and types and signatures, but also concepts related to object implementations, including methods, execution engines, and activation. The model is a generic one that provides objects, values, operations, types, classes, and subtype-supertype relationship among types. An object is an abstraction with a state and a set of operations. The operations have well-defined signatures, and the operations together with the signatures form the interface of each object. Each object and operation has a type. The communication between objects is by means of sending requests, whereby a request is an operation call with one or more parameters, any of which may identify an object (multitargeting). The arguments and results are passed by value.

The reference model identifies and categorizes the components, interfaces, and protocols that constitute the OMA. Figure 7.1 depicts four categories of components: object services, common facilities, domain interfaces, and application interfaces. These are linked by an object request broker (ORB) component, which enables transparent communication between clients and objects. The functions of each of these categories of components are described here. They are discussed in more detail in the subsequent sections.

Figure 7.1

Object Management Architecture.

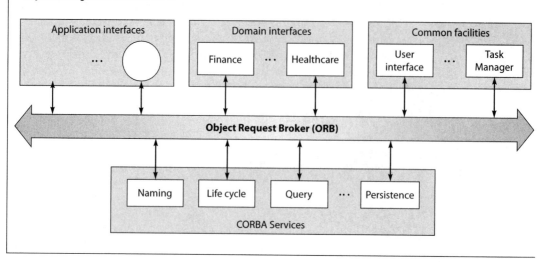

- The ORB component of the OMA is the communications infrastructure of the architecture, with a standard programming interface (OMG 1999c). The interface is used by both the clients and the server objects. ORB allows objects to communicate transparently in a distributed environment, independent of the specific platforms. Its objective is to provide portability and interoperability of objects over a heterogeneous distributed system. The standard interface is provided by the Interface Definition Language (IDL). The IDL is a strongly typed declarative language that is programming language independent. Language mappings from a variety of languages (currently, mappings have been specified for Ada, C, C++, COBOL, Java, or Smalltalk) enable applications to be written in any of these languages and access CORBA objects.

- Object services (OMG 1998b) are, in a sense, value-added services to facilitate the development of distributed applications. They are general-purpose services that are domain independent and have standard IDL interfaces. Thus, they can be accessed by any client application, just like any other CORBA object. A number of these services have been specified, including life cycle, naming, events, persistence, transactions, concurrency control, relationships, externalization, licensing, query, properties, security, time, collections, and trading. We discuss the details of these services in Section 7.4. They provide object abstractions and operations that are used by the other three classes of CORBA components. In theory, it is possible to put together a component DBMS by "gluing" together various CORBA services.

- Common facilities (OMG 1995b) are interfaces for common (i.e., horizontal) facilities that are applicable to most application domains and may be used by many applications. There are four major collections of common facilities: user interface, information management, system management, and task management. The facilities follow the fundamental OMA principle of providing their operational interfaces via the common IDL language. We discuss facilities in more detail in Section 7.5.

- Domain interfaces are application-domain-specific (i.e., vertical) interfaces that provide abstractions for various application domains. These abstractions are developed by OMG-sponsored industry groups. The ones that have received significant attention so far are finance, health care, manufacturing, telecommunication, electronic commerce, and transportation. In earlier versions of the CORBA specification, these were identified as vertical common facilities.

- Application interfaces are external application interfaces that users develop. These applications do not have to be constructed using an object-oriented pattern or in an object-oriented language. Non-object-oriented applications can be wrapped in objects and can participate in a distributed OMA application in that manner.

7.3   Common Object Request Broker Architecture

CORBA (Figure 7.2) is the key communication mechanism of OMA, in which objects communicate with each other via an ORB that provides brokering services between clients and servers. Brokering involves target-object location, message delivery, and method binding. Clients send a request to the ORB asking for certain services to be performed by whichever server can fulfill those needs. ORB finds the server, passes the message from the client, and receives the result, which it then passes to the client.

Figure 7.2 | **CORBA architecture.**

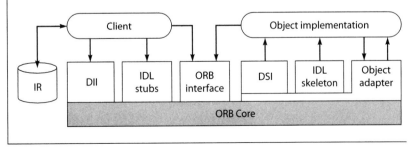

The ORB performs the following functions (which we describe in detail later): requesting dispatch to determine the identity of the callee method, parameter encoding to convey local representation of parameter values, delivery of request and result messages to the proper objects (which may be at different sites), synchronization of the requesters with the responses of the requests, activation and deactivation of persistent objects, exception handling to report various failures to requesters and servers, and security mechanisms to assure the secure conveyance of messages among objects. The clients access the server objects by means of their interfaces. The interfaces are defined by means of the IDL. For each CORBA object that is registered to the system, an IDL specification of its interface is necessary. IDL is a host-language-independent declarative language, not a programming language. It forces interfaces to be defined separately from object implementations. Objects can be constructed using different programming languages and still communicate with one another. IDL enables a particular object implementation to introduce itself to potential clients by advertising its interface. The IDL interface specifications are compiled to declarations in the programmer's own language. Language mappings determine how IDL features are mapped to facilities of a given programming language. There are standardized language mappings for C, C++, Smalltalk, Ada, and Java. IDL language mappings are those in which the abstractions and concepts specified in CORBA meet the real world of implementation. Because of its central role, we first discuss IDL in some detail.

7.3.1 Interface Definition Language

IDL defines the types of CORBA objects by specifying their interfaces. An object's interface is composed of a set of client accessible operations and the arguments to those operations. IDL is purely a declarative language, and, therefore, clients and servers cannot be implemented directly in IDL. The only purpose of the IDL is to define interfaces in a language independent way, which allows applications developed in different programming language to interoperate.

The OMG IDL obeys the same lexical rules as C++, but adds some new keywords (e.g., `any`, `attribute`, `interface`, `module`, `sequence`, and `oneway`) to support distribution concepts. The IDL grammar is a subset of the proposed ANSI C++ standard (supporting only syntax for constant, type, and operation declaration, not any algorithmic structures or variables), with additional constructs to support the operation-invocation mechanism. The restrictions imposed by IDL are that a function return type is mandatory; a name must be supplied with each formal parameter to an operation declaration; a parameter list consisting of the single token `void` is not permitted as a synonym for an empty parameter list; tags are required for structure, discriminated unions, and enumerations; integer types cannot be defined as simply `int` or `unsigned`—they must be declared explicitly as `short`, `long`, or `long long`; and `char` cannot be qualified by `signed` or `unsigned` keywords.

An important feature of the IDL interfaces is that they can inherit from one or more other interfaces. This feature allows new interfaces to be defined from existing ones, and, because a derived interface inherits all attributes and operations defined in all of its base interfaces, objects implementing a new derived interface can be substituted any-where objects supporting the base interfaces are allowed (the well-known substitutability concept in object-oriented programming).

EXAMPLE 1   Consider the following example that defines the interface through which the client can get sets of images from an image DBMS.

```
1   //Example 1 - Filename ``queryagent.idl''

2

3   module DB {

4

5     interface QueryAgent {

6

7       //exception
8       exception SyntaxError {
9         unsigned short position;
10        string errMessage;
11      };

12

13      //user defined types
14      typedef sequence<octet> streamType;

15

16      //content of an image
17      struct imageType {
18        string serverID;
19        string imageID;
20        string imageLabel;
21        streamType imageStream;
22        float similarity;
23      };

24

25      typedef sequence<imageType> imagesType;

26
```

```
27      //operation
28      imagesType getImages (in string queryString)
29                   raises (SyntaxError);
30
31    };//end of interface QueryAgent
32
33 };//end of module DB
```

IDL uses the module construct to create name-space, preventing pollution of the global name-space. Line 3 defines the module DB. The declaration of the interface QueryAgent starts at line 5. Lines 8–11 define the content of the exception this interface may raise. Line 14 defines the type for the image stream, which is an unbounded octet array. Lines 17–23 define the structure of the image type, which includes the server ID indicating which database this image comes from, the imageID (an octet sequence that uniquely identifies the image in the database where it comes from), the imageLabel (name), and the imageStream (real image data); and the similarity between the target image and the query image. Line 25 defines the return type of the query (i.e., a set of images). Lines 28–29 declare an operation (method) called getImages. The input parameter is a query string that will be passed along to the image database; the output is a set of result images matching the query.

EXAMPLE 2 This example, about interfaces to bank account transactions, covers most of the features of the IDL, although some operations are not realistic. The example also demonstrates the substitutability principle previously discussed. The AccountTransaction interface is derived from the Account interface. Anything dealing with objects of type Account can also use an object supporting the AccountTransaction interface, because such an object also supports the Account interface.

```
1   //Example 2 - Filename "bank.idl"
2
3  //establish a unique prefix for interface repository IDs
4   #pragma prefix "bank.com"
5
6   module BANK {
7
8      //types
9      enum AccountType {CHECKING, SAVING};
10     //constant
11     const unsigned long MAX_LENGTH = 20;
```

```
12    typedef sequence<char, MAX_LENGTH> AccountNum;
13
14    interface Account {
15      //attributes
16      readonly attribute AccountNum check_account_num;
17      readonly attribute float check_account_balance;
18      readonly attribute AccountNum save_account_num;
19      readonly attribute float save_account_balance;
20      readonly attribute string pin;
21              attribute string address;
22    };//end of interface Account
23
24    //interface inheritance:
25    //AccountTransaction inherits attributes of Account
26    interface AccountTransaction : Account {
27
28      //exceptions
29      exception account_invalid {
30        string reason;
31      };
32      exception incorrect_pin {};
33
34      //operations and raising exceptions
35      float balance (in AccountType account_type,
36                     in AccountNum account_num,
37                     in string pin)
38            raises (account_invalid, incorrect_pin);
39
40      void deposit (in AccountType account_type,
41                    in AccountNum account_num,
42                    in float amount,
43                    out float new_balance)
44            raises (account_invalid);
45
46      //one-way
47      oneway void withdraw (in AccountType account_type,
48                            in AccountNum account_num,
```

```
49                                    in float amount,
50                                    in string pin);
51
52   };// end of interface AccountTransation
53
54 };// end of module BANK
```

CORBA provides an interface repository (IR) that allows runtime access to the IDL definition. The IDL compiler assigns a repository ID as a unique name for each IDL type into the IR. The prefix pragma adds a unique prefix to a repository ID to ensure its uniqueness. Line 4 defines a prefix `bank.com`. Line 9 declares an enumerated variable `AccountType` with `CHECKING` and `SAVING` representing types of bank accounts. Lines 11–12 define the type of account number, which is a bounded sequence with maximum length of 20. Lines 14–22 define an interface `Account`, which includes the primary information of a bank account, such as pin number, home address, account numbers, and account balances.

An `attribute` defines read and write operations on a variable. A `readonly` attribute defines a single read operation on a variable. Line 20 is semantically equivalent to

```
string get_pin ();
```

Line 21 is semantically equivalent to

```
string get_address();

void set_address (in string address);
```

Even though attribute definitions look like variables, in fact they are just shorthand for the definition of a pair of operations (or a single operation for `readonly`).

Lines 26–52 define an interface `AccountTransaction` and include some basic transactions related to a bank account (e.g., checking, balance, deposit, and withdraw). Lines 29–32 define the contents of `exceptions`. Lines 35–38 define a method `balance`, and lines 40–44 define a method `deposit`. Lines 47–50 define the `oneway` operation `withdraw`. Note that the oneway operation cannot return any values, nor can it raise exceptions.

As indicated, multiple interfaces are supported by means of inheritance. The newly proposed CORBA-3 standard extends this functionality by allowing a composite object to manage independent interfaces that are not supported via inheritance.

7.3.2 Client-CORBA Object Communication

The basic communication between two CORBA objects is accomplished by the ORB core. OMG does not place any restriction on how ORBs are implemented. In most ORB implementations, existing IPC (interprocess communication) methods, such as Unix socket libraries, shared memory and multithreaded libraries, are used to achieve actual communication among clients, servers, and the ORB. Yet the ORB can be as simple as a library that supports communication among objects and their clients, which are co-resident in the same process space.

To make a request, the client needs to know the operations that it is going to request of an object. In other words, it needs to know the interface of the object that will respond to the request. From here, the client can determine the reference of the target object that will service the request. This can be obtained either from the ORB as the reference of an existing object that is generally created by an object factory, or by using the naming services—one of the CORBAservices modules. The target-object reference, together with the requested operations, constitutes the request.

Clients can communicate (or access) CORBA objects in one of two ways. The first way, known as static invocation, establishes the linkage between the client and the server at compile time. To facilitate this linkage, IDL compilers generate client-side stubs and server-side skeletons. These are interface-specific code segments that cooperate to effectively exchange requests and results. A stub is a mechanism that creates and issues requests on the client's behalf. A skeleton is a mechanism that delivers requests to CORBA object implementations.

The alternative is to use dynamic invocation through the dynamic invocation interface (DII) at the client side, and the dynamic skeleton interface (DSI) at the server side. DII allows clients to send requests to servers without the compile-time generation of stubs; DSI allows servers to be written without skeletons. Applications that establish static invocation bindings at compile time execute faster and are easier to program because the programming interface is similar to ordinary object-oriented programs—a method is invoked on an identified object. Furthermore, static invocation permits static type checking, and the code is self-documenting. However, dynamic invocation is more flexible, leading to code genericity, and it allows the runtime addition of CORBA objects and classes, which are needed for various tools such as schema browsers.

For either of these modes, but particularly for dynamic invocation, the client application must have a way to know the types of interfaces supported by the server objects. The CORBA IR allows the IDL type system to be accessed and written programmatically at runtime. IR is itself a CORBA object that has a standard interface. Using this interface, an application can traverse the entire hierarchy of IDL information.

To use or implement an interface, the language-independent interface defined in the IDL must be mapped (using an IDL compiler) into the corresponding type definitions and application program interfaces (APIs) of a particular programming language. These types and APIs are used by the developer to provide application functionality and to interact with the ORB. The generic mapping process is shown in Figure 7.3, although there are differences among various implemented ORBs, as well as among different languages.

IDL definitions of the interfaces of CORBA objects are precompiled to generate skeleton sources (which are server object templates without implementation) and client stub sources. At this stage, the interface definition is also inserted into the IR. The skeleton sources are compiled together with the implementation code to implement the interfaces defined by IDL that generate server-side skeletons (this is the OMG term for server-side stub) and the object-implementation code. The latter is inserted into the implementation repository to keep track of the code. The client stub sources are compiled together with the client-side code to generate client stubs. The two compilers need not be the same and are dependent on the language in which the server object and client application are written.

Figure 7.4 shows the creation process of a client and a server in C++, as implemented in the MICO ORB. After compiling the source IDL file `sample.idl`, the IDL compiler generates two files: `sample.h` and

Figure 7.3

IDL processing.

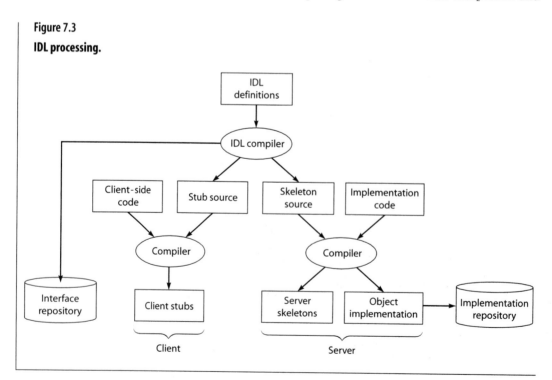

Figure 7.4 | **Creating a CORBA application.**

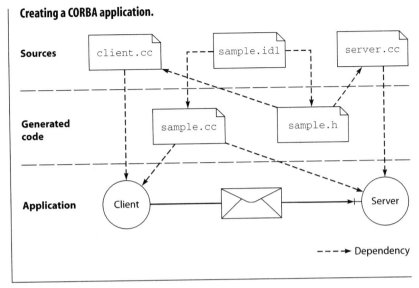

sample.cc. The former contains class declarations for the base class of the sample object implementation and the stub class that a client will use to invoke methods on remote sample objects. The latter contains implementations of those classes and some supporting codes. The client-side file client.cc includes ORB initialization and invocation of the method on a particular interface declared in the IDL file. The files client.cc and sample.h are compiled to create an objective file client.o, using any C++ compiler. The file sample.cc is compiled to an objective file sample.o, which is linked with client.o to create a executable CORBA client. The server-side file server.cc includes the actual implementation codes for the methods. Similarly, the C++ compiler uses the files server.cc, sample.h, and sample.cc together to create an executable CORBA server.

Based on the flow of requests from the client to the server, via the ORB, the following steps occur.

1. A client initiates a request through an object reference by calling stub procedures (the static stub interface) for that particular object or by constructing the request dynamically (using the DII), knowing exactly the type of the object and the desired input-output arguments. Either way, the request is sent to the client ORB core, and the target object cannot tell in which way the request was invoked.

2. If the client ORB core cannot locate the target object for this request, it transmits the request to the ORB core linked with the target-object implementation (the server) by General Inter-ORB Protocol (GIOP) and Internet Inter-ORB Protocol (IIOP) (see Section 7.3.4).

3. The server ORB core dispatches the request to the object adapter that created the target object.

4. The object adapter locates the appropriate object implementation, transmits arguments, and transfers control to the object implementation. As does the client, the server can choose either a static (static IDL skeleton interface) or a dynamic (DSI) dispatching mechanism for its object implementation. While processing the request, the object implementation may obtain some services from the ORB through the object adapter or from the ORB core directly.

5. After the object implementation finishes the request, it returns the control and the output values to the client.

A second issue in client-server communication is the association mode between a client request and a server method. CORBA provides three alternatives for this: one interface to one implementation, one interface to one of many implementations, and one interface to multiple implementations. If there is only one implementation of an interface, all of the requests should be directed to a server that supports this single implementation. If there is more than one implementation of an interface, ORB can direct the requests to a server that supports any one of the existing implementations. In both cases, implementations handle all operations defined in the interface, and after implementation selection, ORB always uses the same implementation for requests to a particular object. If each implementation of an interface does not handle all of the operations defined in the interface—that is, if each implementation provides only a part of the interface—the third method is used for associating a client request with a server method. In this case, ORB directs the requests to a server that supports an implementation of the interface that handles the invoked operation.

Finally, there is the issue of the call communication modes. CORBA versions prior to CORBA-3 define three modes between a client and a server: synchronous, deferred synchronous, and one-way. Synchronous mode refers to blocked communication, where the client waits for the completion of the requested operation. Synchronous mode can be restrictive for clients who issue operations that can be executed in parallel with multiple objects. In deferred synchronous mode, the client continues its execution after server selection and keeps polling the server to get the results until the operation is completed. In one-way mode, a client sends a request without any expectation of getting a reply.

CORBA 2.1 does not support asynchronous mode, which implies that, if a client is to receive asynchronous messages, it should also act as a server that implements an object that can receive requests. In other words, the asynchronous mode of operation can be achieved between two CORBA objects by their sending one-way requests to one another. The only disadvantage of this peer-to-peer approach is the increased complexity of the client code.

With CORBA-3, asynchronous messaging is introduced. In fact, the new standard (OMG 1998a) introduces two new invocation modes: asynchronous method invocation (AMI) and time-independent invocation (TII), both of which can be used in static and dynamic invocations. Clients can use either polling or callback methods to get the results of invocations. Upon receiving these invocations, routers handle the passing of messages between clients and target objects, and communicate with them. Some policies are specified to control the quality of service (QoS) of asynchronous invocations.

7.3.3 Object Adapters

Object implementations access most of the services provided by the ORB via object adapters (OAs). Each OA is an interface to the ORB, allowing it to locate, activate, and invoke operations on an ORB object. The OA is the glue between CORBA object implementation and the ORB itself, adapting the interface of another object to the interface expected by a caller. The OA uses delegation to allow a caller to invoke requests on an object, even though the caller does not know the object's true interface. The fundamental functions that an OA performs are the generation and interpretation of object references, method invocation, security of interactions, object and implementation activation and deactivation, mapping of object references to the corresponding object implementations, and registration of implementations.

Until recently (i.e., until CORBA 2.1), only the Basic Object Adapter (BOA) was defined and had to be provided by all commercial ORBs. The BOA is designed to be used with most object implementations and provides for the generation and interpretation of object references; method invocation; registration, activation, and deactivation of object implementations; selection of proper object implementation for a given object reference; and authentication.

With CORBA 2.2, OMG released an alternative to BOA. This standard, called the Persistent Object Adapter (POA), provides ORB portability. Some CORBA products already include POA as part of their basic system offering. There are expectations that, in the future, OMG will publish another standard for object DBMSs. Because object DBMSs provide some ORB-like services, such as object reference generation and management, this adapter will be tuned to integrate object DBMSs with ORB distribution and communication. Library OAs will be tuned for implementations resident in the client's process space. With the introduction of POA, OMG has removed the BOA specification from CORBA, even though many ORBs continue to support it.

POA is responsible for the entire life cycle of a CORBA object—from its creation to its destruction. When a request is received by the POA (via the ORB) for the invocation of an object, the POA creates the

CORBA object that will service that request. Creation of an object associates a servant with it. A servant is a programming-language object or entity that implements requests on one or more objects, providing bodies or implementations for those objects. Servants generally exist in the context of a server process. A request made on an object through its reference is interpreted by the ORB and transformed into an invocation on a specific servant (Hoque 1998). A created object is activated by its servant. The object must be incarnated by a servant to have requests delivered to it. When the servant is finished with the CORBA object, the servant is etherealized and its linkage to the object is broken (Henning & Vinoski 1999). The object is then deactivated. A created object can alternate between the active and deactive modes during its life cycle. Eventually, the object is destroyed, which completes its life cycle.

Figure 7.5 shows the abstract POA model while a request sent from the client is dispatched to a servant. The process is as follows.

1. The server exports an object reference for an object. Only as a result of this export does the object become known to the system.

2. A client accesses this object by its object reference. The client may obtain this object reference in a number of ways; OMA provides two services (see Section 7.4) that can be used: the naming service and the trader service.

3. The client ORB uses the object reference to dispatch the request to the server ORB.

4. The server ORB then dispatches the request to the OA.

5. The OA dispatches the request to the appropriate servant (identified by object ID) that incarnates the target object.

Figure 7.5 | **Abstract POA model (adapted from Henning & Vinoski 1999).**

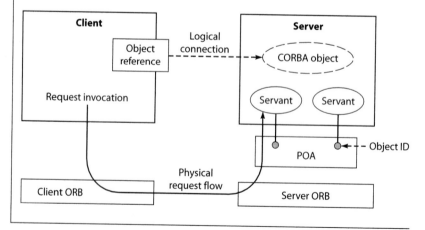

In the case of POA, this process is slightly modified. This is due to a feature of POA that allows a server to have more than one POA. Thus, in step 4, the ORB has to find and dispatch the request to the particular POA instance that services the server object. In the case of multiple POAs, each one represents a set of objects that have similar properties. These properties are controlled via POA policies that are specified when a POA is created. Each server application has at least one POA, called root POA, that stores a standard set of policies. POAs can be defined as specializations of other POAs from which they inherit policy values. The POA policies are as follows.

Thread policy. A POA can either have the ORB control its threads or be single-threaded.

Life-span policy. The objects created in a POA are specified as transient or persistent. Transience is defined with respect to the lifetime of the server process in which the object is created.

Object ID uniqueness policy. A servant can be associated either with only a single object or with multiple objects. The servants associated with multiple objects can reduce the server's memory use.

ID assignment policy. Objects created with that POA are assigned object IDs only by the POA; otherwise, object IDs are assigned only by the server.

Servant retention policy. A POA can either retain the associations between servants and objects across request boundaries or establish a new association for each incoming request.

Request processing policy. When a request arrives for a specific object, the POA can act in one of three ways.

- If the object ID is not among the currently active objects, an exception is returned to the client.

- If the object ID is not among the currently active objects or the nonretention policy is chosen for the servant and a default servant has been registered with the POA, that servant can be used to service the request.

- If a servant manager has been registered with the POA, it is invoked by the POA to locate a servant or raise an exception.

Implicit activation policy. A POA can activate a servant implicitly. This is useful for registering servants for transient objects.

When registering objects to CORBA, it is necessary to specify an activation policy for the implementation of each kind of object that will be used by the object adapter. This policy identifies how each implementation gets started. An implementation may support shared, unshared, server-per-method or persistent activation policies. Whereas a server that uses a shared activation policy can support more than one object, a server that uses an unshared activation policy can support only one object at a time for an implementation. In the server-per-method activation policy, a new server is used for each method invocation. The persistent activation policy is similar to the shared activation policy, except that the server is never started automatically.

7.3.4 ORB Interoperability

Earlier versions of CORBA (prior to version 2.0) suffered from a lack of interoperability among various CORBA products, caused by the fact that earlier CORBA specifications did not mandate any particular data formats or protocols for ORB communications. CORBA 2.0 specifies an interoperability architecture based on the GIOP, which specifies transfer syntax and a standard set of message formats for ORB interoperation over any connection-oriented transport. CORBA 2.0 also mandates the IIOP, which is an implementation of GIOP over TCP/IP transport. With IIOP, ORBs can interoperate with one another over the internet.

7.4 Common Object Services

Object services provide the main functions for implementing basic object functionality using ORB. Each object service has a well-defined interface definition and functional semantics that are orthogonal to other services. This orthogonality allows objects to use several object services at the same time without confusion.

The set of services are diverse and in different phases of development. Some of these services are fundamental to any distributed application development over CORBA: naming service, event service, lifecycle service, and persistent object service. Some others are also important for the development of component DBMSs. Some of these are important database-related object services, including transaction service, concurrency control service, and query service. Other services defined by OMG include relationship service, externalization service, licensing service, property service, security service, time service, collections service, and trading service. Not only are there differences among these with respect to their level of development as standards, but there are differences in the development of commercial services by each vendor. We discuss these services in this section, giving more emphasis to the fundamental ones and to those that are important for component DBMSs.

The provision of these services and their use by other CORBA objects provide plug-and-play reusability to these objects. As an example, a client can move any object that supports life-cycle services by using the standard interface. If the object does not support the standard life-cycle services, then the user needs to know move semantics for the object and its corresponding interface.

7.4.1 Naming Service

The naming service supports a name-to-object association called a name binding. The binding of a name to an object is done relative to a naming context, which is an object that contains a set of name bindings where each name is unique. Several names can be bound to an object in the same or different contexts at the same time, but each name can only identify exactly one object. The resolution of a name is the determination of the object associated with the name in a given context.

A context is like any other object, and it can be bound to a CORBA object or another context object. This results in a hierarchy of contexts and bindings known as a naming graph (Figure 7.6), which can be supported in a distributed, federated fashion. It is possible to view a naming graph as similar to a file system, in which contexts are analogous to directories that store bindings to either directories (other contexts) or files (objects).

7.4.2 Event Service

The event service supports asynchronous events by decoupling the communication between objects. It allows objects to be invoked when certain events occur. An object can assume either a supplier role, if it produces event data, or a consumer role, if it processes event data.

Figure 7.6 | **A naming graph.**

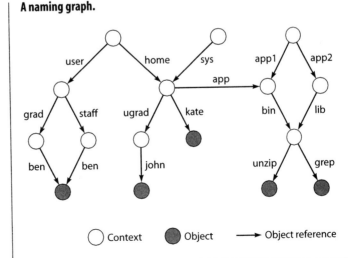

The communication of event data between suppliers and consumers is accomplished by issuing standard CORBA requests through appropriate event-channel implementations. An event channel is an object that facilitates multiple suppliers to communicate to multiple consumers asynchronously. This communication can follow either the push model or the pull model. In the former, the supplier object transfers event data to the appropriate consumer when the corresponding event occurs; in the latter, the consumer periodically requests event data from a supplier.

7.4.3   Life-Cycle Service

The life-cycle service defines a framework composed of services and conventions for creating, deleting, copying, and moving objects. A client is any piece of code that initiates a life-cycle operation for some object. Clients can perform life-cycle operations on objects in different locations under the conventions of the life-cycle service.

A client model of creation is defined in terms of factory objects that provide the client with specialized operations to create and initialize new instances for the implementation. A factory has no standard interface, but instead a generic factory interface. Clients can delete, move, or copy an object by invoking remove, move, or copy requests, respectively on target objects that support `LifeCycleObject` interfaces. The life-cycle service also defines factory finder objects, which support the `find_factories` operation for returning a sequence of factories. Clients pass factory finders to the move and copy operations that invoke the `find_factories` operation to find a factory to interact with. The new copy or the migrated object will be within the scope of the returned factory.

7.4.4   Persistent Object Service

The persistent object service provides common interfaces to the mechanisms used for retaining and managing the persistent state of objects in a data-storage-independent fashion. Objects can be considered in two states: the dynamic state, which is typically in memory and transient, and the persistent state, which is used to reconstruct the dynamic state. The persistent object service is primarily responsible for storing the persistent state of objects.

Each object ultimately has responsibility of managing its own state, but can use or delegate to the persistent object service for the actual work. There is no requirement that any object use any particular persistence mechanism. The persistent object service provides capabilities that support various styles of use and implementation, in order to be useful to a wide variety of objects. The architecture of the persistent object service has multiple components and interfaces. The interfaces allow different implementations of the components to work together to obtain various qualities of service.

7.4.5   Transaction Service

The transaction service supports atomicity, consistency, isolation, and durability (ACID) transactions. Thus, distributed objects that use the transaction service interfaces to cooperate with each other provide the following well-known ACID properties:

> Atomicity. Either all of the actions of a transaction are committed or none are. Thus, if a transaction is interrupted by failure, all efforts are undone (rolled back).
>
> Consistency. A transaction produces consistent results.
>
> Isolation. A transaction is isolated from other transactions. Thus, its intermediate states are not visible to other transactions. Transactions appear to execute sequentially even though they are performed concurrently.
>
> Durability. Once a transaction commits (completes), its effects are persistent and survive future system failures.

Transaction-service implementations must support flat transactions, and the standard specification has provisions for supporting nested transactions. This service depends on the concurrency control service to enforce isolation and the persistent object service to enforce durability.

7.4.6   Concurrency Control Service

This service coordinates the concurrent access to shared objects (i.e., resources) by multiple clients so that the object remains in a consistent state. It enforces the well-known serializability criterion for accesses by both transactional and nontransactional clients.

The synchronization approach is based on locking, where a lock is associated with each object. Several lock modes are defined in order to provide flexible conflict resolution.

7.4.7   Query Service

The query service provides query operations on collections of objects and may return collections of objects. The query operations include predicate-based declarative specifications. The standard does not specify a particular query language; queries can be specified by SQL variants that support object-oriented concepts (e.g., SQL:99 or ODMGs Object Query Language, OQL) or any other type of language.

Queries are executed on the source object collections either by the application of predicates or by intermediate collections that are produced by query evaluators. Query evaluators apply a given predicate to collections to generate other collections. They can operate on implicit collections of objects through their IDL interfaces. Thus, the query service supports nested queries of the well-known form.

7.4.8   Collections Service

The collections service provides a uniform way to create and manipulate the most common collections (groups of objects such as sets, queues, stacks, lists, and binary trees) generically. Three categories of interfaces are defined to accomplish this.

- Collection interface and collection factories. A client creates a collection instance of a collection interface that offers grouping properties that match the client's requirements, using a collection factory. A client uses collections to manipulate elements as a group.

- Iterator interfaces. An iterator is created for a given collection, which is the factory for it. An iterator is used to traverse the collection in a user-defined manner, process elements it points to, mark ranges, and so forth.

- Function interfaces. A client creates user-defined specializations of function interfaces using user-defined factories. Instances of function interfaces are used by a collection implementation rather than by a client.

7.4.9   Other Object Services

The trading service facilitates objects collaboration. An object that is available to provide a service registers its availability with the service by describing the service and specifying its location. Objects can then inquire of the trader for any services they need. Thus, the trader matches the available services to the needs of objects.

The externalization service describes protocols and conventions for object externalizing and internalizing. An object is externalized by recording its state in a stream of data (e.g., in memory, on a disk file, or across the network) and then internalizing it into a new object during the same process or a different process.

The relationship service allows entities, represented as CORBA objects, and their relationship to be explicitly represented.

The licensing service provides a mechanism for producers to control the use of their intellectual properties.

The property service is capable of dynamically associating named values with objects outside the static IDL-type system.

The security service consists of the following features: identification and authentication, authorization and access control, security auditing, security of communication, nonrepudiation, and administration.

The time service enables the user to obtain the current time together with an error estimate associated with it to synchronize clocks in distributed systems.

7.5   Common Facilities

Common facilities consist of components that provide services for the development of application objects in a CORBA environment. These are horizontal facilities that consist of those services that are used by all (or many) application objects. Examples of these facilities include user interfaces, systems management, and task management. (We do not discuss these in this chapter.)

7.6   Building Componentized Applications

One of the strengths of distributed computing platforms, such as OMA, is that they facilitate the development of large-scale distributed applications. However, the facilities provided by the OMA are probably too low level to accomplish this aim. It is certainly possible to develop systems using the CORBA infrastructure and the provided services; there are many examples of this. However, application development in this environment still requires writing a significant amount of glue code. Because these are generally proprietary systems, true reusability at the application level is hard to achieve.

What is required is a value-added framework that allows the development of components and the use of these components in other applications. By components, we mean self-contained modules that perform a particular function (usually at a higher level of abstraction than an ordinary object). Components have clear interfaces that allow them to be plugged into other components. In this type of environment, distributed applications are developed by putting together many of these components and enabling them to cooperate with each other over a backplane. CORBA establishes this backplane, but more work is needed to facilitate this view of application development.

This requirement—and shortcoming—was recognized quite early in the OMA development cycle. OLE provided the required functionality in Microsoft's DCOM/OLE environment; there are third-party OLE providers that encapsulate applications to give them component features. Until recently, there was no comparable component framework for OMA. At one point, it was expected that OpenDoc would serve in this capacity, but with the demise of the OpenDoc initiative, the need for the development of component technology became acute. With the recent release of the CORBA-3 specification, this issue is addressed. Even though there are no commercial ORBs that are fully CORBA-3 compliant, products are expected to come to the market in the next 2 to 3 years.

In CORBA-3, OMG has defined two specifications relevant to component technology: CORBAcomponents (OMG 1999a) and CORBA-scripting (OMG 1999b). In CORBA, components are modeled as objects (as most things are). Consequently, CORBAcomponents introduces a new metatype called `Component`, which supports multiple independent interfaces (as indicated earlier, pre-CORBA-3 ORBs only support multiple interfaces by inheritance) and a `CORBAcomponents` container provides infrastructure to navigate among them. Other components can then be defined as subtypes of the `Component` type, providing for the development of a complete component-type system.

The `CORBAcomponents container` environment is persistent, transactional, and secure. For the developers, these functions are pre-packaged and provided at a higher level of abstraction than those of CORBAservices. As discussed previously, this facilitates the development of CORBA middleware as part of the application development. The end result is expected to be an easier system development because the application developers only need to know components and their interfaces, rather than having to know CORBA in an intimate way.

There is also a provision to interoperate with Enterprise JavaBeans (EJB), which allows CORBA components to present themselves as JavaBeans to Java programs or other tools in the JavaBeans environments.

Component Scripting (OMG 1999b) is a standard scripting language to wire all components together, by means of which users can easily modify or upgrade applications constructed using the language. The specification maps component assembly to a number of widely used scripting languages.

We conclude this section by providing sample code to demonstrate how we go about putting together an application over CORBA. Note that our focus is on the main steps and we, by necessity, eliminate many details.

Recall Example 1, our first IDL example. The purpose of the interface `QueryAgent` is to use the method `getImages` to retrieve a set of images from an image database based on the given query. If we implement both the client and the server using C++, the simplified source codes will include Examples 3 and 4.

EXAMPLE 3

The Client

Initialize ORB and connect to naming service.

```
// ORB initialization
CORBA::ORB_var orb = CORBA::ORB_init(argc, argv,
                                     "mico-local-orb" );

...

// Get reference to initial naming context
CORBA::Object_var nobj =
orb->resolve_initial_references ("NameService");

....

// Narrow
CosNaming::NamingContext_var nc =
            CosNaming::NamingContext::_narrow (nobj);

...
```

Using naming service, get the object reference to the remote-image database server object, `serverName` is a string which is the name of the image database.

```
// Construct a server object
name context CosNaming::Name name;
name.length (1);
name[0].id = CORBA::string_dup (serverName);
name[0].kind = CORBA::string_dup ("");

...

// Resolve the name and get the object reference to the
server
object CORBA::Object_var obj = nc->resolve (name);

...

// Narrow
QueryAgent_var client = QueryAgent::_narrow( obj );

...
```

Invoke the `getImage` method in synchronous mode to get the image data. `retImage` is a pointer that points to a set of images; `queryString` is a string that contains the specified query in a certain query language.

```
retImage = client->getImages (queryString);

...
```

EXAMPLE 4 | **The Server**

The IDL wrapped image-database server is registered with the CORBA implementation repository. The ORB automatically delivers the request from the client to the server, specifically on a particular method, `get-Images`. The implementation codes for that method declared in the IDL file are included in a class called `QueryAgent_impl`.

```
class QueryAgent_impl : virtual public POA_QueryAgent {
public: imagesType *getImages(const char * queryString)
{...}
... }
```

Inside the method, the query string is sent to the local database through its call-level interfaces, and results are composed and returned to the invoker. In the `main()` we initialize ORB and root POA, and create the servant that provides the services to the client.

```
// ORB initialization
CORBA::ORB_var orb;
...

// Obtain a reference to the RootPOA and its Manager
CORBA::Object_var poaobj =
orb->resolve_initial_references ("RootPOA");
PortableServer::POA_varpoa =
          PortableServer::POA::_narrow (poaobj);
PortableServer::POAManager_var mgr =
poa->the_POAManager();
...
// Create and activate the servant
QueryAgent_impl *servant = new QueryAgent_impl;
QueryAgent_var oid = servant->_this();
...
```

We also connect to naming service and bind the server name to its object reference.

```
// Connect naming service
CosNaming::NamingContext_var nc;
...
// Bind
appName.length (1);
```

```
appName[0].id = CORBA::string_dup (serverName);

appName[0].kind = CORBA::string_dup ("");

...

nc->rebind (appName, oid);

...
```

After all the initialization, the POA manager is activated and the server waits for requests from the client.

```
mgr->activate();

...

orb->run();

...
```

7.7   CORBA and Database Interoperability

As an object-oriented distributed computing platform, OMA, and in particular CORBA, can be helpful for database interoperability. The fundamental contribution is in terms of managing heterogeneity and, to a lesser extent, autonomy. Heterogeneity in a distributed system can occur at the hardware and operating system (which we can jointly call platform) level, communication level, DBMS level, and semantic level. CORBA deals mainly with platform and communication heterogeneities. It also addresses DBMS heterogeneity by means of IDL interface definitions. However, the real problem of managing multiple DBMSs in the sense of a multidatabase system requires the development of a global layer that includes the global-level DBMS functionality. One issue for which CORBA is not useful is semantic heterogeneity.

Using CORBA as the infrastructure affects the upper layers of a multidatabase system because CORBA and CORBAservices together provide basic database functionality to manage distributed objects. The most important database-related services included in CORBAservices are transaction services, backup and recovery services, concurrency services, and query services. If these services are available in the ORB implementation used, it is possible to develop the global layers of a multidatabase system on CORBA, mainly by implementing the standard interfaces of these services for the involved objects. For example, by using a transaction service, implementing a global transaction manager occurs by implementing the interfaces defined in the transaction service specification for the involved DBMSs.

In this section, we discuss some of the design issues that must be resolved to use CORBA for database interoperability. This discussion is based, to a large extent, on Dogac et al. (1998).

7.7.1 Object Granularity

A fundamental design issue is the granularity of the CORBA objects. In registering a DBMS to CORBA, a row in a relational DBMS, an object or a group of objects in an object DBMS, or a whole DBMS can be an individual CORBA object. The advantage of fine-granularity objects is the finer control they permit. However, in this case, all the DBMS functionalities needed to process (e.g., querying and transactional control) and manage these objects have to be supported by the global system level (i.e., the multidatabase system). If, on the other hand, an entire DBMS is registered as a CORBA object, the functionality needed to process the entities is left to that DBMS.

Another consideration with regard to granularity has to do with the capabilities of the particular ORB being used. In the case of ORBs that provide BOA, each insertion and deletion of classes necessitates recompiling of the IDL code and rebuilding the server. Thus, if the object granularity is fine, these ORBs incur significant overhead. A possible solution to this problem is to use DII. This prevents the recompilation of the code and rebuilding of the server, but suffers from the runtime-performance overhead discussed earlier.

7.7.2 Object Interfaces

A second design issue is the definition of interfaces to the CORBA objects. Most commercial DBMSs support the basic transaction and query primitives, either through their call-level interface (CLI) library routines or their XA interface library routines. This property makes it possible to define a generic database object interface through CORBA IDL to represent all the underlying DBMSs. CORBA allows multiple implementations of an interface. Hence it is possible to encapsulate each of the local DBMSs by providing a different implementation of the generic database object.

7.7.3 Association Mode

The association mode between a client request and server method is another design issue. As specified earlier, CORBA provides three alternatives for this: one interface to one implementation, one interface to one of many implementations, and one interface to multiple implementations. The choice of alternative is dependent both on the data location and the nature of the database-access requests. If the requested data is contained in one database, then it is usually sufficient to use the second alternative and choose the DBMS that manages that data because DBMSs registered to CORBA provide basic transaction management and query primitives for all the operations that the interface definition specifies. If the request involves data from multiple databases, then the third alternative should be chosen.

7.7.4 Call Mode

As discussed earlier, CORBA-3 defines four basic call communication modes between a client and a server: synchronous, deferred synchronous, one-way, and asynchronous. For objects of an interoperable DBMS, synchronous call mode is generally sufficient. Deferred synchronous mode or the asynchronous (peer-to-peer) approach should be used when parallel execution is necessary. For example, in order to provide parallelism in query execution, the global query manager of a multidatabase system should not wait for the query to complete after submitting it to a component DBMS.

7.7.5 Concurrently Active Objects

Some of the objects in a multidatabase system need to be concurrently active. This can be achieved either by using threads on a server that uses a shared activation policy or by using separate servers activated in the unshared mode for each object. Otherwise, because a server can only give service for one object at a time, client requests to other client requests to the objects owned by the same server should wait for the current request to complete. Further, if the server keeps transient data for the object throughout its life cycle, all requests to an object must be serviced by the same server. For example, if a global transaction manager is activated in shared mode, it would be necessary to preserve the transaction contexts in different threads. However, if the global transaction manager is activated in unshared mode, the same functionality can be obtained with a simpler implementation at the cost of having one process for each active transaction.

7.8 Conclusion

In this chapter we discuss the OMA and its components as a possible platform for developing component DBMSs. We focus on the issues that are relevant to the subject matter of this book. More details on CORBA can be found in many books, such as Siegel (1996) and Hoque (1998), as well as in the OMG specifications cited in this chapter.

The term "component database" may mean many things; a classification is given in Geppert & Dittrich (Chapter 1 of this volume). It is clear that OMA can facilitate many of these componentization efforts. Building interoperable DBMSs on top of component DBMSs has been tried many times, and there are working systems. It should also be possible to put together a single DBMS by gluing together the relevant OMA services such as the query, transaction, persistence, and concurrency control services. There are problems in accomplishing this (such as the inability of the current OAs to efficiently deal with fine-granularity objects), but these may well be overcome. The fundamental criticism of this approach has been the performance overhead that CORBA will produce. Even though this is likely to be a problem, there have been no studies that quantify the overhead.

If componentization of DBMSs (using any definition) is to become a reality, then there is clearly a need for distributed computing platforms such as CORBA. From its modest beginnings, OMA has made significant strides to provide the infrastructure for the building of componentized distributed applications—if components are sufficiently large. It is still unclear whether it can support finer-granularity componentization.

8

The Architecture of a Database System for Mobile and Embedded Devices

Heiko Bobzin
POET Software

8.1 Introduction

POET Software, a leading vendor of object-oriented databases, has developed a new database management system—named Navajo—for mobile and embedded devices. Design and development have faced several special challenges: robustness, low-resource consumption, and connectivity.

A database management system for mobile and embedded devices must be able to run nonstop—perhaps for years—because such devices typically are not shut down; instead, they are placed in suspend mode. Obviously, the database must require zero administration. A transaction model that includes full recovery and different models of concurrency is needed to support background updates and synchronization. Low-resource consumption means that the database kernel is restricted in terms of code size, use of main memory, and persistent storage. Apart from technical considerations (e.g., compression, dynamically reconfigurable caches, and swapping algorithms), the problem is tackled on a conceptual level by choosing a strictly modular approach. The application developer or device manufacturer chooses the set of features required for a particular application and assembles the database configuration from the modules that enable these features. For example, all mobile and embedded scenarios require the device and its database to be occasionally connected to a PC, a company network, or the internet. The database system needs to download new data (delivery) or upload data obtained when the device was offline (archiving). More generally, it needs to synchronize with other data stores. Facilities such as logging, import and export, and replication need to be provided as plug-ins to help the application developer solve individual connectivity problems.

The main objectives, low-resource consumption and on-demand application assembly, require a componentized database management system. Components in this system are parts that can be replaced or loaded at runtime and that implement a defined interface. Replacing an implementation can add more functionality or can resolve memory-performance trade-offs.

8.2 The Idea of a Pure Java Database Management System

Shortly after the introduction of the Java programming language, POET decided to add a Java language binding to its existing object-oriented database management system (OODBMS) (Poet 1999). In a first version, a generic interface was added, but it lacked transparency. Every object had to be read by an explicit method call. Later, a database application programming interface (API) to access persistent objects transparently was developed in cooperation with the Object Database

Management Group (ODMG) (Cattell & Barry 1997). To avoid problems that arise from transporting data to different platforms, we began thinking about a pure Java object database solution. As a possible application area, embedded devices seemed to be a good fit for Java. These devices run specialized programs that need no administration, such as telephones or personal digital assistants (PDAs).

The advantages of a Java-based system are evident: write once, run everywhere; small code size; dynamic loading of components; rapid development cycles; and rich runtime libraries. It is possible to develop an application under Unix or Windows NT and transport it easily to the target system. As with workstations, embedded devices are implemented on a variety of different platforms, and, during the development of the embedded system, hardware and platforms might change. This chapter explains the components of POET's pure Java database management system: user API and object model, object management, concurrency management, backend and storage, distributed applications, event service, log service, postprocessing, and on-demand assembly of components.

8.3   User API and Object Model

For the application developer, a persistence model should be as easy to use and as transparent as possible. For persistent objects, the Java language provides serialization to easily stream objects into a disk file or network stream. The developer can implement his or her own methods to store and reload fields of an object and the serialization methods are then capable of storing and loading whole object graphs in a single call. However, serialization has drawbacks. To work correctly, a class has to inherit from the `Serializable` tag interface. Another disadvantage is that single objects cannot be modified on disk. In addition, the whole object graph must be loaded and stored, which is unacceptable for a large amount of data; and a query for specific objects is not possible.

As another option, Java provides a library to access SQL-based, relational databases. By using the Java Database Connectivity (JDBC) interfaces (Sun Microsystems 1999), a developer can open relational databases, iterate through tables, and perform queries. But this means learning a different language (i.e., SQL). Moreover, the relational model does not fit the Java object model. In addition, the code size and resource consumption of a traditional SQL-based system will extend the capacity of an embedded device.

In Navajo, we therefore propose the use of OODBMS technology. A persistent object, stored in an object-oriented database, can reload its state after starting an application. Persistent objects can refer to other persistent objects, allowing traversal of the object graph without having to load all objects of the graph. The source code of persistent classes

Figure 8.1 | **Persistence by reachability.**

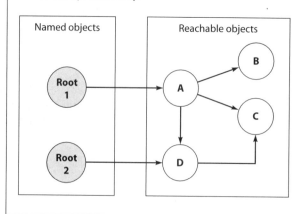

does not differ from other classes. An important concept used by the ODMG is persistence by reachability: If one object is bound to the database, all reachable objects will become persistent, too. During iteration of the object network, only persistent fields of a class are resolved. Starting at a root object, which has a unique name, all other objects can be retrieved by traversing the references (Figure 8.1).

The ODMG Java Binding contains some essential interfaces (which are discussed briefly next). In Java, the `interface` keyword can be used to define classes without fields, state, and implementation. These classes look like C++ classes containing only pure virtual methods. They clearly separate the vendor's implementation from the semantics and the method signatures of a specification. ODMG's Java Binding interfaces specify the minimum requirements that a database vendor has to implement. Since version 3.0 (Cattell et al. 2000), the interfaces are part of the `org.odmg` package and can be downloaded as source code from www.odmg.org.

8.3.1   Implementation

The `Implementation` interface works as an abstract factory. All other objects of the specific ODMG vendor implementation can be instantiated. By using this interface, vendor-independent implementations are possible. The `Implemetation` instance needs only to be created once at a single place in the application.

```
Implementationodmg=newcom.poet.odmg.Implementation();
```

8.3.2   Database

The `Database` interface contains methods to create, open, and close databases. It is also used to insert new objects into the database or delete objects from the database. Certain newly created persistent objects have to be bound to the database by giving them a name. These objects are called root objects. Objects referenced directly or transitively by a root object or some other persistent object become persistent, too.

```
Database db = odmg.newDatabase();
db.open("poet://LOCAL/datafile");
...
Person person = new Person("John Jones");
Address address = new Address(...);
person.address = address;
db.bind(person, "John");
```

8.3.3 Transaction

Transactions are units of atomicity, consistency, isolation, and durability (Härder & Reuter 1983). The Java ODMG Binding specifies that access to persistent objects must be within a running transaction. Therefore a transaction has to be created and started before any persistent object can be read or modified. At the end of an operational unit, the application can decide to commit or abort the current transaction.

```
Transaction txn = odmg.newTransaction();
txn.begin();
... access objects ...
txn.commit();
```

8.3.4 Collections

Collections are used to model one-to-n and n-to-m relationships among objects. As of Java ODMG Binding version 3.0, there are four types of collection interfaces. `DArray` and `DList` contain countable elements and maintain the order in which elements were inserted. `DSet` and `DBag` do not keep the order. `DSet` can contain equal objects only once, while `DBag` allows equal objects to be added several times. Two objects are considered equal if the Java `Object` class methods `hashCode()` returns the same value for them and if the method `equals()` returns true. For example, the following simple code declares a one-to-n relation between a `Person` object and one or more other objects (probably other `Person` objects):

```
public class Person
{
  DSet children;
}
```

A collection can be instantiated by using the abstract factory:

```
children = odmg.newDSet();
children.add(new Person());
```

In the previous version of the ODMG Java Binding `Set`, `Bag`, `Array`, and `List` each had its own interface, compatible with the `Enumeration` and `Vector` interfaces in Java Development Kit (JDK) 1.1, but the latest version lets them inherit from standard Java collection interfaces.

8.4 Object Management

In the Java programming language, objects are accessed by references. Same references always refer to identical objects, but equal objects do not share the same reference at all times. When objects are made persistent in an object database they receive another identity, called object ID (OID). When developing with an ODMG-conforming database, the application developer does not need to know the OID; instead he or she deals with references or named objects. The model explicitly defines that, within the scope of a single transaction, every persistent object maps exactly to one object in memory. Different transactions do not share objects with the same OID, but instead use different Java instances for each object. A transaction cache keeps track of the mapping between objects and OIDs. To understand where objects enter and leave the transaction cache, a life cycle has been defined (see Figure 8.2):

- Transient-new. An object that is instantiated with `new` inside or outside of transaction boundaries.

- Persistent-new. An object that is inserted newly into the database and that has been transient-new before.

- Persistent-hollow. An object that was retrieved from the database, but does not contain valid data.

- Persistent-valid. An object that was persistent-hollow and has had some field read. This will load the data, and the object becomes valid.

- Persistent-dirty. An object that was valid and has been modified by the application.

- Transient-invalid. An object that cannot be accessed; the transaction has terminated.

The transaction cache is responsible for all objects whose state is persistent. For a simple implementation, it is sufficient to use Java class `HashMap` to maintain the active OIDs. In the Navajo system, the OID is defined as a 32-bit integer and the `HashMap` implementation is optimized for integer use.

Figure 8.2 | **Object life cycle.**

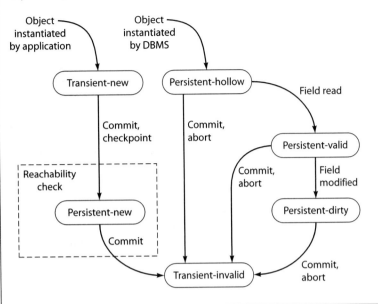

8.5   Transaction Management

In client-server application scenarios, multiple databases or resources are often part of a single transaction. Embedded devices normally never use more than one database in this way. However, because multi-threading is part of the Java programming language, creating a thread is a simple task and it is common to create multiple transactions running in parallel, in different threads. One part of the transaction management keeps track of the assignment among threads, databases, and transactions. The ODMG API specifies that during the executing of a thread exactly one transaction and one database are active.

```
Database db = odmg.newDatabase();

Transaction txn = imp.newTransaction();
// the transaction is assigned to the current data-
base db
txn.begin();
// the transaction is assigned to the current thread

Object obj = db.lookup("Name");
// obj is assigned to the current transaction "txn"
```

Figure 8.3 | **Transaction and object management.**

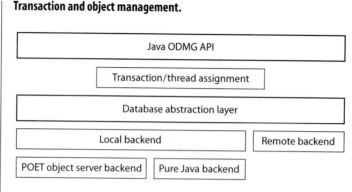

The assignment of a database or transaction to the current thread is possible only by using thread local storage. To get thread local storage, another `HashMap` needs to be implemented. Transaction management is implemented in the top layer of the API (Figure 8.3). Monitoring which objects belong to which transaction and which objects are modified, inserted, or deleted are part of the second layer.

Figure 8.3 illustrates the components that are part of the transaction and object management. The topmost layer implements the ODMG interfaces (database, transaction, and collection interfaces). After selecting the right transaction context, calls are delegated to the abstract database layer. The implementations POET object server and pure Java share a common codebase, called local backend. The remote backend component is discussed later.

8.6   Concurrency Control

To keep data in a consistent state, clients can lock objects against conflicting accesses by other clients. There are three levels of locking: read locks, write locks, and delete locks. A substantial component of the system implements pessimistic locking based on strict two-phase locking (strict2pl). During the first phase, locks are granted to the application; unlocking takes place during the second phase. It has been a great challenge to optimize this with respect to performance and code size. Modular design allows concurrency control to be easily replaced by alternative implementations.

The smallest element that can be locked is a single object. The lock scheduler is based on OIDs, which are kept as long integer values. Another attribute of a lock element is the corresponding transaction. When the transaction commits or aborts, all locks held by the transaction are released. The lock management also supports nested transactions (Moss 1985), where locks are kept until the top-level transaction commits or aborts. The current release of the POET Object Server Suite provides three implementations for concurrency management. They are optimized for different application domains and can be selected during application startup. The first implementation has been developed as a replacement for relational databases' locking management and is used together with POET's object-relational mapper. It is the codebase of the other two implementations. The second implementation can be used via Java Remote Method Invocation (RMI) if the lock service runs on a different machine. The third implementation reduces network traffic in scenarios where read access happens much more often than write-delete access. It also works in concert with an object cache that can be used among multiple transactions.

8.7   Backend

The backend module is used to store and load objects to and from a disk file and to create and manage indices and extents. In object-oriented database systems, an extent can be defined as the set of all currently existing instances of a class. An extent has a special index based on the OID. Other indexes can be defined by the application developer and may contain one or more fields of a class or its parent classes.

Basically, all backend services run under the control of a transaction. It must be possible to roll back all operations performed by a service. For example, if some objects have been inserted into the database and, at the end of the whole transaction, a constraint has been violated (e.g., a unique index condition), all newly stored objects have to be deleted and the index entries have to be rolled back.

The backend is split into the following components, which can be replaced by different implementations.

TreeIndexService. Creation and management of index trees.

NamingService. Lookup of objects by name.

BufferService. Creation and modification of buffer pages used for persistent objects and index trees.

FreeSpaceManager. Management of unused or deleted buffer pages.

For embedded devices, an implementation of a query engine based on the Object Query Language (OQL) was not considered because it would have exceeded the code-size requirements. Instead, an application can use the indexing feature to retrieve ordered collections of objects or to select ranges based on one or more fields of a class.

8.8 Distributed Applications

Traditional database systems provide a client-server interface to allow multiple clients to access a common database from different systems or processes. An object-oriented database server typically falls into one of two types: a page server, which transfers memory pages, or an object server such as POET. Navajo itself does not provide a client-server interface because it is not needed in embedded environments. If the application needs to be as small as possible, for instance to be downloaded from the internet, it can be split into a distributed application. To help application developers write distributed applications, a persistent class can be split into a remote part and a local part. This is called an ultra-thin-client (UTC) application. In addition, the database system provides a server component, which supports the server part of the application. The main application contains applets or other programs running as part of a web browser.

To use the UTC module, all persistent classes must inherit from remote interface declarations.

```
interface Account extends Remote {
    double getBalance() throws RemoteException;
    Person getOwner() throws RemoteException;
}
```

On the server side, these interfaces have to be implemented:

```
Public class AccountImpl implements Account {
    double balance;
    double getBalance() { return balance };
    Person getOwner() { ... };
}
```

The facilities of the Java RMI system are used in this case, but other distribution services such as Common Object Request Broker Architecture (CORBA) could be used. Navajo provides additional classes to invoke ODMG methods remotely via these services and keeps track of remote and local persistent objects. One part of the server component needs to create server-side implementations of the persistent classes and the client side has to get the right stub objects, which implement the remote interface. The stub objects transfer the parameters and return values of the RMI over the network. To achieve persistence by reachability the client- and server-side references have to be kept in synchronization.

8.9 **Event Management**

Sometimes, applications have to react to specific database operations under certain circumstances or they have to initialize transient data of objects when the objects are retrieved. When a class implements the Constraint interface, the appropriate constraint method will be called when a specific database operation takes place.

```
Public class Person implements Constraints {
  Address address;
  Date born;
  transient int age;

  public void postRead() {
    age = ...
  }
  public void preWrite() {

    ...

  }
  public void preDelete() {
    db.deletePersistent(address);
  }
}
```

Here, the age member is not stored in the database, but will be recalculated when the object is loaded into memory.

Although the ODMG model specifies that objects are deleted by a persistent garbage collector if they are no longer reachable by root objects, in reality this is of little use. By overloading the preDelete() method, an application can delete dependent objects or references from lists. If the application can accurately delete dependent objects, garbage-collection operations can be avoided.

The database system triggers events for selected operations based on the Java Beans (Hamilton 1997) event model (java.util.EventListener). The application may subscribe to such events and will receive a callback when the following operations occur:

● Database. Open and close.

● Transactions. Begin, commit, checkpoint, and abort.

● Object management. Activation, deactivation, read, write, and delete during a specific transaction.

● Operations of other clients. Insert, update, and delete operations as part of a database.

- Concurrency. Locking and unlocking.
- Warnings and exceptions.

For example, if the application must listen to all object modifications, the OperationListener callback interface has to be implemented.

```
public class MyEventHandler extends OperationListener
{
    public void inserted(OperationEvent e)
    {
        ... handle inserted objects ...
    }
    public void updated(OperationEvent e)
    {
        ... handle updated objects ...
    }
    public void deleted(OperationEvent e)
    {
        ... handle deleted objects ...
    }
}
```

To register event notification when Person objects are modified, the developer has to acquire an event support interface:

```
OperationEventSupport support =
  EventServices.current().
    getOperationEventSupport(db, Person.class);
```

The following code registers an event-handler instance:

```
MyEventHandler listener = new MyEventHandler();
support.addOperationListener(listener);
```

As opposed to the Constraints interface, modifications of objects in other transactions will be notified as well. For example, a mail application can display incoming messages whenever the message transfer service retrieves new messages.

8.10 Log Service

Connectivity is a very important aspect of embedded devices. Often the devices are connected directly to a PC or another backup media from

Figure 8.4 | **Log service.**

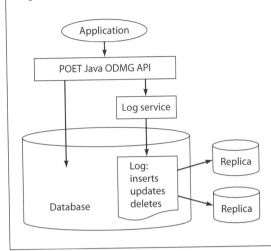

time to time in order to synchronize data and perform other functions. The database system therefore supplies a log service to support synchronization between the embedded device and a PC or network that can be activated by the application.

The log service (Figure 8.4) is based on the event service and saves modifications made during a transaction and the transaction boundaries. The service is not implemented as another process or thread, but will be called at the end of a transaction while data are committed to the backend. The callback interface is registered with the event service in the same manner as regular applications are implemented. All transaction operations, such as updates, inserts, and deletes, can be stored in one or more replicas. At a later time, the replicas can be read to update other media or PCs and the database.

8.11   Postprocessing

To make Java classes persistence-capable in a transparent manner, it is necessary to change the Java source code before compilation takes place (preprocessing) or to change the Java byte code (postprocessing).

The Java source or byte code has to be modified in two ways. First, direct access to persistent fields of any object in memory has to be modified into a method call because the object has to be filled with valid data loaded from the database. When the object's data are changed, the object has to be protected against multiple access (via write lock) and it has to be marked as modified. The second modification is done on persistent classes only. These get some extra fields for persistence information, status, transaction context, and OID. Also, because not all fields of a class may be accessible by the database system—because, for example, they are not declared `public`—these fields have to be accessed by set and get methods such as `_pt_getFlags()`. Another access problem arises if the whole class is declared package visible or local. Therefore, another class is created that works as a factory for instances of a persistent class.

The following code illustrates the annotation or enhancement of the field access.

```
String name = person.name;
```

will become

```
String name = person._pt_preRead().name;
```

The `_pt_preRead` method calls the database API to load the content of the `person` object from the database.

8.12   On-Demand Assembly of Components

The Java language is capable of loading classes at runtime. This feature is used at some key points in POET's Java Binding. A database abstraction layer shown in Figure 8.3 is based on several interfaces and a factory class. While the application opens a database, an instance of the factory must be created.

The protocol part of the database uniform resource locator (URL) defines the factory's class name:

```
String protocol = url.getProtocol();
Class factoryClass = Class.forName("com.poet.database.
                           "+protocol+".Factory");
```

In this case the URL `poet://LOCAL/my_base` results in a class named `com.poet.database.poet.Factory` being loaded.

To create a new instance of the factory, `newInstance` is called. This generic access of Java classes is called reflection.

```
Factory factoryInstance = (Factory)
                           factoryClass.newInstance();
```

A problem arises when parts of the implementation should be reused, but others should not. For this reason all implementations of the database abstraction interfaces must implement a method to return the factory, for example,

```
Factory factoryInstance = database.getFactory();
```

The factory itself can create several different instances of the underlying implementation classes.

```
ITransaction txn = factory.newTransaction();

...

IQuery query = txn.getFactory().newQuery();
query.execute(...);
```

Other components of the database system require just the creation of a single instance to select various implementations. In this case, the implementing class can be created directly. For example, a concurrency control service is selected by

```
String name = ... read from configuration file ...;
ConcurrencyService ccs = (ConcurrencyService)
    (Class.forName("com.poet.ccs."+name+".
    Scheduler").newInstance());
```

Application deployment is difficult if Class.forName is used. By loading classes late, the Java compiler cannot check whether a named class implements the interface. This is done at runtime by typecasting the object to the interface class (ConcurrencyService in this example).

To allow the assembly of components by the application developer, all classes needed for a specific component must be collected in a Java archive file (*.jar). It is hard to cope with dependency checking and deployment of the database system if some components share the same code and if memory consumption is an issue.

8.13 Outlook

In 1999 the ODMG standard was further developed and the new Java collection types were added to the specification. During this process, POET had already developed a first version based on the new specification. Since the beginning of 2000, the new ODMG 3.0 standard (Cattell et al. 2000) has been available and Navajo conforms to this standard, except for OQL. In autumn 1999, the Java group at POET also implemented ODMG 3.0 interfaces for POET's Object Server Suite and shared the codebase with Navajo.

As part of the Java Community Process—an expert group of database vendors, academics, and application developers—a new transparent database API has been specified. The Java Data Objects (JDO) specification has been released to the public in June 2000 (Sun Microsystems 2000).

9 Conclusions and Perspectives

Andreas Geppert
Klaus R. Dittrich
University of Zurich

In this chapter, we summarize achievements, identify open issues, and discuss perspectives for future research.

9.1   Achievements

It is pretty clear that current and future challenging requirements for database technology, as they are currently being formulated, cannot be met any longer by traditional database management system (DBMS) architectures. Any attempt to offer all the required functions in a single monolithic system off the shelf is doomed to failure. Instead, piecemeal enhancements to systems are much more promising for many reasons, including system complexity and maintainability, runtime performance, and cost.

Extensibility, in turn, is a goal easy to state yet difficult to achieve. In order to attain extensibility (and the related objective of software reuse), proven software engineering paradigms and techniques must be adapted. As the chapters in this book show, component orientation is a viable paradigm that renders extensibility and reuse of DBMS artifacts achievable.

The concept "component" is useful in representing extensions in four ways. First, one meaning of component is a DBMS-internal part that implements a new, nonstandard, or specialized DBMS function. The DBMS is then understood as a framework into which these new or adapted components can be plugged. Therefore, the DBMS needs to be componentized at least in those places where new components should be added. This is the approach pursued by universal servers such as DB2 (Chapter 4), Informix (Chapter 2), and Oracle8 (Chapter 3). These three systems are also examples of products that are available in the marketplace. The vendors (and, further, third parties) also already offer numerous extensions.

Second, wrapper-like components can be used to integrate external data stores into a coherent entirety. In this case, the major task of a component is to mediate between the database middleware and the data sources. This is an important task because data sources in practice are very diverse and no assumptions about standard interfaces of data sources can be reasonably made. Database middleware allows components to be pushed between the middleware and the data sources. In this way, data sources can be smoothly integrated into a coherent whole, while the middleware is not required to be aware of the data sources' intricacies. This meaning of component is prevalent in modern database middleware such as Garlic (Chapter 6) and OLE DB (Chapter 5).

Third, a component can be understood as a stand-alone database service providing some unbundled form of database functionality. This approach is exemplified by some of the CORBAservices, which offer database services such as queries and transactions. One possible application of such services is their use for the construction of the integration layer of a multidatabase system (Chapter 7).

Ultimately, we can envision a DBMS as a software system fully built out of components—the fourth meaning of component. If it were possible to build a new DBMS by plugging together several components, one for each required function, then DBMS construction would be much faster and cheaper than it is today. As shown by Navajo (Chapter 8), a stripped-down DBMS to be run on a mobile device can be build in a very cost-effective way using a configurable DBMS.

Summarizing, we consider it as a major achievement in database technology that different forms of component orientation now enable extensions and reuse in many different ways. The extensibility of DBMSs has been investigated for a long time in academia and industry, and we consider it as a great success story for database research that many of the results obtained are now available in products. However, numerous open issues and areas for further research remain. We address some of these in the next section.

9.2 Open Issues

To achieve some purposes, the various approaches represented in this collection can be used. For example, the integration of distributed heterogeneous systems can be done by using CORBA and CORBAservices, using database middleware such as OLE/DB and Garlic, migrating the data to a universal server or using other extensibility features of a universal server (e.g., as in Reinwald et al. 1999). It is currently not yet obvious what the best solution for a specific application scenario would be and whether all these competing approaches will continue to coexist.

Decisive criteria that will impact the outcome of this competition are support for the right set of components, appropriate support for application development, performance, adequate support for the development of components, and management of component libraries.

9.2.1 Adequate Support for Components

Supporting the right set of required components at the right level will have a major impact on the success of component DBMSs (CDBMSs). CDBMSs promise nonstandard functionality in the form of extensions. This means that a system (or an approach in general) is only practicable for users if the right components are available in the first place. This is an issue, for instance, with regard to CORBAservices, for which there is not yet a rich set of implementations of services available in the marketplace. The success of middleware approaches, on the other hand, depends on the availability of a sufficient number of wrappers for commonly encountered data sources.

In addition to offering the right set of components, the components must also offer their functionality in a way that is adequate for their applications' needs. This is a hard problem because requirements for any one component may be varied, and it is hard to foresee all future requirements. In other words, component providers face the design-for-reuse problem. One difficult decision (in the case of plug-in CDBMSs and universal servers) is to distinguish commonly used functionality from functionality used only in special cases. The first should be incorporated into components, while the latter should be left to applications.

9.2.2 Application Development Using CDBMSs

The development of applications also needs to be extended for CDBMSs. In order to use CDBMSs successfully, several open questions must be addressed: How should the right technology and representative of the chosen technology be selected? Can adequate components be found? Can conceptual and logical database design techniques be extended for CDBMSs? Can physical database design techniques be adapted to CDBMSs?

Whenever a new application with nonstandard requirements for the database technology is to be developed, it first has to be decided which technology and platform to use. As described previously, for some tasks several of the approaches represented in this book are applicable. Sound decisions about which approach to pursue require a thorough understanding of the strengths and weaknesses of the various possibilities. Furthermore, guidelines are needed regarding which technology to choose in which case (e.g., database middleware should be used if data cannot be moved to a single data store).

Second, once the technology to use has been chosen, an adequate representative of it needs to be selected. For instance, if it has been decided that universal servers are the way to go, then a concrete DBMS from this class has to be chosen. This kind of decision (if it is not already predefined) depends on new criteria. In particular, depending on the availability, functionality, and performance of these components, we might favor one system over another. Likewise, the possibility of adding home-grown components and the kind of support available for building these components will have an impact on their selection.

Using components requires that the adequate components can be found in the first place—a typical problem in software reuse. As long as the number of candidate components is rather small, this is not a big issue. However, if the number of components is large and many competing providers offer similar components, selecting the best component turns into a major problem in application design.

Moreover, enterprises also have the option to build components themselves. This make-or-buy decision further aggravates the problem of finding components. Such decisions depend on how many requirements candidate components meet, the expected cost of development of home-grown components, their expected reuse potential, and whether the required expertise is actually available. Again, guidelines are required to help users reach an informed decision.

Database design methods also need to be adapted to CDBMSs. In the case of universal servers, the type system is no longer fixed because new components might have been added. Therefore, traditional conceptual database design using the entity-relationship (ER) model (Chen 1976) and fixed transformations into a logical schema are no longer sufficient because then the components and the data types they introduce cannot be optimally exploited. Instead, these transformations must be capable of taking into account the data types and operations provided by the components. Thus, we face the question of how (conceptually and logically) to design schemas in a way that takes extensions into account. One possibility is to adapt object-oriented methods (such as those based on the Unified Modeling Language, UML, Booch et al. 1998) to database design.

Database design for database middleware (and CORBA) is far from being completely understood. Wrappers and the middleware mainly provide the necessary infrastructure for the integration of data sources. The actual integration of data-source schemas into the middleware schema still has to be done by the schema designer. So far, middleware provides little support to that end beyond standard mappings and conversions of data types. There is currently no support whatsoever that takes into account the semantics of the data exported by the involved wrappers. How to represent the semantics of data sources and use it during integration is still an open research issue.

Similar to logical database design, physical database design and tuning have become more complicated. In a traditional database system, tuning guides advise administrators when to define indexes. Some DBMSs are even able to propose the definition of indexes for a given query load (e.g., Valentin et al. 2000). In the case in which multiple kinds of index types such as B-trees and hashing are supported, administrators also can get hints about which kind of index to use in a specific situation. Because index types could also be user-defined, physical database design is more complex because an already existing user-defined index type could be instantiated instead of a built-in one. Moreover, in extreme situations, database administrators could even consider defining their own index type. Thus, database administrators have more options than before and need advice about which option to choose in a concrete situation.

9.2.3 Performance Issues

CDBMSs will only be successful if they are able to deliver their increased functionality with runtime performance comparable to traditional approaches that do not use components.

Therefore, the first open research issue that needs to be addressed is how good or bad the performance of a CDBMS actually is when compared to traditional approaches. Intuitively, we might expect that performance of CDBMS degrades because their extended functionality implies a performance penalty and many code optimizations that are possible in a monolithic approach are not possible in a componentized system. On the other hand, there are also valid reasons to expect performance improvements.

- Universal servers and database middleware allow data that would otherwise have to be collected from multiple stores to be queried using the CDBMS only. This is expected to be more efficient than asking several queries and then combining the results in an application.

- Universal servers and database middleware can optimize queries in a much more sophisticated way.

- Universal servers allow specialized index types to be defined, which also improves query-processing performance.

- Applications become thinner because they are freed from the tasks of integrating nonstandard data and combining results from multiple queries against diverse data sources.

The last point especially indicates that it is not really meaningful to compare the performance of traditional database systems with their componentized counterparts. Instead, entire applications should be considered, and their traditional implementation should be compared to one using a CDBMS. Appropriate benchmarks and performance analyses are still open research problems.

Further performance problems are specific to the kind of CDBMS considered in this book. Because in plug-in CDBMSs internal parts can be extended and modified, robustness becomes an issue. Errors in extensions (such as user-defined functions) should not cause damage to the DBMS kernel. To that end, extensions (optionally) execute in a separate address space so that a crash in an extension cannot take the server down as well. Using different address spaces for the kernel and the extensions, however, implies performance degradations. For this and other reasons, extensions such as user-defined functions incur a high overhead, especially when invoked many times in a single query. Therefore, high performance without compromising robustness is still an open issue in universal servers.

Finally, different ways to implement new index types have been proposed, for example, generalized search trees (GiST) (Hellerstein et al. 1995), index-organized tables (Srinivasan et al. 2000), and general-ized extended secondary indexes (Chen et al. 1999). How these options can be compared with respect to ease-of-use and with respect to achievable performance is another open research issue.

9.2.4   Development of CDBMS Components

Support for the systematic development of components is of para-mount importance for the future of CDBMSs. Three kind of developers can be distinguished.

- Vendors, who have all the information necessary to develop compo-nents, such as internal interfaces.
- Third-party component providers, who can team up with a vendor.
- End users, who have to use a CDBMS as is.

Any group of developers is confronted with the aforementioned design-for-reuse problem. A component must not only meet the requirements at hand, but should also be reusable for future applica-tions (whose requirements might be different from the current ones). Therefore, the problem is to find out which functions are commonly required of the components and which functions are best left to appli-cations. This is a problem particularly for universal servers and config-urable DBMSs. However, it is a problem for database services only when the interfaces of the services have to be defined—once this has been done, the interfaces are standardized and any implementation has to conform to them.

New components usually modify DBMS internals (in the case of plug-in CDBMSs and configurable DBMSs) or at least affect the way a CDBMS processes its requests (e.g., query optimization in database middleware). Therefore, bugs or inconsistencies in components can cause severe damage in the database or DBMS. We have already men-tioned the example of user-defined functions in universal servers that can cause the DBMS to crash when they are incorrect. Protecting the DBMS from new components (as in the fenced mode of user-defined functions) results in performance degradation; so this is not an option for components for applications with high performance requirements. Another example is the optimizer hints (such as cost-model informa-tion) in universal servers or database middleware—if this information is incorrect, the query optimizer is no longer able to determine optimal query-execution plans.

These problems are especially crucial for components developed by end users, for whom adequate support for developing, validating, and testing home-grown components is of utmost importance. Without such support (and the corresponding tools), component development might be possible only for vendors and those third parties who cooper-ate closely with a vendor.

9.3   The End (Is Not Yet Near)

We might ask whether componentization of database functionality has already come to an end, that is, whether every aspect that needs to be and can be componentized has been considered already. If not, what else needs to be componentized—where will componentization end?

For many kinds of componentizations and extensions, a domino effect can be observed—for functional and performance reasons, componentization in one area often implies the need for componentization of other areas as well. An example is concurrency control for indexes. Indexes are hot spots in a database system. Therefore, in order to prevent lock contention on index pages, specialized concurrency control protocols have been devised for indexes such as B-trees (Bayer & Schkolnick 1977). Hence, when a new index type is introduced into the DBMS, it might for performance reasons also be required to adapt concurrency control for this index type. This is, however, only possible if the lock manager is extensible and componentized at least to some degree. The componentization of lock managers in turn affects logging, recovery, and so on. How DBMSs can be componentized further is therefore a challenging research question. On the other hand, extensions to critical parts such as the transaction and lock manager might better be reserved for the vendors. Therefore, another problem is how far componentization and the possibility of users adding their own components can be reasonably pushed.

Database middleware is another typical case where functional reasons demand a higher degree of componentization. Here many questions concerning query processing and optimization have already been solved. How to offer further database functions such as transaction management and consistency-constraint enforcement in such an environment needs much more research. Transaction management is necessary to allow updates of data sources via the database middleware. A particular problem in this respect is that data sources might not be able to participate in a two-phase commit or even that they might not offer transaction management at all on the local level. Therefore, we face the open research question of how to provide data sources with transaction management in such a way that global transactions are possible.

The case of consistency constraints is similar—once database middleware helps to integrate diverse data sources, it should also be possible to formulate, check, and eventually enforce consistency constraints across data sources. Again, the data sources might not be able or willing to contribute to such a task. Hence, how to componentize consistency constraint management and how to use such components in database middleware are two more research questions. Extending database middleware toward the support of all major database functions is a major research challenge. Certainly, it can only be successfully addressed based on some form of componentization.

All approaches to CDBMSs assume there are a fixed part and variable parts that can be extended or customized by components. The fixed part is usually obtained by using (and successively componentizing) an already existing DBMS, and we therefore have to cope with restrictions imposed by the DBMS used as a platform. An alternative construction theory for CDBMSs is based on a kernel DBMS (an analogy to microkernel operating systems), which provides the very basic and commonly used DBMS functions and which also offers hooks to add extensions. Many research questions related to such a construction theory are still open: What is a kernel DBMS? What would it offer right away, and what kind of functionality would have to be added in components? How can components be added so that overall system consistency is maintained?

Using component orientation, database technology has come a long way to meet the new challenges encountered in numerous current applications. Despite the many problems that have already been addressed, many open questions remain that require more research. Therefore, although much has been achieved already and is usable in practice, the good news for the next generation(s) of doctoral students is that interesting and challenging topics are abundant.

Bibliography

Ahmed, R., P. De Smedt, W. Du, W. Kent, M. A. Ketabchi, W. Litwin, A. Rafii, and M.-C. Shan. 1991. The Pegasus Heterogeneous Multidatabase System. *IEEE Computer*, Vol. 24, No. 12, pp. 19–27.

ANSI. 1999a. Information Technology—Database Languages: SQL, 2. Foundation (SQL/Foundation), ANSI/ISO/IEC 9075-2. American National Standards Institute.

ANSI. 1999b. SQLJ, 1. ANSI X3H2-99-284. American National Standards Institute.

Aoki, P. M. 1998. Generalizing "Search" in Generalized Search Trees. *Proceedings of the 14th International Conference on Data Engineering,* Orlando, FL, February, pp. 380–389.

Allen, P., and S. Frost. 1998. *Component-Based Development for Enterprise Systems,* Cambridge University Press, Cambridge.

Astrahan, M. M., M. W. Blasgen, D. D. Chamberlin, K. P. Eswaran, J. N. Gray, P. P. Griffiths, W. F. King, R. A. Lorie, P. R. McJones, J. W. Mehl, G. R. Putzolu, I. L. Traiger, B. W. Wade, and V. Watson. 1976. System R: Relational Approach to Database Management. *ACM Transactions on Database Systems*, Vol. 1, No. 2, pp. 97–137.

Atkinson, M. P., F. Bancilhon, D. J. DeWitt, K. R. Dittrich, D. Maier, and S. B. Zdonik. 1989. The Object-Oriented Database System Manifesto (a Political Pamphlet). *Proceedings of the 1st International Conference on Deductive and Object-Oriented Databases,* Kyoto, Japan, December, pp. 223–240.

Baeza-Yates, R., and G. Navarro. 1996. Integrating Contents and Structure in Text Retrieval. SIGMOD Record, Vol. 25, No. 1, pp. 67–79.

Bancilhon, F., C. Delobel, and P. C. Kanellakis (eds.). 1992. *Building an Object-Oriented Database System.* Morgan Kaufmann Publishers, San Francisco.

Batory, D. S., J. R. Barnett, J. F. Garza, K. P. Smith, K. Tsukuda, B. C. Twichell, and T. E. Wise. 1988a. GENESIS: An Extensible Database Management System. *IEEE Transactions on Software Engineering,* Vol. 14, No. 11, pp. 1711–1730.

Batory, D. S., T. Y. Leung, and T. E. Wise. 1988b. Implementation Concepts for an Extensible Data Model and Data Language. *ACM Transactions on Database Systems,* Vol. 13, No. 3, pp. 231–262.

Batory, D., and S. O'Malley. 1992. The Design and Implementation of Hierarchical Software Systems with Reusable Components. *ACM Transactions on Software Engineering and Methodology,* Vol. 1, No. 4, pp. 355–398.

Bayer, R. 1996. The Universal B-Tree for Multidimensional Indexing. Technical Report I9639. Technische Universität München, Munich, Germany.

Bayer, R., and E. M. McCreight. 1972. Organization and Maintenance of Large Ordered Indices. *Acta Informatica,* Vol. 1, No. 3, pp. 173–189.

Bayer, R., and M. Schkolnick. 1977. Concurrency of Operations on B-Trees. *Acta Informatica,* Vol. 9, pp. 1–21.

Berchtold, S., C. Böhm, and H.-P. Kriegel. 1998. The Pyramid-Technique: Towards Breaking the Curse of Dimensionality. *Proceedings of the ACM SIGMOD International Conference on Management of Data,* Seattle, WA, June, pp. 142–153.

Bernstein, P. A., and E. Newcomer. 1996. *Principles of Transaction Processing for the Systems Professional.* Morgan Kaufmann Publishers, San Francisco.

Biliris, A. 1992. An Efficient Database Storage Structure for Large Dynamic Objects. *Proceedings of the 8th International Conference on Data Engineering,* Tempe, AZ, pp. 301–308.

Biliris, A., and E. Panagos. 1995. A High Performance Configurable Storage Manager. *Proceedings of the 11th International Conference on Data Engineering,* Taipei, Taiwan, March, pp. 35–43.

Blakeley, J. A. 1994. Open OODB: Architecture and Query Processing Overview. In A. Dogac, T. M. Ozsu, A. Biliris, and T. Sellis (eds.), *Computer and System Sciences,* Vol. 130, *Advances in Object-Oriented Database Systems,* pp. 309–325. Springer, New York.

Blakeley, J. A. 1996a. Data Access for the Masses through OLE DB. *Proceedings of the ACM SIGMOD International Conference on Management of Data,* Montreal, Canada, June, pp. 161–172.

Blakeley, J. A. 1996b. OLE DB: A Component DBMS Architecture. *Proceedings of the 12th International Conference on Data Engineering,* New Orleans, LA, February/March, pp. 203–204.

Blakeley, J. A., W. J. McKenna, and G. Graefe. 1993. Experiences Building the Open OODB Query Optimizer. *Proceedings of the ACM SIGMOD International Conference on Management of Data,* Washington, DC, May, pp. 287–296.

Bliujute, R., C. S. Jensen, G. Slivinskas, and S. Saltenis. 1999. Developing a DataBlade for a New Index. *Proceedings of the 15th International Conference on Data Engineering,* Sydney, Australia, March, pp. 314–323.

Booch, G., I. Jacobson, and J. Rumbaugh. 1998. *The Unified Modeling Language User Guide.* Addison-Wesley, Reading, MA.

Box, D. 1998. *Essential COM.* Addison Wesley, Reading, MA.

Brinkhoff, T., H.-P. Kriegel, and R. Schneider. 1993. Comparisons of Approximations of Complex Objects Used for Approximation-based Query Processing in Spatial Database Systems. *Proceedings of the 9th International Conference on Data Engineering,* Vienna, Austria, April, pp. 356–374.

Brinkhoff, T., H.-P. Kriegel, R. Schneider, and B. Seeger. 1994. Multi-step Processing of Spatial Joins. *Proceedings of the ACM SIGMOD International Conference on Management of Data,* Minneapolis, MN, May, pp. 40–49.

Bukhres, O., and A. Elmagarmid (eds.). 1996. *Object-Oriented Multidatabase Systems.* Prentice Hall, Upper Saddle River, NJ.

Carey, M., D. Chamberlin, S. Narayanan, B. Vance, D. Doole, S. Rielau, R. Swagerman, and N. Mattos. 1999. O-O, What Have They Done to DB2? *Proceedings of the 25th International Conference on Very Large Data Bases,* Edinburgh, Scotland, September, pp. 542–553.

Carey, M. J., D. J. DeWitt, D. Frank, G. Graefe, J. E Richardson, E. J. Shekita, and M. Muralikrishna. 1991. The Architecture of the EXODUS Extensible DBMS. In K. R. Dittrich, U. Dayal, and A. P. Buchmann (eds.), *On Object-Oriented Database Systems,* pp. 231–256. Springer, Heidelberg, Germany.

Carey, M. J., D. J. DeWitt, G. Graefe, D. M. Haight, J. E. Richardson, D. T. Schuh, E. J. Shekita, and S. L. Vandenberg. 1990. The EXODUS Extensible DBMS Project: An Overview. In S. B. Zdonik and D. Maier (eds.). *Readings in Object-Oriented Database Systems,* pp. 474–499. Morgan Kaufmann Publishers, San Francisco.

Carey, M. J., D. J. DeWitt, J. E. Richardson, and E. J. Shekita. 1986. Object and File Management in the EXODUS Extensible Database System. *Proceedings of the 12th International Conference on Very Large Data Bases,* Kyoto, Japan, August, pp. 91–100.

Carey, M., and L. Haas. 1990. Extensible Database Management Systems. *SIGMOD Record,* Vol. 19, No. 4, pp. 54–60.

Carey, M., L. M. Haas, P. M. Schwarz, M. Arya, W. F. Cody, R. Fagin, M. Flickner, A. W. Luniewski, W. Niblack, D. Petkovic, J. Thomas, J. H. Williams, and E. L. Wimmers. 1995. Towards Heterogeneous Multimedia Information Systems: The Garlic Approach. *Proceedings of the 5th*

International Workshop on Research Issues in Data Engineering—Distributed Object Management, Taipei, Taiwan, March, pp. 124–131.

Cattell, R. G. G., and D. Barry (eds.). 1997. *The Object Database Standard: ODMG 2.0.* Morgan Kaufmann Publishers, San Francisco.

Cattell, R. G. G., D. K. Barry, M. Berler, J. Eastman, D. Jordan, C. Russell, O. Schadow, T. Stanienda, and F. Velez. 2000. *The Object Data Standard: ODMG 3.0.* Morgan Kaufmann Publishers, San Francisco.

CCA. 1982. An Architecture for Database Management Standards. NBS Special Publication 500-85. Computer Corporation of America.

Chamberlin, D. 1998. *A Complete Guide to DB2 Universal Database.* Morgan Kaufmann Publishers, San Francisco.

Chaudhuri, S., and K. Shim. 1993. Query Optimization in the Presence of Foreign Functions. *Proceedings of the 19th International Conference on Very Large Data Bases,* Dublin, Ireland, August, pp. 529–542.

Chaudhuri, S., and K. Shim. 1996. Optimization of Queries with User-defined Predicates. *Proceedings of the 22nd International Conference on Very Large Data Bases,* Bombay, India, September, pp. 87–98.

Chen, P. P. 1976. The Entity-Relationship Model—Towards a Unified View of Data. *ACM Transactions on Database Systems,* Vol. 1, No. 1, pp. 9–36.

Chen, W., J.-H. Chow, Y.-C. Fuh, J. Grandbois, M. Jou, N. Mattos, B. Tran, and Y. Wang. 1999. High Level Indexing of User-Defined Types. *Proceedings of the 25th International Conference on Very Large Data Bases,* Edinburgh, Scotland, September, pp. 554–564.

Chou, H.-T., D. J. DeWitt, R. H. Katz, and A. C. Klug. 1985. Design and Implementation of the Wisconsin Storage System. *Software—Practice and Experience,* Vol. 15, No. 10, pp. 943–962.

Chow, J.-H., J. Cheng, D. Chang, and J. Xu. 1999. Index Design for Structured Documents Based on Abstraction. *Proceedings of the 6th International Conference on Database Systems for Advanced Applications,* Taipei, Taiwan, April, pp. 89–96.

Chrysanthis, P. K. and K. Ramamritham. 1994. Synthesis of Extended Transaction Models Using ACTA. *ACM Transactions on Database Systems,* Vol. 19, No. 3, pp. 450–491.

Codd, E. 1970. A Relational Model for Large Shared Data Banks. *Communications of the ACM,* Vol. 13, No. 6, pp. 377–387.

Cohera. 1999. *Cohera System Administrators Guide.* Cohera Corporation, Hayward, CA.

Comer, D. 1979. The Ubiquitous B-Tree. *ACM Computing Surveys,* Vol. 2, No. 11, pp. 121–137.

Consens, M. P., and T. Milo. 1994. Optimizing Queries on Files. *Proceedings of the ACM SIGMOD International Conference on Management of Data,* Minneapolis, MN, May, pp. 301–312.

Dadam, P., K. Kuespert, F. Andersen, H. Blanken, R. Erbe, J. Guenauer, V. Lum, P. Pistor, and G. Walch. 1986. A DBMS Prototype to Support Extended NF2 Relations: An Integrated View on Flat Tables and Hierarchies. *Proceedings of the ACM SIGMOD International Conference on Management of Data,* Washington, DC, May, pp. 356–367.

Davis, J. R. 2000. IBM DB2 Universal Database: Building Extensible, Scalable Business Solutions. Whitepaper. http://www.software.ibm.com/data/pubs/papers, February.

Deßloch, S., and N. M. Mattos. 1997. Integrating SQL Databases with Content-Specific Search Engines. *Proceedings of the 23rd International Conference on Very Large Data Bases,* Athens, Greece, August, pp. 528–537.

Deux, O. 1990. The Story of O_2. *IEEE Transactions on Knowledge and Data Engineering,* Vol. 2, No. 1, pp. 91–108.

Dittrich, K. R., W. Gotthard, and P. C. Lockemann. 1986. DAMOKLES —A Database System for Software Engineering Environments. In R. Conradi, T. M. Didriksen, and D. H. Wanvik (eds.), *Lecture Notes in Computer Science,* Vol. 244, *Advanced Programming Environments,* pp. 353–371. Springer, Heidelberg, Germany.

Dittrich, K. R., U. Dayal, and A. P. Buchmann (eds.). 1991. *On Object-Oriented Database Systems.* Springer, Heidelberg, Germany.

Dogac, A., C. Dengi, and M. T. Özsu. 1998. Distributed Object Computing Platforms. *Communications of the ACM,* Vol. 41, No. 9, pp. 95–103.

Drew, P., R. King, and D. Heimbigner. 1992. A Toolkit for the Incremental Implementation of Heterogeneous Database Management Systems. *VLDB Journal,* Vol. 1, No. 2, pp. 241–284.

D'Souza, D. F., and A. C. Wills. 1999. *Objects, Components, and Frameworks with UML: The Catalysis Approach.* Addison Wesley, Reading, MA.

Eddon, G., and H. Eddon. 1998. *Inside Distributed COM.* Microsoft Press.

Elmagarmid, A. K. (ed.). 1992. *Database Transaction Models for Advanced Applications.* Morgan Kaufmann Publishers, San Francisco.

Elmagarmid, A., and C. Pu (eds.). 1990. Special Issue on Heterogeneous Databases. *ACM Computing Surveys,* Vol. 22, No. 3.

Elmagarmid, A. K., M. Rusinkiewicz, and A. Sheth (eds.). 1999. *Management of Heterogeneous and Autonomous Database Systems.* Morgan Kaufmann Publishers, San Francisco.

Elshiewy, N. 1995. MAKBIS: Coordinated Access to Heterogeneous and Autonomous Information Systems. *Proceedings of the 5th International Workshop on Research Issues in Data Engineering—Distributed Object Management,* Taipei, Taiwan, March, pp. 92–99.

ESRI. 2000. Environmental System Research Institute (ESRI). http://www.esri.com.

Extensible Markup Language (XML). 1997. http://www.w3.org/TR/WD-xml-lang.

Faloutsos, C., R. Barber, M. Flickner, J. Hafner, W. Niblack, D. Petkovic, and W. Equitz. 1994a. Efficient and Effective Querying by Image Content. *Journal of Intelligent Information Systems,* Vol. 3, pp. 231–262.

Faloutsos, C., M. Ranganathan, and Y. Manolopoulos. 1994b. Fast Subsequence Matching in Time-series Databases. *Proceedings of the ACM SIGMOD International Conference on Management of Data,* Minneapolis, MN, May, pp. 419–429.

de Ferreira Rezende, F., and K. Hergula. 1998. The Heterogeneity Problem and Middleware Technology: Experiences with and Performance of Database Gateways. *Proceedings of the 24th International Conference on Very Large Data Bases,* New York, August, pp. 146–157.

Fritschi, H., S. Gatziu, and K. R. Dittrich. 1998. FRAMBOISE—An Approach to Framework-Based Active Database Management System Construction. *Proceedings of the 7th International Conference on Information and Knowledge Management,* Washington, DC, November, pp. 364–370.

Fuh, Y.-C., S. Deßloch, W. Chen, N. Mattos, B. Tran, B. Lindsay, L. DeMichiel, S. Rielau, and D. Mannhaupt. 1999. Implementation of SQL3 Structured Types with Inheritance and Value Substitutability. *Proceedings of the International Conference on Very Large Data Bases,* Edinburgh, Scotland, September, pp. 565–574.

Gaede, V., and O. Günther. 1998. Multidimensional Access Methods. *ACM Computing Surveys,* Vol. 30, No. 2, pp. 170–231.

Georgakopoulos, D., M. Hornick, P. Krychniak, and F. Manola. 1994. Specification and Management of Extended Transactions in a Programmable Transaction Environment. *Proceedings of the 10th International Conference on Data Engineering,* Houston, TX, February, pp. 462–473.

Geppert, A., and K. R. Dittrich. 1994. Constructing the Next 100 Database Management Systems: Like the Handyman or like the Engineer? *ACM SIGMOD Record,* Vol. 23, No. 1, pp. 27–33.

Geppert, A., and K. R. Dittrich. 1995. Strategies and Techniques: Reusable Artifacts for the Construction of Database Management Systems. *Proceedings of the 7th International Conference on Advanced Information Systems Engineering,* Jyvaskyla, Finland, June, pp. 297–310.

Geppert, A., and K. R. Dittrich. 1998. Bundling: Towards a New Construction Paradigm for Persistent Systems. *Networking and Information Systems Journal,* Vol. 1, No. 1, pp. 69–102.

Geppert, A., S. Scherrer, and K. R. Dittrich. 1997. KIDS: A Construction Approach for Database Management Systems based on Reuse. Technical Report 97.01. Department of Computer Science, University of Zurich.

Goland, Y., J. Whitehead, A. Faizi, S. Carter, and D. Jensen. 1999. HTTP Extensions for Distributed Authoring—WEBDAV. http://www.ics.uci.edu/~ejw/authoring/protocol/rfc2518.txt, February.

Goldman, R., and J. Widom. 1997. DataGuides: Enabling Query Formulation and Optimization in Semistructured Databases. *Proceedings of the International Conference on Very Large Data Bases,* Athens, Greece, August, pp. 436–445.

Gordon, S. R., and J. R. Gordon. 1993. Factors That Affect the Adoption of Distributed Database Management Systems. *Proceedings of the ACM Conference on Computer Personnel Research,* St. Louis, MO, April, pp. 151–167.

Graefe, G. 1993. Query Evaluation Techniques for Large Data Bases. *ACM Computing Surveys,* Vol. 25, No. 2, pp. 73–170.

Graefe, G. 1995. The Cascades Framework for Query Optimization. *Bulletin of the Technical Committee on Data Engineering,* Vol. 18, No. 3, pp. 19–29.

Graefe, G., and D. J. DeWitt. 1987. The EXODUS Optimizer Generator. *Proceedings of the ACM SIGMOD International Conference on Management of Data,* San Francisco, May, pp. 160–172.

Graefe, G., and W. J. McKenna. 1993. The Volcano Optimizer Generator: Extensibility and Efficient Search. *Proceedings of the 9th International Conference on Data Engineering,* Vienna, Austria, April, pp. 209–218.

Gray, J., and A. Reuter. 1992. *Transaction Processing: Concepts and Techniques.* Morgan Kaufmann Publishers, San Francisco.

Griffel, F. 1998. *Componentware.* dpunkt.Verlag, Heidelberg, Germany.

Güting, R. H. 1993. Second-Order Signature: A Tool for Specifying Data Models, Query Processing, and Optimization. *Proceedings of the ACM SIGMOD International Conference on Management of Data,* Washington, DC, May, pp. 277–286.

Guttman, A. 1984. R-trees: A Dynamic Index Structure for Spatial Searching. *Proceedings of the ACM SIGMOD International Conference on Management of Data,* Boston, June, pp. 47–57.

Haas, L. M., W. Chang, G. M. Lohman, J. McPherson, P. F. Wilms, G. Lapis, B. Lindsay, H. Pirahesh, M. J. Carey, and E. Shekita. 1990. Starburst Mid-Flight: As the Dust Clears. *IEEE Transactions on Knowledge and Data Engineering,* Vol. 2, No. 1, pp. 143–160.

Haas, L. M., J. C. Freytag, G. M. Lohman, and H. Pirahesh. 1989. Extensible Query Processing in Starburst. *Proceedings of the ACM SIGMOD International Conference on Management of Data,* Portland, OR, May/June, pp. 377–388.

Haas, L., D. Kossmann, and I. Ursu. 1999. Loading a Cache with Query Results. *Proceedings of the 25th International Conference on Very Large Data Bases,* Edinburgh, Scotland, September, pp. 351–362.

Haas, L., D. Kossmann, E. Wimmers, and J. Yang. 1997. Optimizing Queries Across Diverse Data Sources. *Proceedings of the 23rd International Conference on Very Large Data Bases,* Athens, Greece, August, pp. 276–285.

Hamilton, D. (ed.). 1997. *Java Beans. Version 1.01.* Sun Microsystems.

Härder, T., and E. Rahm. 1999. *Datenbanksysteme. Konzepte und Techniken der Implementierung.* Springer, Heidelberg, Germany.

Härder, T., and A. Reuter. 1983. Concepts for Implementing a Centralized Database Management System. *Proceedings of the International Computing Symposium on Application Systems Development,* Nuremberg, Germany, March.

Hellerstein, J. M., J. F. Naughton, and A. Pfeffer. 1995. Generalized Search Trees for Database Systems. *Proceedings of the 21st International Conference on Very Large Data Bases,* Zurich, Switzerland, September, pp. 562–573.

Hellerstein, J. M., and M. Stonebraker. 1993. Predicate Migration: Optimizing Queries with Expensive Predicates. *Proceedings of the ACM SIGMOD International Conference on Management of Data,* Washington, DC, May, pp. 267–276.

Henning, M., and S. Vinoski. 1999. *Advanced CORBA Programming with C++.* Addison Wesley Longman, Reading, MA.

Homer, A., and D. Sussman. 1998. *Professional MTS and MSMQ Programming with VB and ASP.* Wrox Press.

Hong, E. K. 1993. Performance of Catalog Management Schemes for Running Access Modules in a Locally Distributed Database System. *Proceedings of the 19th International Conference on Very Large Data Bases,* Dublin, Ireland, August, pp. 194–205.

Hoque, R. 1998. *CORBA 3.* IDG Books.

Hornick, M. F., and S. B. Zdonik. 1987. A Shared, Segmented Memory System for an Object-Oriented Database. *ACM Transactions on Office Information Systems,* Vol. 5, No. 1, pp. 70–95.

IBM. 1995. DB2 Relational Extenders. White Paper, IBM Corp.

IBM. 1999. *IBM DB2 Text Extender Adminstration and Programming Guide.* IBM Corp.

Illustra Information Technologies. 1995. *Illustra User's Guide.* Illustra Information Technologies, Oakland, CA.

Informix. 1998. Developing DataBlade Modules for Informix Dynamic Server with Universal Data Option. White Paper, Informix Corp., Menlo Park, CA.

Informix. 2000. *INFORMIX Internet Foundation 2000 Product Documentation.* Informix Software Inc., Menlo Park, CA, http://www.informix.com/answers/english/iif2000.htm, February.

Jagadish, H. V. 1990. Linear Clustering of Objects with Multiple Attributes. *Proceedings of the ACM SIGMOD International Conference on Management of Data,* Atlantic City, NJ, May, pp. 332–342.

Kabra, N., and D. J. DeWitt. 1999. OPT++: An Object-Oriented Implementation for Extensible Database Query Optimization. *VLDB Journal,* Vol. 8, No. 1, pp. 55–78.

Kapitskaia, O., A. Tomasic, and P. Valduriez. 1997. Dealing with Discrepancies in Wrapper Functionality. INRIA Technical Report RR-3138. INRIA.

Kim, W. (ed.). 1995. *Modern Database Systems: The Object Model, Interoperability, and Beyond.* ACM Press and Addison-Wesley, Reading, MA.

Knuth, D. 1998. *The Art of Computer Programming.* Volume 2. *Sorting and Searching,* 3rd ed. Addison-Wesley, Menlo Park.

Kornacker, M. 1999. High-Performance Extensible Indexing. *Proceedings of the 25th International Conference on Very Large Data Bases,* Edinburgh, Scotland, September, pp. 699–708.

Kornacker, M., C. Mohan, and J. M. Hellerstein. 1997. Concurrency and Recovery in Generalized Search Trees. *Proceedings of the ACM SIGMOD International Conference on Management of Data,* Tucson, AZ, May, pp. 62–72.

Krieger, D., and R. M. Adler. 1998. The Emergence of Distributed Component Platforms. *IEEE Computer,* Vol. 31, No. 3, pp. 43–53.

Krueger, C. W. 1992. Software Reuse. *ACM Computing Surveys,* Vol. 24, No. 2, pp. 131–183.

Lamb, C., G. Landis, J. Orenstein, and D. Weinreb. 1991. The Object-Store Database System. *Communications of the ACM,* Vol. 34, No. 10, pp. 50–63.

Levy, A., A. Rajaraman, and J. J. Ordille. 1996. Querying Heterogeneous Information Sources Using Source Descriptions. *Proceedings of the 22nd International Conference on Very Large Data Bases,* Bombay, India, September, pp. 251–262.

Lienert, D. 1987. *Die Konfigurierung modular aufgebauter Datenbanksysteme.* Informatik Fachberichte 137. Springer, Heidelberg, Germany.

Lindsay, B., J. McPherson, and H. Pirahesh. 1987. A Data Management Extension Architecture. *Proceedings of the ACM SIGMOD International Conference on Management of Data,* San Francisco, May, pp. 220–226.

Linnemann, V., K. Küspert, P. Dadam, P. Pistor, R. Erbe, A. Kemper, N. Suedkamp, G. Walch, and M. Wallrath. 1988. Design and Implementation of an Extensible Database Management System Supporting User Defined Data Types and Functions. *Proceedings of the 14th International Conference on Very Large Data Bases,* Los Angeles, August/September, pp. 294–305.

Lohman, G. M. 1988. Grammar-like Functional Rules for Representing Query Optimization Alternatives. *Proceedings of the ACM SIGMOD International Conference on Management of Data,* Chicago, June, pp. 18–27.

Lu, H., and M. Carey. 1985. Some Experimental Results on Distributed Join Algorithms in a Local Network. *Proceedings of the 11th International Conference on Very Large Data Bases,* Stockholm, Sweden, August, pp. 292–304.

Lynch, C. A., and M. Stonebraker. 1988. Extended User-Defined Indexing with Applications to Textual Databases. *Proceedings of the 14th International Conference on Very Large Data Bases,* Los Angeles, August/September, pp. 306–317.

Mackert, L., and G. Lohman. 1988. R* Optimizer Validation and Performance Evaluation for Distributed Queries. *Proceedings of the 12th International Conference on Very Large Data Bases,* Kyoto, Japan, August, pp. 149–159.

Manber, U., S. Wu, and B. Gopal. 2000. Glimpse. http://glimpse.cs.arizona.edu/.

McHugh, J., S. Abiteboul, R. Goldman, D. Quass, and J. Widom. 1997. Lore: A Database Management System for Semistructured Data. *ACM SIGMOD Record,* Vol. 26, No. 3, pp. 54–66.

McKenna, W. J., L. Burger, C. Hoang, and M. Truong. 1996. EROC: A Toolkit for Building NEATO Query Optimizers. *Proceedings of the 22nd*

International Conference on Very Large Data Bases, Bombay, India, September, pp. 111–121.

Melton, J., and A. R. Simon. 1996. *Understanding the New SQL: A Complete Guide.* Morgan Kaufmann Publishers, San Francisco.

Microsoft. 1966. *OLE DB Programmer's Reference. Version 1.0,* Vol. 2. Microsoft Corp.

Microsoft. 1997a. *Automation Programmer's Reference: Using ActiveX Technology to Create Programmable Applications.* Microsoft Press.

Microsoft. 1997b. *ODBC 3.0 Programmer's Reference and SDK Guide.* Microsoft Press.

Microsoft. 1998. *Microsoft OLE DB 2.0 Programmer's Reference and Data Access SDK.* Microsoft Press.

Microsoft. 1999a. Microsoft Data Access Components (MDAC) 2.0. Microsoft Corp. http://www.microsoft.com/data.

Microsoft. 1999b. *Microsoft OLE DB 2.5 Programmer's Reference.* Microsoft Corp. http://msdn.microsoft.com.

Moss, J. E. B. 1985. *Nested Transactions: An Approach to Reliable Distributed Computing.* MIT Press, Cambridge, MA.

Niblack, W., R. Barber, W. Equitz, M. Flickner, E. H. Glasman, D. Petkovic, P. Yanker, C. Faloutsos, and G. Taubin. 1993. The QBIC Project: Querying Images by Content Using Color, Texture and Shape. *Proceedings of the SPIE Conference,* San Jose, CA, February, pp. 173–187.

Nierstrasz, O., and L. Dami. 1995. Component-Oriented Software Technology. In O. Nierstrasz and D. Tsichritzis (eds.), *Object-Oriented Software Composition,* pp. 3–28. Prentice Hall, London.

Nierstrasz, O., and T. D. Meijler. 1998. Beyond Objects: Components. In M. P. Papazoglou and G. Schlageter (eds.), *Cooperative Information Systems: Trends and Directions,* pp. 49–78. Academic Press, San Diego, CA.

Nittel, S., and K. R. Dittrich. 1996. A Storage Server for the Efficient Support of Complex Objects. *Proceedings of the 7th International Workshop on Persistent Object Systems,* Cape May, NJ, May, pp. 205–221.

OMG. 1995a. *CORBAservices: Common Object Services Specification.* Object Management Group.

OMG. 1995b. *Common Facilities Architecture. Revision 4.0.* Object Management Group.

OMG. 1997a. *The Common Object Request Broker: Architecture and Specification. Revision 2.1.* Object Management Group.

OMG. 1997b. *A Discussion of the Object Management Architecture.* Object Management Group.

OMG. 1998a. CORBA Messaging. Object Management Group. http://www.omg.org/cgi-bin/doc?orbos/98-05-05, May.

OMG. 1998b. *CORBAservices: Common Object Services Specification.* Object Management Group.

OMG. 1999a. CORBA Components. Object Management Group. http://www.omg.org/cgi-bin/doc?orbos/99-02-05, March.

OMG. 1999b. CORBA Component Scripting. Object Management Group. http://www.omg.org/cgi-bin/doc?orbos/99-08-01, August.

OMG. 1999c. *The Common Object Request Broker: Architecture and Specification. Revision 2.3.1.* Object Management Group.

Olson, S., R. Pledereder, P. Shaw, and D. Yach. 1998. The Sybase Architecture for Extensible Data Management. *Bulletin of the Technical Committee on Data Engineering,* Vol. 21, No. 3, pp. 12–24.

Oracle. 1997. *Oracle8 Server Concepts,* Vols. 1–2. Part Nos. A54644-01 and A54646-01. Oracle Corporation.

Oracle. 1999a. All Your Data: The Oracle Extensibility Architecture. Oracle Technical White Paper. Oracle Corporation.

Oracle. 1999b. *Oracle8i Application Developer's Guide. Release 8.1.5.* Part No. A68003-01. Oracle Corporation.

Oracle. 1999c. *Oracle8i Concepts: Release 8.1.5.* Part No. A67781-01. Oracle Corporation.

Oracle 1999d. *Oracle8i Data Cartridge Developer's Guide. Release 8.1.5.* Part No. A68002-01. Oracle Corporation.

Oracle 1999e. *Oracle8i Enterprise JavaBeans and CORBA Developer's Guide. Release 8.1.5.* Part No. A64683. Oracle Corporation.

Oracle. 1999f. *Oracle8i interMedia Text Reference. Release 8.1.5.* Part No. A67843-01. Oracle Corporation.

Oracle 1999g. *Oracle8i Java Stored Procedures Developer's Guide. Release 8.1.5.* Part No. A64686. Oracle Corporation.

Oracle 1999h. *Oracle8i JDBC Developer's Guide and Reference. Release 8.1.5.* Part No. A64685. Oracle Corporation.

Oracle. 1999i. *Oracle8i Spatial Cartridge User's Guide and Reference. Release 8.1.5.* Part No. A67295-01. Oracle Corporation.

Oracle 1999j. *Oracle8i SQLJ Developer's Guide and Reference. Release 8.1.5.* Part No. A64684. Oracle Corporation.

Oracle. 1999k. *Oracle8i Visual Information Retrieval Cartridge User's Guide. Release 8.1.5.* Part No. A67293-01. Oracle Corporation.

Oracle 1999l. *PL/SQL User's Guide and Reference. Release 8.1.5.* Part No. A67842. Oracle Corporation.

Orenstein, J. A., and F. Manola. 1988. PROBE Spatial Data Modeling and Query Processing in an Image Database Application. *IEEE Transactions on Software Engineering,* Vol. 14, No. 5, pp. 611–629.

Orfali, R., D. Harkey, and J. Edwards. 1996. *The Essential Client/Server Survival Guide,* 2nd ed. John Wiley & Sons, New York.

Özsu, M. T. 1996. Future of Database Systems: Changing Applications and Technological Developments. *ACM Computing Surveys,* Vol. 28, No. 4.

Özsu, M. T., A. Munoz, and D. Szafron. 1995. An Extensible Query Optimizer for an Objectbase Management System. *Proceedings of the 4th International Conference on Information and Knowledge Management,* Baltimore, MD, November/December, pp. 188–196.

Özsu, M. T., and P. Valduriez. 1999. *Principles of Distributed Database Systems,* 2nd ed. Prentice Hall, Upper Saddle River, NJ.

Papakonstantinou, Y., H. Garcia-Molina, and J. Widom. 1995a. Object Exchange across Heterogeneous Information Sources. *Proceedings of the 11th International Conference on Data Engineering,* Taipei, Taiwan, March, pp. 251–260.

Papakonstantiou, Y., A. Gupta, H. Garcia-Molina, and J. Ullman. 1995b. A Query Translation Scheme for Rapid Implementation of Wrappers. *Proceedings of the International Conference on Deductive and Object-Oriented Databases,* Singapore, December, pp. 161–186.

Papakonstantiou, Y., A. Gupta, and L. Haas. 1996. Capabilities-based Query Rewriting in Mediator Systems. *Proceedings of the International IEEE Conference on Parallel and Distributed Information Systems,* Miami, FL, December, pp. 170–181.

Patel, J. M., and D. J. DeWitt. 1996. Partition Based Spatial-Merge Join. *Proceedings of the ACM SIGMOD International Conference on Management of Data,* Montreal, Canada, June, pp. 259–270.

Paul, H. B., H.-J. Schek, M. H. Scholl, G. Weikum, and U. Deppisch. 1987. Architecture and Implementation of the Darmstadt Database Kernel System. *Proceedings of the ACM SIGMOD International Conference on Management of Data,* San Francisco, May, pp. 196–207.

Perry, D. E., and A. L. Wolf. 1992. Foundations for the Study of Software Architectures. *ACM SIGSOFT Software Engineering Notes,* Vol. 17, No. 4, pp. 40–52.

Pirahesh, H., J. M. Hellerstein, and W. Hasan. 1992. Extensible/Rule Based Query Rewrite Optimization in Starburst. *Proceedings of the ACM*

SIGMOD International Conference on Management of Data, San Diego, CA, June, pp. 39–48.

POET. 1999. *Poet Java Programmer's Guide.* POET Software Corp., Hamburg, Germany, http://www.poet.com.

Ram, S. (ed.). 1991. *IEEE Computer Special Issue on Heterogeneous Distributed Database Systems,* Vol. 24, No. 12.

Ramakrishnan, R. 1997. *Database Management Systems.* McGraw-Hill, New York.

Reinwald, B., H. Pirahesh, G. Krishnamoorthy, G. Lapis, B. T. Tran, and S. Vora. 1999. Heterogeneous Query Processing through SQL Table Functions. *Proceedings of the 15th International Conference on Data Engineering,* Sydney, Australia, March, pp. 366–373.

RFC2068. 1997. RFC2068: Hypertext Transfer Protocol. http://info.internet.isi.edu/in-notes/rfc/files/rfc2068.txt.

Richardson, J. E., and M. J. Carey. 1987. Programming Constructs for Database System Implementation in EXODUS. *Proceedings of the ACM SIGMOD International Conference on Management of Data,* San Francisco, May, pp. 208–219.

Röhm, U., and K. Böhm. 1999. Working Together in Harmony—An Implementation of the CORBA Object Query Service and Its Evaluation. *Proceedings of the 15th International Conference on Data Engineering,* Sydney, Australia, March, pp. 238–247.

Rosenberg, R., and T. Landers. 1982. An Overview of MULTIBASE. In H. Schneider (ed.), *Distributed Databases,* pp. 153–184. North-Holland, New York.

Roussopoulos, N., S. Kelley, and F. Vincent. 1995. Nearest Neighbor Queries. *Proceedings of the ACM SIGMOD International Conference on Management of Data,* San Jose, CA, May, pp. 71–79.

Schek, H.-J., H.-B. Paul, M. H. Scholl, and G. Weikum. 1990. The DASDBS Project: Objectives, Experiences, and Future Prospects. *IEEE Transactions on Knowledge and Data Engineering,* Vol. 2, No. 1, pp. 25–43.

Schek, H.-J., and M. H. Scholl. 1986. The Relational Model with Relation-Valued Attributes. *Information Systems,* Vol. 11, No. 2, pp. 137–147.

Selinger, P. G., M. M. Astrahan, D. D. Chamberlin, R. A. Lorie, and T. G. Price. 1979. Access Path Selection in a Relational Database Management System. *Proceedings of the ACM SIGMOD International Conference on Management of Data,* Boston, MA, May/June, pp. 23–34.

Seshadri, P. 1998. Enhanced Abstract Data Types in Object-Relational Databases. *VLDB Journal,* Vol. 7, No. 3, pp. 130–140.

Shaw, M., and D. Garlan. 1996. *Software Architecture: Perspectives on an Emerging Discipline*. Prentice Hall, Upper Saddle River, NJ.

Sheth, A. P., and J. A. Larson. 1990. Federated Database Systems for Managing Distributed, Heterogeneous and Autonomous Databases. *ACM Computing Surveys*, Vol. 22, No. 3, pp. 183–236.

Shivakumar, N., H. Garcia-Molina, and C. S. Chekuri. 1998. Filtering with Approximate Predicates. *Proceedings of the International Conference on Very Large Data Bases*, New York, August, pp. 263–274.

Siegel, J. 1996. *CORBA Fundamentals and Programming*. John Wiley & Sons, New York.

Silberschatz, A., and S. B. Zdonik. Strategic Directions in Database Systems—Breaking out of the Box. *ACM Computing Surveys*, Vol. 28, No. 4, pp. 764–778.

Singhal, V., S. V. Kakkad, and P. R. Wilson. 1992. Texas: An Efficient, Portable Persistent Store. *Proceedings of the 5th International Workshop on Persistent Object Systems*, San Miniato, Italy, September, pp. 11–33.

Skarra, A. H., S. B. Zdonik, and S. P. Reiss. 1991. ObServer: An Object Server for an Object-Oriented Database System. In K. R. Dittrich, U. Dayal, and A. P. Buchmann (eds.), *On Object-Oriented Database Systems*, pp. 275–290. Springer, Heidelberg, Germany.

Srinivasan, J., R. Murthy, S. Sundara, N. Agarwal, and S. DeFazio. 2000. Extensible Indexing: A Framework for Integrating Domain-Specific Indexing Schemes in Oracle8*i*. *Proceedings of the 16th International Conference on Data Engineering*, San Diego, CA, February/March, pp. 91–100.

Stonebraker, M. 1986. Inclusion of New Types in Relational Data Base Systems. *Proceedings of the International Conference on Data Engineering*, Los Angeles, CA, February, pp. 262–269.

Stonebraker, M., P. Brown, and M. Herbach. 1998. Interoperability, Distributed Applications and Distributed Databases: The Virtual Table Interface. *Bulletin of the Technical Committee on Data Engineering*, Vol. 21, No. 3, pp. 25–33.

Stonebraker, M., P. Brown, and D. Moore. 1999. *Object-Relational DBMSs. Tracking the Next Great Wave*, 2nd ed. Morgan Kaufmann Publishers, San Francisco.

Stonebraker, M., and G. Kemnitz. 1991. The Postgres Next Generation Database Management System. *Communications of the ACM*, Vol. 34, No. 10, pp. 78–92.

Stonebraker, M., W. B. Rubenstein, and A. Guttman. 1983. Application of Abstract Data Types and Abstract Indices to CAD Data Bases.

SIGMOD 1983: Engineering Design Applications, San Jose, CA, May, pp. 107–113.

Stout, R. 1995. EDA/SQL. In W. Kim (ed.), *Modern Database Systems: The Object Model, Interoperability, and Beyond,* pp. 649–663. ACM Press and Addison-Wesley, Reading, MA.

Sun Microsystems. 1999. *JDBC 2.1 API.* Sun Microsystems Inc., Redwood Shores, CA.

Sun Microsystems. 2000. *Java Data Objects.* Version 0.8. Sun Microsystems Inc., Redwood Shores, CA, http://access1.sun.com/jdo/, June.

Swank, M., and D. Kittel. 1997. *Designing & Implementing Microsoft Index Server.* Sams.Net Publishing.

Szyperski, C. 1997. *Component Software: Beyond Object-Oriented Programming.* Addison-Wesley, Reading, MA.

Thomsen, E., G. Spofford, and D. Chase. 1999. *Microsoft OLAP Solutions.* John Wiley & Sons, New York.

Tomasic, A., L. Raschid, and P. Valduriez. 1998. Scaling Access to Heterogeneous Data Sources with DISCO. *IEEE Transactions on Knowledge and Data Engineering,* Vol. 10, No. 5, pp. 808–823.

Tork Roth, M., F. Ozcan, and L. Haas. 1999. Cost Models DO Matter: Providing Cost Information for Diverse Data Sources in a Federated System. *Proceedings of the 25th International Conference on Very Large Data Bases,* Edinburgh, Scotland, September, pp. 599–610.

Tork Roth, M., and P. Schwarz. 1997. Don't Scrap it, Wrap it! A Wrapper Architecture for Legacy Data Sources. *Proceedings of the 23rd International Conference on Very Large Data Bases,* Athens, Greece, August, pp. 266–275.

Unland, R., and G. Schlageter. 1992. A Transaction Manager Development Facility for Non-standard Database Systems. In A. K. Elmagarmid (ed.), *Database Transactions for Advanced Applications,* pp. 399–466. Morgan Kaufmann Publishers, San Francisco.

Valduriez, P. 1987. Join Indices. *ACM Transactions on Database Systems,* Vol. 12, No. 2, pp. 218–246.

Valentin, G., M. Zuliani, D. C. Zilio, and G. Lohman. 2000. DB2 Advisor: An Optimizer Smart Enough to Recommend Its Own Indexes. *Proceedings of the 16th International Conference on Data Engineering,* San Diego, CA, February/March, pp. 101–110.

Vaskevitch, D. 1994. Database in Crisis and Transition: A Technical Agenda for the Year 2001. *Proceedings of the ACM SIGMOD International Conference on Management of Data,* Minneapolis, MN, May, pp. 484–489.

Vaskevitch, D. 1995. Very Large Databases. How Large? How Different? *Proceedings of the 21st International Conference on Very Large Data Bases,* Zurich, Switzerland, September, pp. 677–685.

Wang, Y., G. Fuh, J.-H. Chow, J. Grandbois, N. M. Mattos, and B. Tran. 1998. An Extensible Architecture for Supporting Spatial Data in RDBMS. *Proceedings of the Workshop on Software Engineering and Database Systems.*

Weikum, G. 1991. *Principles and Realization Strategies of Multilevel Transaction Management. ACM Transactions on Database Systems,* Vol. 16, No. 1, pp. 132–180.

Wells, D. L., J. A. Blakeley, and C. W. Thompson. 1992. Architecture of an Open Object-Oriented Database Management System. *IEEE Computer,* Vol. 25, No. 10, pp. 74–82.

Index

Figures are indicated by *f* following the page number and tables are indicated by *t* following the page number.

About the Authors

Sandeepan Banerjee is currently a Director of Product Management in Oracle's Server Technologies division. He has been involved with component technologies for over 10 years—first in plug-and-play operating systems, then in distributed object technologies, and recently in extensible databases. Sandeepan Banerjee holds a bachelor's degree from the Indian Institute of Technology, Kanpur.

José A. Blakeley joined Microsoft in 1994 and is currently an architect in the SQL Server product working on server-side programmability and extensibility. Along with Michael J. Pizzo, he shared responsibility for the technical direction and delivery of OLE DB, Microsoft's component-based architecture for Universal Data Access. Before joining Microsoft, José was a member of the technical staff of Texas Instruments, where he developed an object database management system. José A. Blakeley has authored several book chapters and journal articles on design aspects of relational and object database management systems, and on data access. He has a doctorate in computer science from the University of Waterloo, Canada.

Heiko Bobzin graduated in electronic design (Dipl. Ing.) in 1994. His work experience includes extensive software engineering projects with C, C++, and Java since 1980, including client/server connectivity tools, terminal emulation software, design and implementation of a universal communication development toolkit and a TCP/IP stack. He joined POET Software in April 1999 and is development project manager of the Java Software Development Kit group. He is an active member of the Java Data Objects (JDO) specification group, which is part of SUN's Java Community Process.

Paul Brown is INFORMIX's "Chief Plumber." He has worked in the INFORMIX Chief Technology Office for 5 years, since joining INFORMIX from Illustra, the pioneering object-relational startup. Before that, he worked at the University of California, Berkeley, on the Postgres and Sequoia 2000 projects. He is the co-author of *Object-Relational DBMSs: Tracking the Next Great Wave* and the author of the forthcoming book *Developing Object-Relational Database Applications* and of numerous research papers and technical reports.

Weidong Chen received a doctoral degree in computer science from the State University of New York at Stony Brook in 1990. He is currently with LinkAir Communications, Inc., creating new wireless technologies for high-capacity voice and high-speed data services. Previously Weidong Chen was with IBM Santa Teresa Laboratory in San Jose, California, and a tenured associate professor at the Department of Computer Science and Engineering, Southern Methodist University. His research interests include mobile and wireless communications, mobile computing, and database and knowledge-base systems.

Jyh-Herng Chow graduated from the University of Illinois at Urbana-Champaign in 1993 with a doctoral degree in computer science. He then joined IBM and had been working on compiler optimization, runtime systems, and database technologies. He worked on various parts of the DB2 Universal Database engine and the XML Extender, and was a team leader for the DB2 Everywhere product, a lightweight relational database engine for mobile devices. Jyh-Herng Chow is currently a principal software engineer at Oblix, Inc.

Stefan Deßloch is a senior software engineer in IBM's Database Technology Institute at Santa Teresa Laboratory in San Jose, California. He is working on object-relational extensions, application-server integration, and application-development support for IBM's DB2 products; and is representing IBM in the SQLJ standardization effort. Previously, he was a chief architect of the DB2 Text Extender product that integrates full-text search capabilities into DB2 by exploiting its object-relational features. He has also been involved in the development of the SQL3 standard as IBM's representative to the German DIN SQL committee and as a DIN representative to the International Organization for Standardization (ISO) Committee for database. Stefan Deßloch received his master's and doctoral degrees in computer science from the University of Kaiserslautern in 1988 and 1993, respectively. He has published numerous papers on object-relational and object-oriented databases, knowledge-base management, and application areas in various magazines and conferences.

Klaus R. Dittrich has been a full professor at the Department of Information Technology of the University of Zurich since 1989 and heads the Database Technology Research Group there. He is the current secretary of the VLDB Endowment and is a past member of the ACM SIGMOD Advisory Committee. He also has been nominated as a Distinguished Speaker under the IEEE Computer Society European Distinguished Visitors Program and is on the executive board of SI, the Swiss Informaticians Society. He has held visiting scientist or guest professor positions at IBM Almaden Research Center, San Jose, California; Hewlett-Packard Laboratories, Palo Alto, California; Stanford University; and the University of Aalborg, Denmark. Prior to his current appointment, Klaus R. Dittrich held various junior research positions at the University of Karlsruhe and was head of the Database Group at Forschungszentrum Informatik (FZI) there. He holds a diploma (comparable to a master's degree) and a doctoral degree in computer science from the University of Karlsruhe. His research interests stretch across many aspects of advanced database technology, including object-oriented, object-relational, and active database systems; database system architecture (e.g., database federations and data warehouses); database security; and nonstandard database applications. In these areas he has led and/or participated in many national and international projects. He has over 100 scientific publications in these areas, and has followed and influenced the development of object database technology in particular from the very beginning.

You-Chin (Gene) Fuh received a doctoral degree in computer science from the State University of New York at Stony Brook in 1989. Since then he has worked in the area of compiler development for various programming languages, such as VHDL (Very High-Scale IC [hardware] Description Language), Verilog, Fortran 90, and Object-Relational SQL. He is currently a technical leader for IBM Database Technology Institute/System 390, supervising the research and development activities of the query-optimization team. Prior to joining IBM in 1993, You-Chin Fuh held several technical management positions in the electronic CAD (computer-aided design) industry. His recent technical interests are compiler construction, language design, object-relational database technology, client/server debugging methodology, and query optimization.

Andreas Geppert has been a senior research staff member at the Department of Information Technology, University of Zurich, since 1994. He received a diploma (comparable to a master's degree) in computer science from the University of Karlsruhe in 1989 and a doctoral degree in computer science from the University of Zurich in 1994. From 1998 to 1999, he was a visiting scientist at the IBM Almaden Research Center, San Jose, California. His current research interests include active and object-oriented database systems, workflow management, database middleware, and the architecture of database management systems.

Jean Grandbois is a senior developer with Environmental Systems Research Inc. (ESRI), a leading provider of Geographic Information Systems. Jean graduated with a degree in applied mathematics from the University of Waterloo, and has over 10 years experience in developing spatial database software using commercial DBMS engines such as DB2, SQL Server, Oracle, and Informix. He spent the last 4 years designing and implementing ESRI's core data management facility, the Spatial Database Engine (ArcSDE). ESRI and IBM collaborated to implement ArcSDE using DB2's object and user-defined indexing extensions.

Laura Haas is a research staff member and manager at IBM's Almaden Research Center, San Jose, California. She joined IBM in 1981 to work on the R* distributed relational database management project and subsequently managed the Starburst extensible query-processing work that forms the basis of the DB2 UDB query processor. Laura Haas then headed the Exploratory Database Systems Department at Almaden for $3^1/_2$ years. She returned to project management to start the Garlic project on heterogeneous middleware systems. Laura Haas has a doctoral degree and was vice-chair of ACM SIGMOD from 1989–1997. She has served as an associate editor of the ACM journal *Transactions on Database Systems* and as program chair of the 1998 ACM SIGMOD technical conference. She has received IBM awards for Outstanding Technical Achievement and Outstanding Contributions and a YWCA Tribute to Women in Industry (TWIN) award.

Michelle Jou is currently working at the IBM Santa Teresa Laboratory in San Jose, California. She has worked in the UDB development for the last 8 years, primarily focusing on query processing. Michelle Jou received her bachelor's degree in computer science from Washington State University in 1989.

Vishu Krishnamurthy is the director of development in Oracle's Server Technologies Division, overseeing the development of XML, object-relational extensions, and component database technology. He holds a master's degree from the University of Florida and has over 10 years of industry experience in object-oriented and distributed database technologies.

Nelson Mattos is an IBM distinguished engineer at the IBM Santa Teresa Laboratory in San Jose, California. He is the manager of Advanced Business

Intelligence and Database Technology, including solutions such as DB2 OLAP Server, DB2 Warehouse Manager (formerly Visual Warehouse), QMF, Intelligent Miner, Data Replication, DataJoiner, and other BI products. Previously Nelson Mattos was in IBM's Database Technology Institute, which combines resources from the Almaden Research Laboratory and the Santa Teresa Laboratory. He is the chief architect for Object-Relational, leading the integration of SQL and object-relational extensions for IBM's DB2 products as well as the development of various Extender products that exploit the object-relational features of DB2. He works on adding object semantics, event management, support for multimedia, and constructs to increase the expressive power of SQL. He has also been heavily involved in the development of the SQL:99 standard as IBM's Standard Project Authority for SQL. Nelson presents IBM's representation to different standard forums, including the ANSI SQL committee, the International Organization for Standardization (ISO) Committee for database, W3C, CWMI, and SQLJ. He has contributed extensively to the design of SQL:99 through more than 300 accepted proposals. Prior to joining IBM, Nelson Mattos was an associate professor at the University of Kaiserslautern, where he was involved in research on object-oriented and knowledge-base management systems. Nelson received his bachelor's and master's of science degrees from the Federal University of Rio Grande do Sul, Brazil, in 1981 and 1984 respectively, and a doctoral degree in computer science from the University of Kaiserslautern in 1989. He has published over 75 papers on database management and related topics in various magazines and conferences and is the author of the book *An Approach to Knowledge Base Management.*

Ravi Murthy is a principal software developer at Oracle Corporation, Redwood Shores, where he works on extensible and object-relational database technology. He holds a master's degree in computer science from the University of Wisconsin, Madison, and a bachelor's degree from the Indian Institute of Technology, Madras.

Raiko Nitzsche graduated from the University of Rostock in 2000, earning a master's degree in computer science. In 1998, Raiko completed an internship at the IBM Santa Teresa Laboratory, San Jose, California, where he worked on DB2 UDB index extensions and wrote a prototype that demonstrated the use of index extension in connection with the DB2 Text Extender. After the internship, his work focused mainly on the integration of object-relational databases and information-retrieval tools. During his studies he also worked as a database programmer and administrator.

M. Tamer Özsu is a professor of computer science and faculty research fellow at the University of Waterloo. Previously, he was at the University of Alberta for 16 years. His research interests are on distributed data and object management, multimedia data management, and interoperability issues. He was visiting scientist at GTE Laboratories during 1990–1991 and spent 1997–1998 visiting INRIA Rocquencourt (France), GMD-IPSI (Germany), the University of Jyväskylä (Finland), the Technical University of Darmstadt (Germany), the University of Udine (Italy), and the University of Milano (Italy). M. Tamer Özsu has a doctoral degree and is the author, co-author, and co-editor of five books. He is an editor-in-chief of *The VLDB Journal* (VLDB Foundation) and is on the editorial boards of *Distributed and Parallel Databases* (Kluwer Publishers), *Information Technology and Manage-*

ment (Baltzer Scientific Publishers), *Internet and Web Information Systems* (Kluwer Academic Publishers), *SIGMOD DiSC* (Digital Symposium Collection), and *SIGMOD Digital Review*. He also served (1992–1996) on the editorial board of *Concurrency* (IEEE Computer Society).

Michael Pizzo is a senior program manager in the WebData group at Microsoft Corporation. Along with José Blakeley, he shared responsibility for the technical direction and delivery of OLE DB, Microsoft's component-based architecture for Universal Data Access. Prior to working on OLE DB, Michael Pizzo was one of the technical contributors to, and owner of, Microsoft's Open DataBase Connectivity (ODBC), a standards-based call-level interface for SQL databases. He has been actively involved in database standards at both the US and International level. He has two bachelor's degrees, one in physics and one in mathematics with an emphasis in computer science, from Occidental College.

Mary Tork Roth received a master's degree in computer sciences with a specialization in databases from the University of Wisconsin in 1992. She is currently employed by Propel.com. Previously, Mary Tork Roth was a software engineer at the IBM Almaden Research Center, San Jose, California, where she was a lead designer of the Garlic project described in this volume.

Peter Schwarz is a member of the Exploratory Database Systems group at IBM's Almaden Research Center, San Jose, California, where he has worked on the design and implementation of database systems for over 15 years. He received a doctoral degree from Carnegie-Mellon University in 1984 and a bachelor's degree from the State University of New York at Stony Brook in 1975. His current interests include database middleware and tools for schema mapping.

Brian Tran received his master's degree in computer science engineering from San Jose State University in 1986. He is currently working in the DB2 OS/390 Data Base Technology Institute. Previously, he was a key developer of the Object Relational Team in DB2 Universal Data Base for Unix, Windows, and OS/2.

Yun Wang is a distinguished engineer in the IBM Data Management Architecture and Technology group. Yun Wang has participated many IBM database projects related to query optimization, parallel query execution, heterogeneous distributed database systems, database extensions for user-defined features, and data warehouses. Currently, he leads a Database Technology Institute group, developing advanced technologies for IBM DB2 Universal Database for OS/390. Yun Wang received his master's of science degree from the University of California, Santa Barbara.

Bin Yao is a doctoral student in the department of computer science at the University of Waterloo. He obtained his master's degree in computer science from the University of Alberta in 2000. His thesis project involved building a distributed-image database management system on top of a CORBA platform. His research interests include distributed database systems, distribution architectures, scalability issues over the Internet as well as scalability in pervasive computing environments. He got his bachelor's degree in computer science at Beijing Information Technology Institute.